THE STORY OF THE
THAMES

THE STORY OF THE
THAMES

ANDREW SARGENT

AMBERLEY

First published 2013
This edition first published 2015

Amberley Publishing
The Hill, Stroud
Gloucestershire, GL5 4EP

www.amberleybooks.com

British Library Cataloguing in Publication Data.
A catalogue record for this book is available from the British Library.

ISBN 978 1 4456 4662 6 (paperback)
ISBN 978 1 4456 1201 0 (ebook)

Typeset in 10pt on 13pt Sabon.
Typesetting and Origination by Amberley Publishing.
Printed in the UK.

Contents

Acknowledgements

The author would like to thank the librarians at the English Heritage Archive in Swindon for their friendly welcome and assistance during the research phase of this book.

Thanks are due to Oxfordshire County Council, Oxfordshire History Centre for allowing the use of three photographs by Henry Taunt. Carol Butler kindly provided her photograph of 'The Source of the Thames on Millennium Morning', as did David Lee his photograph of Maunsell Fort. Thanks also to Peter Watson for his photograph of Reculver.

The author would also like to take this opportunity publicly to acknowledge his wife's unstinting support during this project.

1

The Context

Climate, Environment and Human Interference

A 'Natural' River?

The River Thames is ancient; older than England, older than humanity, even older than the British Isles themselves. Its life cycle operates on a geological timescale. The river is almost a living being, writhing sinuously across its flood plain, eroding its banks and altering its channel, constantly changing. Go back far enough and even its general course is no longer fixed.

The proto-Thames flowed across the Vale of St Albans, opening into the North Sea near Harwich.[1] Then the Anglian Glaciation, which at its greatest extent buried the country as far south as London beneath many hundreds of feet of ice, forced it southwards until it carved a new valley along a course that is largely familiar today. This new river flowed out onto what we know as the bed of the North Sea, but at that epoch it was dry land, exposed when the glacial climate locked up vast amounts of seawater in ice. There it became a smaller tributary of the proto-Rhine, before emptying into the long inlet which was to become the English Channel.

Most rivers begin as a vigorous young stream cutting a steep valley through the uplands, before opening out into a mature river that winds across a broadening floodplain where it drops the load of alluvium it gathered in the hills. The Thames is unusual; it seems to start as a young river, already too mature to cut a classic V-shaped valley – though its tributaries rising in the Cotswolds have experienced that stage. But do not be deceived; the Thames has had a violent history. It has hauled and dropped huge cargoes of gravel, building up its valley floor, only to cut through it again, forming the terraces that are a feature of its middle and upper reaches.

Yet the Thames is also new. 'No man ever steps into the same river twice', so said Heraclitus of Ephesus (*c.* 535–475 BC).[2] Those words express the thought that the universe is not fixed but in a constant state of flux: how true that is of the River Thames! At one level, the level intended by Heraclitus, the waters flow past and are gone. That much is self-evident; but if a person was to watch the Thames through a time-lapse, they would see different processes operating as the river carves and shapes its course and valley, constantly remodelling itself. The banks erode; silt is deposited then cut through as the river burrows ever deeper into its bed; bends become meanders before being cut off and infilling; islands and mudbanks appear then vanish; its course braids and alters. It is forever changing, forever new.

If these natural processes of change have – quite literally – moved mountains, the impact of people on the river has arguably been as great. Over the centuries the river has been dammed and harnessed for power, revetted to prevent erosion, dredged, straightened and embanked, had new cuts made, been bridged, polluted and cleaned, its floodplains drained and built over, its catchment cleared of natural vegetation, and its water pumped. Its current and volume of flow have been manipulated, both deliberately and accidentally, time out of mind. Now, global warming is creating a whole new set of circumstances. These human factors would be significant on their own, but they interact with and compound the natural forces in unpredicted ways.

Geological Time

On a geological timescale the differences may justly be described as transformational. Powerful and unpredictable, at times the river has built up the valley floor only to cut through it again, forming the terraces which are a feature of its middle and upper reaches. Nothing can be assumed: it is only half a million years since the proto-Thames forced its way southwards to create a new valley.

The Context

Throughout most of written history – and earlier – the Thames looked very different to the river we are familiar with today. In its natural state it was broader, shallower and more meandering, and its banks were less clearly defined. In many sections the channel was braided, with many more small islands (called aits or eyots) and sandbanks than are currently there. Flowing more slowly, sediment from its upper reaches was dropped lower down; of course, today the river still needs to be dredged for management and navigation. It was a seasonal river, as it still is, capable of sudden destructive fury – flooding is not a new phenomenon.

The geology of the Thames has contributed immeasurably to its character. The underlying strata, laid down by a variety of forces over many millions of years, combined with the drift geology of gravels, has been sculpted by the relentless river. The sharp bends in its upper course reveal where it has negotiated its way around limestone outcrops, while the tight pinch point of the Goring Gap is where it squeezed through a weak point between the Downs and the Chilterns. In its middle section it meanders between the chalk of the Chilterns and the South Downs on a bed of gravel and alluvial deposits. East of London, the underlying clay has created a low landscape of marsh and wide views.

The underlying geology, hidden beneath a layer of soil, also gives local character to the traditional buildings of each section of the valley. The villages of the upper reaches and its tributaries display the distinctive honey-coloured limestone of the Cotswolds or the coarser random rubblestone of coral rag. Medieval Oxford made extensive use of stone from Wheatley and Headington, though the finer facing stones used in later centuries came from further afield. Below Oxford, the ancient houses are mostly of timber and clay, reflecting a shortage of building stone among the broad clay vales and chalk uplands. The chalk of the Berkshire and Buckinghamshire hills is not well suited to construction, and brick or tile-hung timber were traditionally favoured in the valley settlements. The flints that occur with the chalk are used particularly for farm buildings on the hills, but they are also combined with stone to create a patterned effect in a medieval church such as Henley or village churches such as Sonning or Shottesbrooke. In Essex and also in East London, the traditional weatherboarding on a timber frame reflects the lack of solid rock beneath. Half-timber, weatherboard and tile facings were all popular materials in north Kent. Brick was first used for great houses and churches, but by the seventeenth century it was coming down the social scale and finding its way into townhouses and farms. In London, brickmaking received a huge fillip after the Fire of London. As a fire-prevention method, the City was to be rebuilt in brick or stone – brick was by far the cheaper – and wood was not to appear on the exteriors (apart from doors, windows and shop signs). The London clays, specifically 'brickearth', which occur along the estuary are ideally suited for brickmaking. They have satisfied the urban growth of the last three centuries: by 1892 London required an average of 800 million bricks a year! London literally rose from the earth. Over time, colours and finishes for brick were developed, adding variety, along with decorative terracotta to provide ornament.

Under human influence, a number of tributaries of the Thames have been 'lost', particularly in the London area, where they meshed awkwardly with the urban landscape. The Roman town was founded on a river bluff cut by two main streams, the River Fleet, hard against its western walls and the River Walbrook through its very heart. The latter, which rose in Moorfields marsh immediately to the north of the City, had long been paved over by the time the historian John Stow was writing at the end of the sixteenth century.[3] The Fleet was bridged at five points in Stow's day, but had an ignoble history as a common sewer. Today it is entirely culverted: it discharges unceremoniously into the Thames through a drain beneath Blackfriars Bridge. The Tyburn, a stream that was once piped to feed public fountains in the City, originally met the Thames at Westminster. Other small streams, such as the Westbourne, flowed further to the west – a length of this stream survives as the Serpentine in Hyde Park. Watercourses have also been lost on the South Bank. The River Wandle still struggles to the Thames, but the River Effra, the Falcon Brook, the Earl's Sluice and the Neckinger have all disappeared. Many were redesignated as sewers when they were culverted, and help to flush out London's drains. Though invisible, these streams are still active: the Tyburn is piped over the underground line at Baker Street, while the Westbourne passes overhead at Sloane Square station. Built over and forgotten, they can occasionally burst out at times of flood.

Climate, Environment and People

The Thames exists within the context of our planet. Over the last half-million years the world's climate has oscillated between extremes. At times it has been a glacial outflow stream rushing across a barren landscape to a frozen sea. At others, it was fringed by sub-tropical forest with hippopotamuses swimming in its warm waters and lions patrolling its banks. The last ice age to grip Britain, the Devensian Glaciation, reached a peak between 22,000 and 16,000 years ago. Even as warmer conditions began to reassert themselves, the world climate continued to fluctuate. Another cold snap after 13,000 BP saw temperatures plummet once again, before it began to warm up. In Britain a 'climatic optimum' was reached around 4000 BC when conditions were 2 °C – 4 °C warmer than today and also a little drier. This was followed by a downturn. The first millennium BC was a period of climatic deterioration, becoming significantly cooler and damper by the Late Iron Age and Roman periods with a particular impact on low-lying land and farming. Another warm period in the tenth to thirteenth centuries was followed by the 'Little Ice Age', extending from the fifteenth or sixteenth century until the mid-nineteenth century, after which the world began to warm up once again. On several occasions the river froze over and hosted the famous frost fairs. Climatic variation continues, though latterly human behaviour has begun to influence its speed and direction in unforeseen ways.

If communities were the passive victims of a changing climate, they were often much more equal partners when it came to environmental change – though they have seldom realised it. The pollen record for the Neolithic period (which brought the first farming communities) from the Upper Thames reveals a landscape of lighter elm, oak and hazel woodland on the gravels, while the natural vegetation of the floodplain was a scrubby alder woodland crossed by meandering watercourses, some of which had become partially silted pockets of wetland. Pollen deposits near the foreshore to the east of modern London reveal a natural flora of mixed, deciduous woodland, with wetlands beginning to form beside the river. The limited woodland clearances made by the first farmers are surprisingly invisible, though during the fourth millennium BC the floodplain was progressively cleared to create open grassland, which was maintained over the generations by regular grazing. It was fully 2,500 years, around 1600–1200 BC, before a marked decline in woodland cover was matched by a sustained rise in grassland species. The seasonal flooding, which created rich meadowland resources on the floodplain, was not a natural part of the hydrological cycle, but an unforeseen consequence of woodland clearance on the surrounding uplands.

An organised landscape with extensive systems of fields separated by areas of grazing developed in the later Bronze Age, from 1500 BC. By the eve of the Roman conquest an agricultural landscape of fields and hedges was well established throughout the Thames valley, and if anything this was intensified under the economic pressures that accompanied Britain's incorporation into the Roman Empire. Pollen evidence indicates that the landscape during the early Saxon period (the fourth to the eighth centuries) was open and unwooded, but agricultural production was less intensive, with the balance adjusted in favour of grazing over cultivation. The amount of sedimentation in the river is a measure of ploughing, which may have declined by as much as 50 per cent from its Roman peak; though it returned to earlier levels after the eighth century.

The river provided all sorts of resources. It was a valuable economic asset, though some of its uses increasingly came into conflict. It was a source of water for humans and animals alike, a source of power to drive watermills, a source of fish and other riverine produce, and a major transport route. From the later Saxon period onward, the many dams for watermills disrupted the river's flow and caused silting. Various attempts were made to administer the river as a unit, but these foundered on the multiple factors of competing uses, vested interests, private ownership and divided jurisdiction, and added to that was the need for investment and expenditure.

Despite some of its other uses, it served as a conduit for all types of waste. Pollution became an ever larger problem, and public health became a major concern in London. The first real steps to combat these issues were taken in the mid-nineteenth century, but progress could barely keep pace with the growing population. By the mid-twentieth century the tidal Thames was dead.

The British coastline is not fixed. The tide flows in and out twice daily following monthly and annual cycles. At the same time, the south-eastern corner of Britain is sinking at a rate of 0.1–0.2 cm per year. Over the long history of the Thames, fluctuations in sea level due to climate change have had a much more dramatic effect – and may continue to do so into the future. In the depths of the last ice age, so much water was locked up in ice that the sea level fell by up to 150 m, creating a vast frozen tundra in what is today the bed of the southern portion of the North Sea, known as 'Doggerland' (after the Dogger Bank).[4] At the same time, the huge weight of the ice sheet was sufficient to press the land mass down into the core beneath. As temperatures warmed at the close of the ice age, meltwater caused the sea level to rise, while the released weight of the ice sheet allowed the land to 'rebound'; the latter process slightly offsetting the former. Even then, the situation was not straightforward, as periodic dips in temperature halted or even briefly reversed the melting of the ice reserves.

Due to the complexity of the geological factors that contribute to sea level change and the difficulty of precise measurement, estimates of the sea level at different dates can vary widely. The low topography of much of the south-east of Britain and the extensive submerged banks mean that small vertical differences potentially have a significant impact on the balance between dry land and the marine environment.

The sea level in the Thames estuary in 7000 BC may have been more than 5–6 m below its present level, meaning that many square miles of what is today riverbed would have been dry land, with the tidal head somewhere around Tilbury. By around 3500 BC, sea level had climbed to only 4.5–5 m below its present level, and by the turn of BC/AD, MHWS (Mean High Water Springtide) was possibly only 2–3 m below. The drowned remains of woodland at places such as Erith, Southwark, Chelsea and Richmond, which are partially exposed at the lowest tides, are evidence of this. Occasional traces of a human presence within this rich ecology are discovered among the tree stumps. However, the rise was not relentless but tied to small fluctuations in world climate. For example, during the Roman period river levels in London may have fallen by as much as 1.5 m, only to rise again during the Saxon period. Change continues, with tides measured at London Bridge showing an average increase of 60 cm over last century.

A recent study of the Ebbsfleet valley in advance of the Channel Tunnel Rail Link was able to trace the local pattern of marine incursion in response to changing sea level in the estuary. Today, the valley is largely filled by sediment. In the early Mesolithic period around 8500 BC the Ebbsfleet stream flowed beneath the current ground level, through a wooded valley landscape which is now deeply buried, to join the Thames well below the current low-water mark. By the early Neolithic, from around 4300 BC, the northern section of the valley was dominated by freshwater alder carr and peat had begun to form. Around 2400 BC, in the Early Bronze Age, this was replaced by open salt marsh and tidal creeks as the seawaters of the estuary began to penetrate. As the sea level continued to rise, these creeks and salt marshes extended up the valley as far as the Roman sanctuary at Springhead. This sequence was replicated all along the lower reaches of the estuary.

One result of this is that the Thames at London may have been a freshwater river until about 4500 BC, not becoming fully tidal until around 1500 BC. Without the twice-daily ebb and flow of the tide, the river bank would have been a much more stable environment. Even in the Roman period the tidal range at London may have been as little as 1.5 m, while in the fourteenth century it had increased to about 3 m; today it is nearer 7 m. When, in 1285, the City of London erected a stone to mark the upriver limit of their jurisdiction, the tidal head was at Staines. Subsequently, the construction of Teddington Lock in 1811 set a limit on tidal flow.

This process has not been entirely natural. Since the Roman period, people have nibbled away at the river, protecting, consolidating and consciously reclaiming its banks. This was independent of climate and sea level change, though was sometimes in response to it. Out in the estuary, marshy areas such as Canvey Island were drained. Within London, the Victorian embankments were major civic undertakings which canalised the river, in places creating 100 feet or more of new land on either bank.

Half a century of professional archaeology within the City has confirmed that the mid-first-century foreshore and the first Roman riverfront facilities lay just to the north of the present line of Thames Street. By the late Roman period the foreshore had moved southwards through a combination of falling river levels and reclamation to a line south of Thames Street. During the Saxon period rising river levels and increasing tidal activity clawed back these claims right up to the Roman riverside wall, eroding its southern face and depositing a gravel foreshore against it. Parts of the wall appear to have collapsed in the eleventh century, perhaps due to scouring by the tide, and the creation of a new timber waterfront in the twelfth century suggests the wall was either in ruins or was demolished. The area between Thames Street and the river is therefore mostly made ground, reclaimed little by little over 2,000 years. Thames Street generally follows the line of the wall and may have been cut through the vacant space it left in the townscape in order to provide good access to the new wharf facilities.

The consolidation and reclamation of the foreshore was not limited to London and Southwark. Recent archaeological excavations in many of the riverside towns of the Middle Thames have found that economic growth in the medieval period, and more recently, went hand in hand with the creation of wharves, the reclamation of low-lying waste, or simply revetment to protect properties against erosion and flood damage.

Flooding is not a new danger, either on the tidal river or in the riverside towns. Global warming is increasing the risk in both zones, but archaeology has found evidence of flooding in prehistoric and Roman times, while the Anglo-Saxon Chronicle also records unusual floods. River defences and embankments have often been built, though ultimately they have tended to fail. The floods that devastated the east coast on the night of 31 January 1953 spared London, but gave a clear warning. As was the case in 1953, the greatest threat today is a storm surge funneling up the estuary. The government has invested heavily in surge defences, resulting in the Thames Barrier and the Barking Flood Barrier. However, global warming means that these can only be regarded as temporary solutions.

Bridges were victims of the power of the river, requiring regular repair. London Bridge was seriously damaged on several occasions; for example, the Anglo-Saxon Chronicle for 1099 records that it was virtually destroyed by what sounds like a tidal surge. A number of the eighteenth- and nineteenth-century bridges of London were undermined by the scouring current, necessitating either extensive repairs or complete rebuilding. Extreme river conditions were not confined to the lower reaches: the stone bridge at Henley was swept away by floods in March 1774.

What is the Thames?

To think of the Thames as 'natural' is misleading, as humans have had a significant impact on its hydrology for at least the last 3,500 years, contributing to both flooding and water shortage, erosion and silting. What, then, is the River Thames?

The Roman (i.e. Latin) name for the river was *Tamesis*, perhaps itself the Latinising of an earlier British name. Two competing names, Thames and Isis, both appear to be derived from this ancestral original. Antiquarians have argued that the river above Dorchester is properly the Isis, only becoming the Thames downstream. Many writers have compromised with 'Thames or Isis', and even the authoritative Ordnance Survey, unwilling to stick its neck out, follows this convention along the upper river. Popularly, however, it is the Thames from source to mouth, and that nomenclature is followed here.

The river is 215 miles long, from its source in the Cotswolds near Kemble, to the Nore, where it officially meets the North Sea amid the marshes and mudflats of Essex and Kent. Throughout its length it falls about 105 m. It is tidal as far as Teddington Lock, and the forty-four locks above Teddington are indispensable for navigation. An average of 1,145 million gallons of water a day flow over Teddington Lock, varying from a high of over 5,500 million gallons a day in the spring to less than 600 million gallons in the late summer.

For convenience, the river is often divided into three sections, each with its own character. The Upper Thames, from the source to the Goring Gap, is a young, rural river; the Middle Thames, as far as Teddington, is a mature river with a broad floodplain, today lined with Thames-side commuting towns; the Lower Thames is tidal, flowing on to the sea through London and the Kent and Essex marshes, and carrying a weight of shipping.

Yet the Thames is more than just a physical entity, flowing at the whim of human and natural agencies. It can be defined as a cultural artefact. In past periods people have thought about and used the river in very different ways, and it has been an intimate part of the life of the nation. Without realising it, people have always projected the broader concerns and values of society onto the river; the river has almost come to represent society. We are no different: the modern view of the Thames is both leisure-based and green, reflecting our post-industrial affluence, our dependence on the internal combustion engine and our pressing environmental concerns.

Very different perceptions of the river and its valley are frequently in competition, with wide-reaching implications – for example, national politics and the 'big picture' versus more parochial concerns is a conflict that has been personified and enacted in the landscape of the river. This schizophrenia is exemplified in the Anarchy (1135–53) and the English Civil War (1642–49), when opposing armies crossed and re-crossed the valley, vying for strategic control and occasionally clashing, over the heads of local people and communities as they struggled to eke out a living, sowing and harvesting, making and trading. These are just two glaring instances. As always, ordinary people are the losers in such situations.

The source of the Thames lies in the Cotswolds about 2 km north of Kemble. Thames Head, as it is known, is surrounded by the ghosts of the past. This seems appropriate for a river that for so long has flowed through the heart of our national life, witnessing the rise and fall of empires. Trewsbury Fort, a hillfort dating from the Iron Age, stands on rising ground to the north. The Roman road the Fosse Way arrows past to the south, making for Cirencester, Roman *Corinium*, capital of the province of *Britannia Prima*, just 5 km away. To the west the source is overlooked by the remains of the deserted medieval settlement of Hullasey, recorded as a manor in Domesday Book, later the property of Romsey Abbey and finally abandoned in the fifteenth century. Together these ancient sites span two and a half millennia of human activity, an eternity in the life of the nation but the merest blink of an eye in the life of the river.

The source has long held a fascination for sightseers. An illustration in William Combe's book *An History of the River Thames*, published in 1794, shows the spring covered by a dry stone structure from which a stream of water flows.[5] Photographs by the Oxford photographer Henry Taunt show that by the 1870s there was nothing left to mark the spot other than a stone-lined hollow. A statue of Old Father Thames watched over the Thames source from 1958 until 1974, when it was moved to a more secure location beside St John's Lock, Lechlade. One of a series commissioned from the Italian sculptor Rafaelle Monti in 1854 to decorate the fountains at the new site of the Crystal Palace in Sydenham, it was sold off following the disastrous fire of 1936. It was replaced by a granite block inscribed, 'The Conservators of the River Thames 1857–1974. This stone was placed here to mark the source of the River Thames.'

The visitor to Thames Head will usually be disappointed by the complete absence of water. A shallow, dry depression can be traced leading away from the dry spring, but it seldom flows with life. Photographs by Henry Taunt, taken in the 1870s and 1880s, show both a dry spring and extensive flooding, depending on the season and the weather. As early as the 1530s, John Leland, Henry VIII's antiquary, noted that the channel was often dry in the summer. Since then, the volume has decreased further. The blame for this may in part be due to pumping from the water table: first, the Thames & Severn Canal needed constant filling at this, its highest point, if it was not to drain; then, in 1878, a water-pumping station was built to supply the GWR Works in Swindon. In the twenty-first century, aquifers are constantly raided to satisfy the growing thirst of our towns and industries. A more permanent spring, Lyd Well, lies about 1 km below the source. This creates a virtually constant pool from which the young Thames flows as a surprisingly wide stream, lush with water plants. At the bottom of the field, a two-arched stone bridge is needed to carry the A429 over the broadening river.

It should be mentioned that there is a rival claimant for the prized title of source of the Thames. Turn northwards from the

Thames at Cricklade and follow the River Churn deep into the Cotswolds. Just north of the village of Coberley is Seven Springs, source of the Churn. If accepted, this would add 15 miles to the length of the river and would make the source a further 400 ft above sea level. However, historically the Churn has always been regarded as a mere tributary, not the main river.

Does a river lend or borrow character? Indeed, can a river have character, personality? Does it just wash the feet of its greater sister, a self-effacing servant? Or is the river a spirit of the ancient world, forgotten at our peril? How often a river defines a city! What would Paris be without the Seine? Or Florence without the Arno? Vienna dances to the strains of the 'Blue Danube' waltz. A river can also define a country. The Danube is the icon of the Czech nation, passionately portrayed in music by Bedřich Smetana in his symphonic cycle *Má Vlast*. The Nile is and always has been the spine and lifeblood of Egypt, the very reason for its existence, its unpredictable floods dictating years of feast or famine. The great rivers of China are almost synonymous with Chinese art as they erode the landscape into fantastic shapes. Slow, meandering and silted, populated with paddle steamers, the Mississippi seems to capture the essence of the Deep South, the natural home of jazz bands. The Ganges goes beyond merely symbolising a nation; it is a focus for religious practice and identity.

Despite its comparatively small physical size, the Thames has stature. It stands proudly alongside other world rivers. It has defined the character of London for two millennia, and in the process has been the beating heart at the core of the Empire. Historically, it has also been the river of the nation – at least of southern England. It has been dominant in war and peace, in spiritual life and the imagination, in the British psyche. And it has changed with the temper of the age: working river, leisured river; defended river, abandoned river; dead river, river reborn.

2

The Ancient River

The First Inhabitants, from 500,000 to 5000 BP

A Moment in Time

Britain would have been unrecognisable 500,000 years ago.[1] It was a peninsula, joined onto north-west Europe by a broad chalk ridge across what is today the Strait of Dover: the Channel then was no more than a large bay or inlet. The mighty Bytham River flowed eastwards across the Midlands and East Anglia to the North Sea. The Thames broadly followed its current course – an ancient channel has been found near Caversham – before turning north-east near Marlow and striking across the Vale of St Albans to the coast near Harwich.

This was a warm period when southern Britain enjoyed a Mediterranean climate with summer temperatures 3–8 °C higher than today, and mild winters with seasonal rainfall in the winter months. Large herbivores, such as elephant, buffalo, giant deer, horse and rhinoceros, and carnivores such as lion, wolf and hyena thrived. Early hominids were part of this ecosystem. Groups of *Homo heidelbergensis* would have crossed this land bridge and then followed the coast to the west or east in pursuit of game, pushing up the major river valleys into the interior. They left their signature in the stone tools which they discarded.

Excavations at Boxgrove (Sussex) have provided an astonishing insight into the lives of these distant ancestors.[2] Very rare for this remote period, the artefacts and animal bones still lay where they had fallen and had hardly been disturbed by geological or other processes. These ancestors were clearly skilled hunters capable of taking down large and dangerous prey. The Boxgrove archaeologists identified two sites where animal carcasses were dismembered. At one, a horse had been butchered, while the other preserved the butchered remains of a rhinoceros. Study of the bones reveals that, where the tooth marks of wolves or hyenas overlap with cut marks made by flint tools, the cut marks were made first. The group was near the top of the food chain, able to fend off powerful competitors until they had eaten their fill.

Controversially, *Homo heidelbergensis* was not 'human' as we understand that concept. The species appears to have occupied a position between humans and animals that is not seen today. However, it should not be thought that they were unintelligent, any more than a lion or chimpanzee is thought unintelligent. The species clearly flourished and was well adapted to the environment in which it lived, not just existing on the margins. This may have been achieved as much through instinct as through planned behaviours, just as a pride of lions or a pack of wild dogs knows how best to stalk its prey. The physiological evidence implies that they could not speak, though they could have communicated using a wide range of vocal sounds and gestures. A lack of language suggests a limited ability to plan or reason; if so, the group would have functioned at a largely instinctive level.

Almost the only artefacts excavated from sites of this period are stone (usually flint) axes and the waste flakes – 'debitage' – created in their manufacture. These 'hand axes', named Acheulian after the type site in France, were a multipurpose tool; the Swiss Army knife of their day. In shape they are remarkably uniform – oval or shaped like a teardrop, thin, with a razor-sharp edge running round it and usually of a size to be used with one hand; they were not hafted. They are found in their thousands over a period of hundreds of thousands of years: over 300 were recovered from Boxgrove alone. It appears that hand axes were not carried around, but made as required and then discarded once the immediate task was complete. Experiments suggest that a skilled knapper could have produced a hand axe in only fifteen minutes.

Despite the high profile of sites like Boxgrove in literature, the Britain of more than 500,000 years ago was an empty land, barely visited by early hominids as they moved in family groups in search of game: peninsular Britain was very much on the margins of Europe. Any estimate of population density would be meaningless as groups would have been constantly on the move in the resource-rich major river valleys and coastal plains dictated by the rhythm of the seasons. To pluck a figure from the air, perhaps no more than a dozen families of between twenty-five and fifty individuals penetrated southern Britain at any one time; and that figure could on occasion have been as low as zero. Camps may have been used for no more than a night or at most a few days before the group moved on, while a kill site such as Boxgrove may have been a focus of activity for no more than an afternoon.

Climate Change

The history of the Thames has, on one scale, reflected the history of climate change. As the world's climate has oscillated to and fro like a see-saw, southern Britain has swung between arctic and Mediterranean climates. At its extreme, during the glacial periods nothing lived in north-west Europe, while the warmest periods saw hippopotamuses in the Thames. Humans and their ancestors followed the animals.

One key to understanding the nature and extent of climatic change lies in deep sediments on the ocean floor. It was realised that the shells of microorganisms that lived and died in the oceans preserved the ratio of two stable isotopes of oxygen that are found in seawater: 16O and 18O. The indicator of warm oceans is 16O, while 18O indicates cool ones, so that their ratio in the shells of fossil microorganisms provides a snapshot of the temperature of the seas during their brief lifetime. Deep-sea cores have allowed a sequence of temperature change to be built up. This is conventionally displayed as Oxygen Isotope Stages (OIS). The OIS gives a series of relative dates, each stage being older and younger respectively than its neighbours. Absolute calendar dates have been calculated for each stage using different forms of radiometric dating. Of course, smaller fluctuations in temperature occurred within each stage, but the scheme provides a working framework.

Table 1: A simplified correlation of Oxgen Isotope Stages[3]

OIS	Age '000s years	Geological phase	Climate
1	0–12	Flandrian	Warm
2	12–25	Devensian	Cold
3	25–50	Devensian	Cold
4	50–70	Devensian	Cold
5a-d	70–110	Devensian	Cold
5e	110–130	Ipswichian	Warm
6	130–186	Wolstonian	Cold
7	186–245	Wolstonian	Warm
8	245–303	Wolstonian	Cold
9	303–339	Wolstonian	Warm
10	339–380	Wolstonian	Cold
11	380–423	Hoxnian	Warm
12	423–478	Anglian	Cold
13	478–528	Cromerian	Warm

The Mediterranean climate did not last. By about 470,000 BP, Britain was in the grip of an extreme ice age known as the Anglian Glaciation (OIS-12), which lasted for over 50,000 years. At its greatest extent, a vast ice sheet covered the whole of Britain as far as a line between the Severn and Thames estuaries and extending across the North Sea. North of that was an empty polar waste similar to Antarctica today; to the south was a frozen wilderness of permafrost, exposed rock and outwash gravels where few plants could survive. Under these harsh conditions Britain and Northern Europe were abandoned.

When the ice finally retreated, it revealed a hugely remodelled landscape. The ancient Bytham River had been scoured away and a new drainage pattern had to develop. The earlier route of the River Thames through the Vale of St Albans had been blocked, pushing the river southwards to find a new course along its present valley. The huge volumes of crushed rock that were deposited in front of the ice sheet have been re-worked continually by the Thames to create the system of gravel terraces (the remnants of successive flood plains) that line the valley.

It was probably towards the end of the Anglian Glaciation that the high chalk land bridge between Britain and north-west Europe was broken. It seems likely that meltwater ponded up between the ice sheet and the chalk ridge, eventually catastrophically breaking through. Even so, for much of the next 400,000 years these islands remained a peninsula jutting out from the Continent. During cold phases, so much water was tied up in the vast ice masses that the sea level was significantly reduced, exposing extensive plains, dubbed Doggerland, which are now drowned beneath the North Sea. These plains fluctuated in area as warming or cooling temperatures caused the sea level to rise or fall, but it is thought that Britain was not finally separated from the Continent until perhaps 5500 BC.

When the climate eventually began to warm up again, a new hominid species, ancestral to the Neanderthals, colonised the empty land. In 1935 the first of three bones from the skull of an adult female in her twenties was found in a gravel pit near Swanscombe in Kent. This has since been dated to around 400,000 years ago, placing it early in the Hoxnian interglacial (OIS-11), which followed the Anglian Glaciation. At this time the Thames around Swanscombe meandered in a wide and marshy valley. Woodlands along the river banks were backed by a grassy floodplain, and the whole environment was rich in plant, animal, fish and bird life. The larger mammals included wild boar, wolf, red, roe and fallow deer, horse, bison and giant deer, but also elephant, rhinoceros and lion.

In the long years since Britain had last been occupied, it seems that at least some groups of the new ancestral Neanderthals had learned to control fire, particularly important for warmth in a cold environment. It also opens the possibilities of cooking and of protection from non-human predators, and offers a communal focus for the group to gather around. Language was another vital tool.

There is enigmatic evidence that a few adventurous hominids may have ventured up the Thames valley at this period. In 1996 a hand axe and flake were recovered near Culham Hill in Oxfordshire from the gravels of the Hanborough Terrace, one of the higher terraces of the Thames. Although this terrace was laid down in OIS-10, a cold phase, the tools show signs of having been rolled and redeposited by the river, which would allow them to be dated to the preceding warm phase, the Hoxnian interglacial (OIS-11).

Two further hand axes which could possibly date to this period have come from the gravels of the Hanborough Terrace. However, three hand axes would represent only the briefest of visits.

Over the next 300,000 years, from 380,000 to 70,000 BP, the climate continued to oscillate, dipping into glacial phases separated by warmer interglacials. The evidence for hominid activity in Britain during this long time period is rather slight, and it seems likely that hominid groups withdrew southwards to warmer areas in the face of each colder climatic period, while at the peak of each warmer stage the rising sea level may have severed Britain from the Continent.

A survey of Lower Palaeolithic stone tools from the river valleys of southern Britain listed a large number of Acheulian hand axes from the river gravels throughout the length of the Thames. As these have all been carried and worn by river action, they can give little information about the groups who used them, but by dating the gravel terraces in which they are found it is possible to suggest a chronological sequence. It seems most were probably used in the two warm interglacials OIS-9 (339,000–303,000) or OIS-7 (245,000–186,000). Evidence from the surrounding uplands is rare at this period, showing that these groups focused on the rich resources of the Thames valley.

An important though ambiguous find was made in a brick clay pit at Wolvercote, near Oxford, which was worked out by the end of the 1920s. Sixty flint and quartzite hand axes, together with the bones of straight-tusked elephant, rhinoceros, red deer, aurochs, bison and horse were preserved in an ancient river channel. The hand axes are of an unusual type, making it impossible to date them by comparison with tools found elsewhere. The fauna indicates a warm, interglacial period; however, due to the conditions in which the material was recovered and to geological complications it has proved difficult to assign the assemblage to an Oxygen Isotope Stage, though the Purfleet interglacial (OIS-9) now seems to be favoured.

The Lower Thames and Essex seem to have been more densely occupied during OIS-7, though 'dense' is a relative term. A disused tramway cutting serving Lion Pit, West Thurrock (Essex), produced an important assemblage of the Levallois tools that are characteristic of Neanderthals, associated with the remains of brown bear, straight-tusked elephant, mammoth, horse, rhinoceros, red deer, bison and aurochs. Fish bones and freshwater molluscs were also recovered. This suggests a rich environment with open water and wetland forming a mosaic with woodland and grassland, though it was a little cooler than today, with mean summer temperatures no lower than 18 °C. A number of other sites are known from the region including Aveley, Belhus Park, Crayford, Grays Thurrock, and Ilford.

An excavation at Dix Pit near Stanton Harcourt in the Upper Thames valley produced a well-preserved assemblage of insect and environmental material. Most importantly, animal bones, including a small species of mammoth, straight-tusked elephant, bison, red deer, horse, bear, lion and hyena, were associated with twenty-three stone tools (mostly hand axes) some of which were fresh and unworn. This material came from an ancient watercourse and the excavator believed the context had been largely undisturbed. Although no evidence of butchery was identified, hominids and animals were clearly moving in the same environment. Over eighty flint and quartzite hand axes, axe fragments and flakes of similar date have been recovered from Gravelly Guy Pit, only 1 km away. A hand axe from Station Pit, Eynsham, was apparently associated with hippopotamus bones.

With the return of a cold climate around 186,000 years ago (OIS-6) Britain was once again abandoned; though as the climate became harsher the ancestral Neanderthals may have hung on for a while at Crayford, where flakes of the Levallois technique are found embedded in the jaw of a woolly rhinoceros. The succeeding Ipswichian interglacial (OIS-5e) was warm and lush, but surprisingly there is no evidence for a renewed colonisation of Britain. A likely explanation is that the rapid sea level rise associated with the start of the interglacial cut Britain off from the Continent before it could be re-colonised.

Neanderthals (*Homo neanderthalenis*) reappeared in Britain around 60,000 years ago (OIS-4/OIS-3).[4] This was a period of cooler climate, building to the peak of the last (Devensian) glaciation. The mean summer temperature in south-east Britain may have reached 13 °C with mean winter temperatures falling below -10 °C. However, classic Neanderthals had developed many physiological adaptations for the cold. The function of their prominent brow ridges is uncertain, but large noses are thought to have warmed the air as they breathed. Their bodies were shorter and more compact than our own, again to minimise heat loss. Their bones were robust, and their teeth were large and heavy, adapted for chewing. Surely they made clothing and shelters against the extreme cold.

Traces of Neanderthal activity are sparse but widespread across central and southern England and Wales. Most of the sites are caves, probably reflecting the better preservation of deposits rather than a genuine preference for cave dwelling. Total population numbers for Britain were very low, perhaps measured in the hundreds. In this cool-temperate environment Neanderthals hunted medium-sized herd animals – reindeer and horse – as well as hunting or scavenging occasional larger prey such as mammoth and woolly rhinoceros: there was little edible plant life. These species all migrate seasonally over long distances, so the Neanderthal groups must have followed them, moving south to more sheltered and warmer areas in winter and covering many hundreds or even thousands of miles in a year. A few scattered artefacts from the Thames gravels are sufficient to show that Neanderthals did penetrate the region, however fleetingly.

Modern Humans Arrive

Recent studies using mitochondrial DNA point towards a single emergence of *Homo sapiens* in Africa around 150,000–200,000 years ago. About 40,000 years ago the first *Homo sapiens*, fully modern humans, appeared in Europe, and almost simultaneously their first 'signature' stone tools are found in Britain. These are leaf points accompanied by a specialised toolkit of blade tools, chisels, gouges and burins (fine scraping or engraving tools) related to the industries of the Aurignacian and Gravettian peoples who were found widely in Europe. At this time modern humans shared the landscape with Neanderthals, competing for resources in a severe and deteriorating climate that supported a largely treeless steppe-tundra of grasses and low shrubs. How they interacted is not known, but Britain may have been sufficiently empty for them to avoid one another most of the time in the same way that they avoided other dangerous predators such as wolf and brown bear.

A flint 'leaf point' – a tell-tale cultural signature – was found at Temple Mills on the River Lea, and another was dredged from the Thames in Long Reach. A single 'leaf point' from near Osney Lock and some long flakes from a gravel quarry near Sutton Courtenay (both in Oxfordshire) are the only evidence that these first humans ventured up the Thames valley.

Then, once again, the occupation of Britain came to a full stop. As the climate became increasingly severe, both the Neanderthal and human populations withdrew. After around 25,000 BP their trail disappears despite the fact that the falling sea level meant that the land bridge across Doggerland remained open. The Devensian Glaciation (OIS-2) reached its peak between 22,000–16,000 BP. Although this was not as extreme as the Anglian Glaciation had been, the ice sheet covered northern England and the whole of Wales. The Midlands and East Anglia would have experienced permafrost, while the south of England and the steppe to the east remained very inhospitable, even during the summer months.

When the ice began to loosen its grip, the Neanderthals had died out, leaving modern humans in sole charge. From around 16,000 BP the climate suddenly began to warm up and plentiful herds of game migrated across the new grazing lands. In their wake, groups of hunters re-colonised north-west Europe, reaching Britain by perhaps 15,000 BP. Immediately post-glaciation, Britain was still a bleak place. Although summer temperatures may have been comparable with those of today, winters were much colder and drier. The landscape was largely treeless, with sheltered stands of birch or willow. Animal species included reindeer, red deer, horse, aurochs and rare mammoth, wolf, and smaller mammals such as arctic hare and lemming.

The first post-glacial human populations were sparse but widespread and highly mobile, following herds on which they depended on their seasonal migrations. Most evidence for their way of life comes from cave sites which would have provided some protection from the elements (and, incidentally, attracted the later attentions of antiquaries), such as Gough's Cave in Cheddar Gorge (Somerset). Isotope analysis carried out on human bones from the cave has shown, unsurprisingly, that animal protein made up the majority of the diet. Small wolf bones have been tentatively interpreted as evidence for the first domesticated dog, which would have been a useful hunting tool. The bow and arrow had certainly been invented; on the eve of the Second World War, excavation at a kill site at Stellmoor, near Hamburg (Germany), recovered a remarkably preserved group of 105 arrows of pine wood among bones of a large number of reindeer. These sophisticated arrows were designed to separate so that the shaft could be reused with a new stone tip.

A buried river channel was investigated as part of larger-scale excavations in advance of the Thames Water pipeline at Gatehampton Farm, Goring. Two flint scatters were recovered from the upper fill of the channel deposits, one of which was slightly older than the other. They are attributed to the 'long blade' industry of the late Upper Palaeolithic, broadly dated to 13,000–10,000 BP. These were interpreted as flint knapping sites where tools had been made. The flakes were in situ and it was possible to 'refit' some of the larger blades and smaller waste fragments to recreate the flint cores from which the blades had been struck.

A cluster of sites is known from the valley of the Kennet, a tributary of the Thames that cuts through the chalk downs, and a date somewhere around 10,000–9300 BP has been suggested. At this time the landscape was open, with few trees, but with plentiful grazing for herd animals such as horse and reindeer, while rich riverine resources might have offered an added attraction. Two short-lived camps were excavated at Church Lammas, Staines, where aurochs, wild horses and reindeer were butchered and flint tools made. Two camps with a similar assemblage of tools were found on the floodplain of the River Colne at Uxbridge. A site at Wey Manor Farm, Addlestone (Surrey), was dated to the twelfth millennium BC and produced almost 400 struck flints, though no bone was preserved. Flint blades have been picked up at Shoeburyness (Essex) and Oare (Kent). The traces left by these people are slight and difficult to detect; the sites mentioned above are just the tip of the iceberg.

After about 11,500 BP the climate began a sustained period of warming, reaching the Holocene Optimum between 9000 and 5000 BP when Britain was warmer and moister than today. The change would have been very noticeable, taking just two or three lifetimes to reach modern temperatures. At the beginning of the period, pollen from a tree throw hollow at Littlemore on the Upper Thames, dated around 9900 BP, revealed a cold climate supporting tundra-like vegetation with a few isolated stands of birch, pine and willow. Other pollen analyses from the area allow the change in vegetation due to climate change to be traced in some detail. Gradually an open woodland developed, dominated by elm, oak and hazel broken up by areas of grassland. This is important because the vegetation cover reflects the types of foods and other resources available.

At the start of this warm period the sea level was still perhaps more than 60 m lower than today, with the Thames flowing out onto what is now the seabed to join the Rhine. As the climate warmed up, the sea level rose, drowning the low-lying plains. As the lowlands were lost, the Thames estuary began to take shape; at the same time blocking the movements of human and animal populations. Britain was finally separated from the Continent sometime around 5500 BC.

Due to the amelioration of the climate, deciduous woodlands spread over much of lowland Britain. The herd animals of the open grasslands that had been the staple foods for the Upper Palaeolithic populations – horse, reindeer and mammoth – were replaced by woodland species – red deer, aurochs and wild boar – as well as many plant foods, and the way of life for human populations changed completely. This period is known as the Mesolithic. In the woodlands, individual hunters or small bands could stalk and bring down smaller game using bows and arrows. A new 'microlithic' stone tool technology was developed to create the specialised composite tools such as arrows and harpoons required for these new hunting techniques. Fire may also have been used to manage the landscape, creating open areas where woodland animals could graze. Ecologically rich environments such as wetlands, river valleys and coastal plains were particularly favoured.

Mesolithic populations are likely to have been territorial, with their way of life built around an intimate knowledge of resource availability and the routes between resources – a mental calendar and map. Although they travelled to find resources, complementary and often quite distant locations (or 'base camps') were linked to form the group's annual territory. Territory size would depend on many factors: a study at Star Carr (Yorkshire East Riding) has suggested that the group moved between low-lying wetlands in the Vale of Pickering and the North Yorkshire Moors, a distance of little more than 10 km. Communities may have linked resources in the Thames valley with the surrounding uplands or coastal areas in the same way.

Scatters of flint tools are found in almost all areas and show that Mesolithic populations were widespread throughout Britain. This can give the impression of a heavily populated landscape, though many of the find spots probably represent no more than the temporary activity areas of small groups that were constantly on the move. Bearing this in mind, attempts have been made to put reasoned population estimates against time slices. One study divided the country south of Scarborough into 10 km squares and recorded the presence or absence of Mesolithic material in each square, where possible using radiocarbon dates (of which only 197 were available) to give a degree of chronological control. The results show a progressively increasing population, from 1,100–2,200 at 11,000 BP to 2,750–5,500 at 7000 BP. These figures are surprisingly low and are qualified with many caveats, but are a corrective to impressions based on numbers of find spots alone.

Any attempt to reconstruct the social structure of Mesolithic groups must be highly speculative, as there is so little settlement or burial evidence. Group size had probably changed little since the Palaeolithic and regional population densities were perhaps as low as 0.01–0.02 people per km. Ethnographic studies have found that groups of this type are frequently bound by kinship, with authority following the same lines. Elders may have enjoyed status as individuals who had gained knowledge and wisdom through experience. The low-density population would mean that neighbouring groups need seldom meet accidentally, making competition and conflict unlikely. They may, on the contrary, have formed part of a larger social network, gathering at predetermined places and times to share and celebrate their perceived bonds.

Evidence of a Mesolithic presence survives widely as a scatter of material with no archaeological context, and hence difficult to interpret. In the estuary, large numbers of artefacts have been recovered from the area around Southend and on the opposite shore from the Isle of Grain. Finds from the bed of the Thames, for example around Thurrock, may be from drowned woodland rather than having originally been lost in the river itself. Mesolithic flints have been found throughout Greater London. A large quantity have come from the river, for example around Ham, Kew, Mortlake, Richmond and Teddington; these may have eroded out of the banks, with the high rate of recovery due to the history of dredging. Artefacts are also widely known from the Middle and Upper Thames, with a particular concentration around Reading, Newbury and the Kennet valley.

Two concentrations in the Upper Thames have been examined by controlled excavation. In addition to widespread stray finds over many years, a cluster of Mesolithic flints was found at the former Morlands Brewery site in Ock Street, Abingdon. A location near the mouth of the Ock may have been visited regularly, though perhaps only for a few weeks each year, although no hard evidence for such a camp has been found. A second archaeological investigation took place in advance of quarrying on an extensive site at Tubney New Plantation, on the Corallian ridge overlooking the valley, recovering over 6,800 worked flints. Although the flints had unfortunately been disturbed and came from the plough soil, it was still possible to identify three main activity areas. This important discovery was interpreted by the excavators as a 'hunting camp' visited on several occasions.

A base camp in the Abingdon area would represent only a pause in the group's annual rhythm of movement. The size and shape of their annual territory is not known. However, it seems reasonable to suggest that they might have wintered in the Upper Thames valley and spent the summer in the Cotswolds before making the return journey – an annual round trip of perhaps 150–200 km. To the south, it seems probable that the Downs formed part of the annual circuit of neighbouring groups who wintered in the Kennet valley. Similar annual movements by communities along the Thames would link the river with its surrounding hinterland.

3

The Sacred River

Ritual, Ceremony and Power from the Neolithic to the Iron Age

The Environment in Prehistory

The Thames has long been recognised as a valuable asset. People have lived on its banks. It has provided water for human groups and their livestock and offered an easy transport route, while its valley and terraces have been exploited for agriculture and grazing. Yet such prosaic considerations are only part of the story. For over 4,000 years, from at least the time that the first farming communities made their living in these islands, the river was held sacred. By turns it was the venue for ritual actions, was worshipped and was viewed as a portal to the other world. Remarkably, the evidence for these different, though not always distinct, beliefs is still preserved. In short, the Thames helped these societies to make sense of their world.

What sort of landscape did these pioneers find along the Thames valley? As late as the nineteenth century, Charles Dickens could present the marshes edging the Lower Thames, just a few miles outside London, as a remote and mysterious landscape where the escaped criminal Magwitch could hide from justice. These low-lying lands were vulnerable to small changes in sea level. Indeed, a modern map of the estuary is very misleading. For example, around the Isle of Sheppey a strip of land perhaps 5 km wide has been lost to the rising sea since the Neolithic period. These lowlands supported a mosaic of rich and valuable resources: areas of damp woodland, wet grassland and open marsh. Extensive areas of woodland along the estuary around Tilbury and Purfleet were drowned by successive fluctuations of the river level, finally being overcome by peat in the early third millennium BC. Occasional finds of stone tools show that their rich resources were exploited in a non-intensive fashion; as these areas became damper, their value decreased. Tangles of roots, stumps and fallen trunks are still dug up in the peat today, and ancient tree stumps are seen at low tide as far upstream as Chelsea and Richmond.

Given the right conditions of preservation, several types of organic evidence allow the vegetation and environment to be reconstructed on a local scale. Pollen from deposits along the foreshore to the east of modern London reveals a natural flora of mixed, deciduous woodland, with wetlands beginning to form beside the river. In some locations, peat had started to develop as early as the late fourth millennium BC in response to a deteriorating climate and a rising sea level. The gravel terraces of the Upper Thames supported a light elm, oak and hazel woodland in the mid-fifth millennium BC, while the natural vegetation on the edge of the Chilterns was dominated by lime woodland on better-drained soils and alder on wetter soils. By contrast, the Thames floodplain carried a scrubby alder woodland crossed by meandering watercourses, some of which had become partially silted pockets of wetland.

The pollen record shows what little impact these early farmers had on the vegetation. Limited woodland clearance began in the earliest phases, but was apparently abandoned and the woodland was allowed to regenerate. Only a small amount of cereal was grown and grass pollen suggests localised areas of grazing were created. It was fully 2,500 years, around 1600–1200 BC, before a marked decline in woodland cover was matched by a sustained rise in grassland species. The floodplain was progressively cleared during the fourth millennium BC to create open grassland, which was maintained over the generations by regular grazing. Historically, a high water table on the floodplain combined with seasonal flooding created rich meadowland resources such as the Port Meadow on the edge of Oxford. However, recent excavation projects have discovered that this was not always the case. During the Neolithic the water table was lower than today; river flooding only became common much later as an unforeseen consequence of woodland clearance on the surrounding hills. For example, major disruption to the woodland on the Chiltern flanks only began around 1800 BC.

The first millennium BC was a period of climatic deterioration, becoming significantly cooler and damper. However, the human manipulation of the vegetation and landscape over the previous centuries still coloured the region. A rising water table meant that occupation on the floodplain was generally abandoned, although the grazing may have become more lush.

The First Farmers

A series of innovations swept across Europe from the Middle East in the sixth millennium BC that carried huge implications for the future of the Continent. Known as the Neolithic, this period was initially defined by archaeologists on the basis of changes in technology: new stone tools with ground and polished cutting edges made their appearance and the first pottery was made. However, the period quickly came to be defined by another innovation that was destined to have far-reaching consequences: the adoption of mixed farming. This is closely connected with the start of a sedentary way of life, leading in due course to further developments in lifestyle and social organisation.

The first farming groups in Britain left a light footprint. Only slight traces of their settlements survive, suggesting that they were quite mobile, seldom stopping anywhere for long. They appear predominantly to have been pastoralists, tending cattle and sheep; wheat and barley formed only a small fraction of their diet. Their material culture was also restricted, as might be expected of groups who were constantly on the move. The general distribution of their remains indicates that they favoured the well-drained gravel terraces along the Thames, sometimes leading their flocks and herds into the neighbouring uplands – the Cotswolds, Chilterns and Downs – to find grazing.

Although communities chose not to live and farm on the damp and wooded foreshore, favouring instead the drier areas flanking the valley, its unique resources were exploited. Stone tools are found among the roots of the submerged woodlands along the Essex shore. Two trackways or platforms dating from the early fourth millennium BC were examined on the south bank near Woolwich. The first consisted simply of split timbers laid directly onto the peat. This was overlain by a more complex structure made of brushwood held in place by two lines of logs. Excavations at Fort Street, Silvertown (London Borough of Newham), identified a similar trackway leading across the wet alder carr to a small eyot. Two lines of planks held in position by stakes were packed with a mat of unworked branches to form a dry surface. Its construction was dated to 3340–2910 BC. Further upstream, Chiswick Eyot also appears to have been a focus for activity during the Neolithic, though no trackway linking it to the river bank has been reported.

The River Lea offered an easy route northwards from the Lower Thames into the fertile region that is now Essex and Hertfordshire. Investigations on the site of the Olympic Park found more evidence for the use of the river bank. Three timber posts, dated to around 3640–3360 BC, had been driven into the edge of a slow-moving watercourse. Perhaps they formed part of a landing stage for the simple log boats which are known to have been in use at this time.

Spiritual life also thrived. Uniquely, a burial dated to around 4220–3970 BC was discovered in the sand of the foreshore at Yebsey Street, Blackwall (London Borough of Tower Hamlets). An adult had been laid in a loosely flexed position on her left side in a grave lined with oak planks. A broken bowl, a flint knife and other flint tools were placed with her. Further potsherds and charred plant remains scattered near the grave were interpreted by the excavator as traces of a campsite. A remarkable object known as the Dagenham Idol, a wooden figure 48 cm tall, was found in marshy deposits beside the Thames in 1922. Dated to 2351–2139 BC, it was presumably a 'cult' object, but its purpose and meaning remain impenetrable.

After 500 years of near-invisibility in the archaeological record, a burst of monument building exploded within these Neolithic farming communities, at a time when domestic structures were still slight and transient, creating the first substantial monuments seen in these islands. The three main types of monument are known to archaeologists as long barrows, cursus monuments and causewayed enclosures, all of which focused around ritual and ceremonial life. These were significant civil engineering projects involving a considerable investment in resources. Did they want to make their mark, changing the landscape in ways that would last?

The Upper Thames became something of a 'ritual powerhouse'. A much greater density of major monuments was constructed here than almost anywhere else in Britain. Several sites remained centres of ritual over several generations, though the nature of that ritual activity changed. A glance at a distribution map shows that monuments tended to cluster into what have been described as 'complexes', of which the three most enduring are focused around Dorchester, Drayton (perhaps including Abingdon), and Lechlade/Buscot. These complexes would have been fixed points in an otherwise mobile world, with ritual or ceremonial providing the focus for the social groups that exploited the Upper Thames. As social, ritual and spiritual life changed over the centuries, these complexes were places where the old and the new could be integrated. They might best be thought of as ceremonial landscapes, where current monuments in use were built in deliberate relationship to older, venerated monuments in various states of decay; and several continued to attract burials in the succeeding Early Bronze Age period.

The treatment of the dead was clearly regarded as of the utmost importance, in complete contrast to the early Neolithic for which almost no burials are known. The three key monument types all appear to have been related in different ways to the treatment of the dead. This is most evident in the case of the long barrow, of which over 600 are known from England. These are thought to have served as communal burial places, in some ways like family crypts; this may indicate an ancestor cult. In southern England a long barrow is typically a mound of earth or chalk rubble, taller and broader at one end. They vary in length, averaging perhaps 30–40 m, though some are as long as 100 m, with a ditch running parallel down each side. Classic examples are West Kennet near Avebury (Wilts.) and Waylands Smithy (on the Berkshire Downs), both of which have a massive facade of sarsen stones at one end and behind it, within the mound, a stone-built passage and series of chambers.

Although they have often been described as *communal* burial places, it is apparent that far fewer individuals were buried in long barrows than were needed to build them, and they certainly do not represent an entire community over several generations. If burial in long barrows was a restricted privilege, interments may represent people of special status within the community, perhaps a leader or shaman (or priest). The gender and age balance of burials shows that access was not confined either to men or to adults, which may mean that respected roles were open to both sexes or that families shared their status. The precise details of the burial rites are much debated and are likely to have varied anyway. Human remains found in the long barrows are jumbled, sometimes with body parts being grouped together. Many bones, and particularly the small bones of the hands and feet, are frequently missing, which may be a result of the practice of excarnation – exposing bodies in trees or on scaffolds until the flesh has decayed before the bones are collected for burial. Ancestral bones may have had an important ceremonial role beyond burial, with individual bones often found outside a funerary context.

A class of major monument which is truly enigmatic is the cursus. In form, these earthworks are defined by parallel ditches, often with internal banks. They may be open-ended or their terminals may be closed off by a ditch. They vary considerably in size, being up to 100 m wide and from a few hundred meters to several kilometres in length. Usually surviving only as cropmarks visible in aerial photographs, they are consequently elusive, with only around sixty recorded in England. Detailed excavation seldom finds any evidence for the contemporary use of these structures, which early antiquaries interpreted by analogy with the race tracks of Classical Greece and Rome! Human remains are, however, sometimes recovered.

Causewayed enclosures fit into this picture, generally dating to between 3700 and 3300 BC, though only about sixty probable examples are known in England. In form, they consist of one or more enclosing ditches dug in sections like a dashed line (the spaces between known as 'causeways'), usually backed by a low bank. They often have two or three circuits, and vary in size from small enclosures of under 1 hectare to large ones of more than 10 hectares. Their internal banks were often supplemented by palisades, and where these can be traced they appear to close off some of the causeways leaving just one or two main entrances. The first to be recognised and excavated was Windmill Hill, overlooking Avebury (Wilts.). Initially they were interpreted as settlements, but more recent analysis of the finds suggests a ceremonial or 'ritual' function. The presence of fragmentary human remains at many causewayed enclosures may indicate a funerary connection.

A cluster of causewayed enclosures are known along the Upper Thames. A key excavated example on the outskirts of Abingdon, situated on a spur bounded by two small streams, had been severely damaged by gravel working. Two curving segmented ditches defined the area, although the excavator suggested that the inner ditch had been levelled when the outer was dug. Much of the interior had been destroyed, but a number of pits, postholes and gullies survived in the space between the ditches. A 10.5 m length of the inner ditch produced a surprising density of cultural material – animal bone, pottery and flints. Aerial photography has identified a remarkable string of possible causewayed enclosures upstream from here: at Radley, Eynsham, Aston, Buckland (on the floodplain near Rushy Lock), Broadwell and Langford, Down Ampney and Eastleach.

Downstream, another has been confirmed at Etton Wick near Windsor. In 1961–3 a causewayed enclosure was excavated at Yeoveney near Staines (Surrey). It was positioned on a low ridge set among the network of channels at the confluence of the River Colne with the Thames. Another excavated example, at Orsett (Essex), lies on the edge of the terrace overlooking the Thames, and consisted of three incomplete circuits of interrupted ditches. Recently, two new examples were identified only 300 m apart on higher land on the Isle of Sheppey in the Thames estuary. Excavation found that the northern of the two was constructed around 3710–3635 BC and may have been used for 185 years, while the southern enclosure dates from 3660–3580 BC and was in use for about 150 years. This phenomenon of 'paired' sites has been recognised elsewhere.

This urge to express themselves in exuberant ritual and ceremonial rather than in material goods can give the impression that Neolithic peoples were preoccupied with ritual activity to the neglect of everyday life. Over the last thirty years it has widely come to be recognised that the division of the world into 'religious' and 'secular' simply imposes a Western mode of thought. As anthropologists have shown, many non-Western societies do not make a clear distinction between the religious and the secular so that few activities are seen as purely one or the other – though even that may be a misrepresentation, as many societies would not see these as two separate, albeit plaited, strands. It is a reminder that the world views of past societies were very different from our own; indeed, the more familiar an artefact or activity appears, the greater the potential for misunderstanding. This insight reveals a new dynamic for prehistoric communities, recognising the reality of their spiritual, religious and ceremonial lives.

Metal is Power

As the Neolithic drifted into the Bronze Age, small communities of farmers continued to be dominated by the needs of their livestock, moving around the landscape in search of fresh grazing and growing only small quantities of grain. The marks of late Neolithic and Early Bronze Age ards, a primitive form of plough, are being increasingly identified in archaeological excavations. These simple tools had gouged into the ancient land surface at several sites around Bermondsey in London, but no corresponding settlements have been found.

The rich resources of the damp foreshore of the Lower Thames clearly continued to be attractive to nearby communities. At Rainham (Essex) a trackway dated 1680–1260 BC led down to the River Ingrebourne, a tributary of the Thames. Another track at Beckton (East Ham) was traced for 80 m, while a sequence of timber tracks, revetments and a possible jetty were seen at Barking. A track at Dagenham unusually consisted of a pebble surface 30 cm thick which the excavators followed for almost 40 m. Several of these tracks were quite sophisticated, with retaining stakes driven at an angle to form either a V or an X to hold bundles of brushwood. On the opposite bank, at Erith, four or five rows of stakes with a wattle infill may have supported a platform. Upstream, at Westminster, on marshy ground at the edge of

Thorney Island, a timber beam and upright lay directly on the peat. This was dated by radiocarbon to 830–414 BC, the Late Bronze Age or Early Iron Age. A scoop in the sand of the foreshore at Yabsley Street, Blackwall, marked the spot where an Early Bronze Age fisherman had built a fire.

Around the middle of the second millennium BC society experienced something of a step change. The mobile lifestyle that had prevailed since farmers first appeared in these islands three millennia earlier gave way to a more fixed and rooted way of life. Permanent settlements were seen for the first time, and large enclosed – apparently defensive – sites appeared. The landscape was divided up as extensive field systems were laid out. The treatment of the dead changed, with individual burial under barrows being replaced by cremation cemeteries. All along the Thames valley these archaeological developments are echoed in pollen evidence for significant and sustained clearance of woodland and a corresponding rise in grassland species and cereal cultivation. Population numbers had reached a threshold, and what had been an expansive pioneer landscape was beginning to fill up. Taken together, these lines of evidence indicate a more consciously intensive use of the land, and imply a greater degree of organisation and control.

In the Upper Thames, small settlements that may best be interpreted as farmsteads sprang up within the field systems – permanent fields required year-round attention. An example at Corporation Farm, Abingdon, consisted of three interlinked ditched enclosures. The central enclosure, with its surrounding bank and palisade, measured 36 m by 33 m and contained a post-built roundhouse. Several fence lines were probably part of a system to control livestock. Spiritual life is attested by a number of carefully placed deposits of human and animal bone within the compounds and ditches. At Eight Acre Field, Radley, a roundhouse stood in a similar location among paddocks next to a waterhole, while pits were associated with field enclosures and waterholes at Appleford Sidings. Circular and semi-circular settings of postholes at Yarnton represent roundhouses and related structures.

By the Late Bronze Age (after around 1000 BC) settlement evidence had become widespread along the Thames and its hinterland. Most of these sites were simple farmsteads, perhaps occupied by members of a single extended family and concerned with little more than making their own livelihoods. A Late Bronze Age settlement dated to the ninth or eighth century BC is inferred at Heathrow on the basis of a large density of pottery and a few shallow pits. A scatter of middle Bronze Age pottery and a possible later Bronze Age enclosure were found beneath the later Iron Age Uphall Camp, Ilford (London Borough of Redbridge). Unenclosed middle and Late Bronze Age occupation sites are known around North Shoebury (Essex).

These settlements may have been at the base of a short social hierarchy. Two neighbouring Late Bronze Age sites, named the North and South Rings, were explored at Mucking (Essex) where they overlooked the Thames estuary. Surrounded by circular ditches 48 m and 83 m in diameter respectively, and producing, among other cultural materials, mould fragments from bronze casting, ceramic debris from salt production and spindle whorls for textile production, they may represent local, perhaps tribal, centres of focus and power. A comparable circular enclosure or 'ring fort' was found at Queen Mary's Hospital, Carshalton. The enclosure under Uphall Camp may be a further example.

The new focus for communal and religious life at the start of the Bronze Age appears to have been the barrow cemeteries which had grown up over the previous few centuries. It is here that confirmation of the rise of a bronze-using elite may be sought. Today many thousands of barrows (or burial mounds) survive, often as grassy bumps, but when first constructed they would have stood out as mounds of fresh earth or shining white chalk on the Downs. The most common type is the round barrow, a simple earthen mound and ditch, though a variety of different forms have been identified. They vary considerably in size from a few meters in diameter to 50 m or more, though their original height is harder to gauge. Unlike the earlier long barrows, they usually cover the burial of a single individual, who was then permanently sealed beneath a mound. This new emphasis on single burial is often taken to imply that the importance of the individual was gaining ground over the role of the community; in other words, that leaders were rising to prominence.

Barrows gave way to cremation cemeteries; in fact, for the

middle Bronze Age, archaeologists have discovered rather more cemeteries than settlements. Typically they contain perhaps one or two dozen burials. They are found along the full length of the Thames. For example, two cemeteries containing seven and twenty-five cremations respectively were excavated near the much earlier causewayed enclosures on the Isle of Sheppey, and dated by radiocarbon to the middle and late years of the second millennium BC. Their location close to the Neolithic sites may just be coincidence; alternatively, the remains may have been visible and attracted attention. In the Middle Thames, twenty cremations were buried in urns at Ashford Common, twenty-three at Sunningdale, and over fifty at Oatlands (near Weybridge, Surrey). Other examples have been excavated in the Reading area. In the Upper Thames, cremation cemeteries were often drawn to earlier burial sites. Eight cremations associated with Deverel-Rimbury-style pottery were inserted into Barrow 16 at Barrow Hills, Radley, while an unusually large cremation cemetery of seventy-eight burial pits focused around a ring ditch at Standlake Down. Were these the resting places for a whole community, or just for a leading family that validated its position with reference to the ancestors?

The seeds of radical change were, surprisingly, borne by metal rather than farming. Initially, the pattern of life for ordinary people hardly changed as the first bronze objects were proudly displayed in the Thames valley. Towards the close of the third millennium BC the few small copper objects in circulation may have been regarded in much the same light as 'traditional' exotic materials such as amber and gold. People soon learned that the addition of around 10 per cent of tin to the copper makes a much stronger metal that keeps its edge for longer. Over the next 1,000 years, the techniques of bronze working became increasingly sophisticated.

The rise of this new raw material, which quickly came to define the period, was paralleled by the emergence of a leadership class. The two may have progressed hand in hand. As the new elite competed for bronze, it appears to have been prized not so much as a superior technology for tools and weapons but as a marker of value. In a world of stone tools, copper and bronze were in a different category, one to which gold and other exotic materials could be added. Its raw materials were rare, and the almost magical technology required to turn rock into finished objects was probably a closely guarded secret. The fact that bronze takes a high polish certainly added to its attractions: bronze was for public display.

Copper occurs quite widely in Western Europe, with sources in Spain, Cornwall, North Wales, Scotland and Ireland. Tin is a much rarer commodity, known only from Spain, Brittany and Cornwall. (Both ores are also found in Central Europe, the Balkans and the Eastern Mediterranean.) This geological accident made Britain a key player within a European network of contact and exchange.

Raw materials and finished items were exchanged widely, both within Britain and with the Continent. There is, for example, considerable archaeological evidence that Mount Batton, a peninsula near Plymouth (Devon), was a port of trade in the earlier first millennium BC. Metallurgical analysis demonstrates that, by the close of the middle Bronze Age, Britain was importing much of its raw metal from Europe; though what types of goods passed in the other direction is a matter for speculation. In confirmation, two shipwrecks have been discovered that were carrying cargoes of ingots and scrap destined for these shores. In Langdon Bay, Dover, 189 winged axes, palstaves, sword and dagger blades, spearheads, socketed chisels and pins, all of French design, were recovered from the seabed 500 m offshore. Although no remains of a boat were found, this material is convincingly interpreted as the cargo of a vessel which foundered near its destination. A much smaller group of seven bronze objects of French types, also interpreted as a cargo, was discovered on Moor Sand, about 3 km off Salcombe (Devon). These items would have been melted down and recast.

Bronze quickly became the engine powering British society. In order to acquire this new material, society had to be organised and productivity increased. In this competition there were winners and losers, as ambitious individuals or communities rose to dominance. Then, as the period progressed, inflation took hold and ever larger quantities of bronze were required.

The River Thames was the major highway carrying the raw metal and finished products into the heart of southern Britain, and presumably transporting some equally valuable, possibly perishable, products the other way. It would be anachronistic to think of this as 'trade' in a commercial sense, though there was no doubt a balance in perceived value. Instead, it is more helpful to think of it as an exchange network, access to which was restricted according to kinship or social criteria.

In 1978 an ancient site was discovered on the bank of the Thames at Runnymede, right in the path of the M25. A rescue excavation found it to be unique. Located on a former eyot in the river, it was unusually large, covering around 2 hectares. Layers of occupation debris and midden deposits testify to intensive use over a considerable period during the ninth and eighth centuries BC. There was plentiful evidence for craftwork such as metalworking and textile manufacture, and the remains of 'feasting'. Perhaps the most significant feature, however, was its developed waterfront of revetments and jetties. This was obviously far more than an ordinary domestic settlement – it is widely believed that it was one of a handful of 'high-status' sites, controlling the movement of bronze and other prestige goods along the river.

Other riverside sites further upstream appear to have acted as local focuses for exchange, dominating and controlling communities and resources in their turn. Three possible candidates in the Middle Thames, all wealthy and possibly defended sites on the river bank, are Water Oakley near Bray, the Eton Rowing Lake site near Dorney and Marshall's Hill near Reading. In the case of Dorney, a series of revetments and jetties around and between the small islets is reminiscent of Runnymede and provide clear evidence of the importance of water transport.

Between 1985 and 1992 a remarkable riverside site was excavated on the line of the Wallingford bypass. Like Runnymede, the site was originally a small gravel eyot; the narrow channel between it and the river bank gradually silted up. During the Late Bronze Age the western edge of the island was protected or defined by a revetment or palisade, and two jetties were constructed. Postholes on the island have proved difficult to reconcile into structures, but midden deposits and a range of craft activities – metalworking, skinning and butchery, leather working, textile working, woodworking, flint knapping – show the site was intensively used. At least thirty-seven bronze items have been recovered from the site over many years; most of the metalwork is of the Ewart Park tradition (1000–800 BC). This site may have been the focus for river-borne exchange for communities in this section of the Upper Thames valley, but compared with Runnymede it was very small and little bronze may have reached this fringe of the exchange network.

A similar pattern of riverside sites presumably existed downstream of Runnymede, towards the estuary. A concentration of tools and weapons dredged from the Thames between Richmond and Mortlake suggests a lost entrepôt in that area. At Vauxhall, twenty substantial timbers were set into the bed of the river in two parallel rows, reaching at least 18 m into the Thames. They have been dated to the middle Bronze Age, so could represent the remains of another key riverside site.

Late in the period a group of enclosed sites appeared, often in prominent locations on hilltops or the edge of terraces. Castle Hill, Little Wittenham, one of a pair of isolated hills that command a section of the river around Dorchester, is a well-excavated example. Another excavated example at Taplow, opposite Maidenhead, contained plentiful evidence for occupation. The site was first established on the edge of the terrace overlooking the Thames in the eleventh century BC, and its bank and ditch, which were remodelled at least three times over the next 300 years, enclosed an area of 1.2 hectares.

These enclosures are most easily understood as the strongholds of an emerging class of local leaders. Their use overlapped with riverside sites such as Runneymede and Wallingford Eyot, so it seems likely that they were key places within a single exchange network. Perhaps these prominent sites served as gathering points for local produce in order to exchange it for the prestigious bronze? It takes little imagination to suggest that the leading people organised surplus production, collecting it in the form of customary tribute, and using their privileged access to bronze to maintain and enhance their political dominance.

What were these Thames communities or their leaders able to offer in exchange for metal? The region has no valuable mineral resources, so their convertible wealth must have been in perishable form. The clue may be found in the development of the ordered systems of fields which first appeared in the middle Bronze Age, from around 1500 BC. They represent a conscious and planned decision to intensify agricultural productivity, and imply a controlling authority. The sites at Water Oakley, Dorney and Marshall's Hill each lay at the centre of an area of field systems, and between these major sites are 'blank' areas without field systems. Perhaps it was their potential that was harnessed to acquire bronze?

Aerial photography, backed up by excavation, has allowed huge acreages of Bronze Age field systems to be identified in the Thames valley. Remarkably, traces of these buried landscapes still survive beneath our feet after 3,000 years. The layout of field systems often betrays a preoccupation with livestock. Trackways (interpreted as drove ways) lead through the complex of small fields or paddocks to more extensive areas of grazing beyond, with gates and pinch points for inspecting and sorting stock. River meanders are sometimes cut off by long ditches to create large areas of riverside grazing; such as at Fullamoor Farm, Clifton Hampden, where a ditch was traced for over 500 m on aerial photographs enclosing 200 hectares of riverside pasture. Two pairs of parallel ditches set at right angles at Northfield Farm, Long Wittenham, are part of a field system that aerial photography has shown covered 6 hectares. Waterholes were dug within the fields. Sometimes their sides were revetted with wooden stakes or lined with wattle to prevent collapse, and occasionally ramps were dug to allow access for animals. The remains of dung beetles from a waterhole at Appleford Sidings provide independent confirmation that livestock were watered there. However, cereals and other crops were certainly cultivated. The charred remains of plant foods are routinely recovered in excavation, as are saddle querns and grain rubbers. The tip of a wooden ard was found at Staines Road Farm, Shepperton. Even more direct evidence for cultivation is provided by a set of ard marks sealed beneath the South Oxfordshire Grim's Ditch at Mongewell. This may have been what kept the cycle of bronze moving. It must have been an effective solution as field systems were adopted simultaneously in many regions of Britain, from Dartmoor to the Cambridgeshire fens.

All this adds up to a series of important sites plugged into an exchange network which followed the Thames. In each case an apparently wealthy and possibly defended site on the river bank lay at the centre of an area of field systems, while significant numbers of bronze artefacts have been dredged from the corresponding section of the Thames. These communities or their leaders gathered resources from their hinterlands which they used to acquire valuable bronze objects. Some of these may have been passed on as gifts to cement relations with neighbouring, but less powerful, groups or leaders, extending the network thinly across the Thames valley and the surrounding uplands. This was a dynamic social landscape of competition, offering ambitious leaders the chance to move up the scale and engage more fully with the network.

The value of bronze was not limited to its use as a precious object or as a rare gift to forge alliances. Archaeologists know about bronze artefacts because so many were deposited in different ways. Some accompanied burials, while a very large number were buried in 'hoards'. Still others have been found in 'watery places' such as rivers or bogs. Significantly, thousands of bronze items have come from the Thames and museums are well stocked. Jill York examined 302 objects dredged from the non-tidal river by the Thames Conservancy.[1] She found that most were from specific sections of the river, rather than being found randomly along its length. It seems implausible that this pattern could be the result of casual loss; deliberate deposition in the river in certain places is a more natural explanation. She also found that 21 per cent of middle Bronze Age items and a huge 70 per cent of Late Bronze Age items from the Thames had been damaged (probably deliberately) prior to deposition – for example, the tips of spears were broken off and swords were bent or broken in half. This has been interpreted as symbolically putting an object out of commission in the context of a ceremony or offering. This pattern of deliberately casting valuable bronze objects into the Thames can best be interpreted as a 'ritual' act. Objects buried in hoards could, in principle, be dug up again. By contrast, the conspicuous disposal of wealth in a river is definitive, as there is no chance of recovery. The items have been 'given' to the river or have passed into another world. Such an act may gain credit with supernatural forces and be a source of prestige in this world.

The practice of ritual deposition in the Thames was not novel in the Bronze Age. The distribution discovered by York replicates the distribution of earlier stone axes, suggesting that the tradition of depositing valued items in the river had begun at least by the Neolithic. The deposition of metalwork was just the latest manifestation of a long-standing practice; even though the precise beliefs may have changed, the practice was deeply ingrained.

Another, more gruesome, class of object has been recovered from the Thames in vast numbers – human skulls! More than 100 were recorded at Strand-on-the-Green by antiquaries, now all lost, while 'numerous crania' were found during the construction of Battersea Bridge, and many others are mentioned in the literature. By their nature, stray skulls from the river could be of any date, even when they are available to study. Richard Bradley and Ken Gordon were intrigued, and examined almost 300 in museum collections for which reasonable documentation of their provenance survives.[2] They found that this essentially random sample did not reflect a natural human population: 140 were male and ninety-two female, while the vast majority were aged 25–35 years. Next they arranged for six skulls to be radiocarbon dated. Four came out in the range of 1388–800 BC, placing them firmly in the middle and Late Bronze Age, with the other two falling much earlier and much later. They also noted that only a handful of jaw bones and few other human bones had been collected, suggesting they were not present. The inescapable conclusion is that the skulls of adults in the prime of life were selectively deposited in the river at certain locations, the flesh probably having been first removed. While the detailed beliefs and motivations surrounding this behaviour are inaccessible, it can only be described as 'ritual'.

Tribes and Kingdoms

The Iron Age traces the beginnings of a sophisticated indigenous social order, cut short by Imperial Rome before it could reach its full flowering. It fits into the time frame 800–700 BC to AD 43. As the period progressed, the scale and ambition of a tribal society and its leaders was transformed, and by the first century BC the expanding tribal groups had turned into 'kingdoms' which were developing towards full-blown states with towns, coinage, international trade and diplomacy, and other trappings of civilisation copied from their Classical neighbour. Julius Caesar recorded a brief glimpse of this rapidly emerging and increasingly sophisticated society in his autobiography, *The Gallic War* (*De Bello Gallico*).

As with the previous periods, the Iron Age is named after a technological innovation. Iron has three major advantages over bronze: its raw materials are widely available, the technology for forging iron is less complex than that for bronze-making, and iron is a more robust material for tools. Even so, iron must have been imported into the region in ingot form. Recent excavations have found that iron working was widespread and took place on most sites, though it is possible that this was undertaken by travelling smiths rather than the resident community. Hammerscale from Berrick Salome is direct evidence of ironworking, while even an apparently ordinary farmstead such as Mingies Ditch (near Hardwick, Oxon) had a smithing hearth where simple agricultural tools could be repaired. A forge requires large quantities of charcoal, so local woodland must have been managed for its production.

Aerial photography on the gravels of the Upper Thames has revealed a remarkable buried landscape of small settlements and field systems, often joined by trackways, though the presence of Iron Age remains on the gravel terraces has long been known as a result of discoveries made during quarrying. The nature of these sites has, however, only recently begun to be understood. It seems that the agricultural base of the economy was consciously intensified. The floodplain of the Thames was rapidly colonised by small 'farmsteads' enclosed by a bank and ditch, rather than simply being grazed from distant settlements on the gravel terraces. Each farmstead may have supported just one or two families and have served as specialist stock-management camp associated with one of the larger 'villages' on the gravels. And this pattern is replicated time and again from Lechlade to Goring. In this way, efficient use was made of the rich summer grazing of the floodplain.

A key site is Gravelly Guy, on the gravel terrace near Stanton Harcourt, where Oxford Archaeology conducted a long-running programme of excavation. The most immediately striking feature of this site was its compact and strongly linear layout, 160 m long (north-west to south-east) by 30 m wide. Its western edge was partially defined by a ditch; but the boundaries of this tightly demarcated settlement were not marked on the ground but embedded in the minds and behaviour of the community. Within this confined area was a dense concentration of around

700 Early Iron Age pits and some thirty roundhouses. Despite the dense concentration of excavated features, Gravelly Guy has been interpreted as quite a small settlement of no more than five or six households at one time and possibly fewer – the permanently occupied site of a community practising a mixed pastoral and arable economy. The many pits and structures are the result of continued occupation and rebuilding over several generations, resulting in a slow 'settlement creep' along the terrace. This provides a model for understanding other open sites in the region.

But Gravelly Guy revealed a second secret. To the east of the settlement lay an apparently empty zone. On closer inspection, this zone had a long history as a Neolithic and Bronze Age ceremonial and funerary space focused on the Devil's Quoits henge monument. This ancient space was clearly still respected in the Early Iron Age, forming a sort of central 'green' around which Gravelly Guy and four other open settlements – Linch Hill Corner, Beard Mill, Vicarage Field and Stanton Harcourt Aerodrome – were grouped. All five sites were notably linear in form, and in each case their arable fields lay on the side of the settlement away from the central area. The excavators interpreted this as the 'fossilisation' of a traditional land-use pattern and suggested that the central area had gradually transformed from a sacred communal arena to common grazing. If true, this is a remarkable example of continuity and adaptation over not just centuries but millennia.

Another important site was excavated on the First Terrace and floodplain at Farmoor in 1974–6 in advance of reservoir construction. Here a sequence of three groups of enclosures was examined, and environmental evidence clearly shows that they were subject to winter flooding. It seems likely that these farmsteads were not contemporary but successive, so that as one was abandoned a replacement was built on a fresh location a short distance away. With their animal bone dominated by cattle and sheep, these were seasonal camps designed to exploit the rich grazing of the low-lying lands as a summer pasture component within a wider system and were abandoned during the regular winter floods. Dung beetle and the snail *Lymnaea truncatula* (which is associated with liver fluke in sheep) were both present, while finds include a triangular loom weight and a polished sheep tibia which may have been used in weaving.

A number of rural settlements are known in the Middle Thames around Staines and Chertsey. A typical farmstead at Lower Mill Farm, Stanwell, consisting of three linked circular enclosures, compares well with many Upper Thames examples, while two clusters of occupation features were investigated at Thorpe Lea Nurseries on the gravel terrace south of the river. Several unenclosed settlements have been explored within a short distance of Heathrow; for example, four roundhouses and other structures at Stockley Park, Dawley, the middle Iron Age hut groups at East Bedfont, or the sixth- to fourth-century BC settlement beneath the western end of Runway 1. Others are known from aerial photographs. A large rectangular enclosure, traditionally known as 'Caesar's Camp', was excavated in 1944 in advance of airport construction. Enclosed by a single bank and ditch, it measured 100 m by 110 m, making it unusually large for a rural settlement. Eleven roundhouses were squeezed into the interior, some of which clearly pre-dated the bank if not the ditch. But the outstanding feature was a rectangular building described by the excavator as a temple. This was post-built, 5.34 m by 4.42 m in dimensions, and probably with a thatched roof. Within this was a smaller room or cell – quite probably a shrine. The whole site was middle Iron Age in date, though some Late Iron Age pottery suggests continuing activity nearby. A superficially similar square, triple-ditched enclosure at Launders Lane, Rainham, measuring 78 m by 84 m, was first identified as a crop mark. Excavation confirmed it was a farmstead occupied from the first century BC, which overlaid a typical settlement and enclosures and possibly continued in use into the early Roman period. Elsewhere, on the site of the Olympic Park beside the River Lea, a small farmstead of the middle Iron Age was also replaced by a square enclosure.

A substantial square ditched enclosure at Gun Hill, West Tilbury, proved to have been short-lived and was apparently defensive in purpose. Sited commandingly on a spur, the large bank inside the ditch has been reconstructed as supporting a palisade. Created in the mid-first century AD, it was being levelled within just a few years. Before the enclosure, the area had already seen activity throughout the Iron Age. A series of shallow linear ditches formed field boundaries and a drove road, while the curved foundation slots of two roundhouses indicate a middle Iron Age farmstead. Similar enclosures are known within the region at Orsett and Mucking. The threat they faced may have been tribal unrest, or perhaps a Roman invasion was anticipated.

Spiritual or religious life is often revealed archaeologically in the use of monuments, in burial practice and in the special deposition of artefacts. In the early–middle Iron Age these indicators become very faint. This does not mean that the Iron Age people were any less spiritual than their predecessors, but rather that their acts of observance left a less visible archaeological trace.

After millennia of use and reverence, the ceremonial and funerary sites of the Neolithic and Bronze Age finally ceased to act as foci for society. In fact, formal burials were rare over much of Britain during the Iron Age, only becoming frequent once more in the first century BC; and few are known in the Thames valley. A Late Iron Age tradition of wealthy cremation burials, extending from Hertfordshire via Essex and into Kent, is interpreted as the signature of a warrior ancestry. Elsewhere, a small number of skeletons have been found in pits within settlements, while stray human bones are frequently unearthed. For example, some twenty burials, mostly of infants, came from early and middle Iron Age contexts at Gravelly Guy, together with a number of stray bones. Burial on this scale cannot account for the population; consequently it has been suggested that corpses, whether or not cremated, were placed in the Thames together with goods which might include metalwork.

Recently a rare inhumation cemetery was recognised at Worton Rectory Farm, Yarnton, where thirty-five crouched burials were laid in two groups. As they were not accompanied by datable grave goods they would usually have been catalogued as 'of unknown date', but radiocarbon determinations on nine of the skeletons found they died between the early fourth and the early third centuries BC. Another small cemetery at Spring Road, Abingdon, has also been dated by radiocarbon to the fourth to third centuries BC. These cemeteries, which could each represent two or three generations of a family, may help to explain why Iron Age burials outside settlements are so seldom identified, and so reduce the need to postulate mass burial in the Thames.

However, another line of evidence shows that the Thames

certainly did continue to act as a focus for ritual activity. The famous Battersea Shield was found in 1857 during the construction of Battersea Bridge. It is too thin for serious military use and, with its gilded surface inlaid with red glass 'jewels', it was probably intended as part of a set of flamboyant parade armour, perhaps making it an ideal candidate for ceremonial destruction in the river. It was far from unique. Two ornate shield bosses were recovered from the Thames at Wandsworth, while the Waterloo Helmet, found near Waterloo Bridge in 1868, was another parade item consisting of a bronze cap with two attached horns of sheet bronze.

While the above items were of outstanding quality, a considerable amount of metalwork of the 'second tier' has been recovered from the Thames throughout its length. The 'Mayer' mirror, one of several decorative bronze mirrors dredged from the river near London, is now in Liverpool Museum. The Thames at Days Lock has produced a unique amount of metalwork, including three swords. Among many examples, a unique bronze shield was recovered from an abandoned channel at Abbey Meads (near Chertsey), while a sword and scabbard came from confluence of the River Wey at Shepperton Ranges.

These objects, and perhaps also foodstuff and items of perishable material, may have been deposited during ceremonies which had developed from the tradition of the preceding Bronze Age. Alternatively it is often suggested that they accompanied the river burials of leading members of their communities.

As the Iron Age progressed, a new class of enclosed site appeared – the traditional term 'hillfort' is repeated here for convenience without wanting to make possibly unwarranted assumptions about the nature of their society. Following a period of abandonment at the start of the period, the hilltop enclosure at Taplow was re-fortified. Occupation evidence is limited, and activity focused on the defences, which were extended, more than doubling the area. Similarly, a hillfort was dug on Castle Hill, Little Wittenham, following the abandonment of the earlier enclosure. Not all these sites were prominently positioned on hills or elevations. The poorly understood site of Cassington Big Enclosure overlooked the River Evenlode, its single ditch 9.6 m wide and 4 m deep encircling an area

355 m by 250 m. First recognised as a crop mark, this substantial site was patchily recorded during destruction by gravel working in the 1950s. The enclosure was created in the first century BC/AD and, although the defences were soon levelled, occupation continued well into the Roman period.

The enclosures (or hillforts) on St Anne's Hill and St George's Hill command opposite banks of the Middle Thames near Chertsey. Archeological investigations on these two sites suggest they were very different. St Anne's Hill has revealed a dense pattern of postholes and other occupation evidence, while very little evidence has come from St George's Hill.

Uphall Camp, Ilford, is the largest hillfort in the London area, covering 24 hectares. It sits on a well-drained rise on the edge of marshland overlooking the River Roding. The enclosing bank and ditch has since mostly been levelled and the site built over. Activity is dated to the later second century BC and consisted of a settlement of roundhouses and four-poster 'granaries' with evidence for textile production and metal working. The misleadingly named Caesar's Camp stands on Wimbledon Common.

These large defensive sites suggest a society in which warfare was rife. In contrast, the many small farmsteads of the Thames valley give the appearance of a settled way of life in which people farmed their fields in safety. The solution to this puzzle may be that the hillforts were more were about making a statement than actual conflict – reminiscent of the Cold War philosophy of the nuclear deterrent. They do, however, argue for a social hierarchy in which an established warrior leadership exercised authority from behind their prestigious ramparts.

Julius Caesar was responsible for subjugating Gaul, and the reason he gave for invading Britain was that the close relations between the two peoples meant that the Gauls were receiving military aid from the Britons. When Caesar visited Britain in 55 BC and 54 BC at the head of an expeditionary force, he found a way of life (at least in the region of Kent, which he saw) which was similar to that of Gaul. He also found a land divided between tribal groupings ruled by 'kings'. The system of tribes (more correctly 'chiefdoms') and tribal rulers (chieftains or 'kings') which he describes seems to leap fully formed into history. In reality such a system must have developed over a period of time, but somehow remains hidden from the archaeologists' gaze.

The nature of the tribal units that Caesar encountered is uncertain. His account hints at a mosaic of smaller tribal groupings, each with their own identities and leaders, which may have been allied or federated into larger units. These sub-divisions may have gone down to a local level. He records that Cassivellaunus, king of the Catuvellauni, sent to the four kings of Kent to raise their military levies. This appears to mean that the tribe later known as the Cantiaci was at this time composed of four independent sub-tribes. Caesar named five tribes in what was to become the heartland of the Catuvellauni – the Cenimagni, Segontiaci, Ancalites, Bibroci and Cassi – which are never heard of again. Another major tribe to the south of the Thames was divided into the (northern) Atrebates and the Regni (or southern Atrebates).

It is evident that certain tribes or their rulers pursued aggressive policies of amalgamation and expansion during the century between Julius Caesar's campaigns of 55 BC and 54 BC and the Roman conquest of southern Britain in AD 43. British rulers aped those on the Continent. Gold coins were first minted in Britain around 70 BC, inspired by Gallic originals, themselves modelled on the gold stater issued by Philip II of Macedonia. The fashion was widely copied, and within two or three decades both gold and silver coinage was being produced by the southern tribes. Inscriptions begin to reveal the names of individual rulers, and the use of titles reveals much about the structure and ambition of the British tribes. Around 25–10 BC the Trinovantian ruler Tasciovanus was the first to add a royal title to his coinage, describing himself as *rignon* or 'high king': this implies a system of client kings who recognised an overlord. The title of *rex* or 'king' was subsequently used by a number of rulers.

This was a time of upheaval and rapid state formation. The most successful was the Catuvellauni, with its heartland in Bedfordshire and Hertfordshire. Following the alliance made with Rome in 54 BC, this tribe seems to have enjoyed trade with Roman Gaul: exotic imports are found in rich graves, such as Italian amphorae (and presumably their liquid contents). Perhaps fuelled by this wealth, the Catuvellauni seem to have exerted their authority over the Cantiaci and the northern Atrebates. The distribution of its coinage shows that its influence extended westwards across Buckinghamshire and Oxfordshire to the River Cherwell and possibly into the Upper Thames. Their ruler, Cunobelin, was described by the Roman author Suetonius as 'king of the Britons', acknowledging Catuvellaunian overlordship of the south-eastern region of the country. Following Cunobelin's death in around AD 40, his sons Caratacus and Togodumnus appear to have divided his lands between themselves. This dynamic process of state formation, which looked as if it could have only one winner in the Catuvellauni, was cut short in AD 43 by the Roman conquest.

Caesar described the tribal strongholds of south-east Britain as areas of woodland fortified with a rampart and trench. Unlike the earlier hillforts, the rampart did not completely enclose the defended area but instead formed strategic lines incorporating natural features such as marshes. Over the following century among the tribes of the South East, this system of strongholds developed into defended centres known as *oppida* or 'proto-towns'. *Camulodunum*, a massive dyke complex on the River Colne near modern Colchester, was probably the capital of the Catuvellauni under King Cunobelin. The three major sub-divisions of the Atrebates each appear to have maintained an *oppidum* – at *Calleva* (modern Silchester), at *Venta* (modern Winchester), which under Roman administration became the capital of the Belgae, and a lost site in the Selsey/Chichester area, which was in Regni territory. A Dobunni *oppidum* at Bagendon, near Cirencester, has been investigated. A small *oppidum* may have commanded the river at Woolwich. Uphall Camp, Ilford, may be another, as may Quarry Wood Camp, Loose, near Rochester. Excavation has shown that this class of site fulfilled many of the functions expected of a town: permanent occupation, centres for international as well as local trade, and a range of craft activities, while the minting of coins implies a political/administrative function.

Two sites in the Upper Thames have been described as *oppida*, though they lacked the extensive outwork of dykes which characterise the later tribal *oppida* discussed above. The centre of modern Abingdon, between the rivers Ock and Thames south of Vineyard was occupied throughout the Iron Age. Two, and in places three, circuits of huge ditches and banks were dug between the two rivers to create an enclosed area of some 33 hectares (which is about the same size as the inner enclosure at *Calleva*) – the dating of this has not yet been refined, but sometime in the first century BC would be likely, with the second ditch possibly being dug at the very beginning of the first century AD. The ditch was first seen during salvage work in 1990 and has since been investigated further on neighbouring plots. Within this area occupation was dense, and population was attracted from neighbouring settlements. Abingdon centre has been claimed as an *oppidum*, and it certainly continued as a small town throughout the succeeding Roman period. Indeed, it gives Abingdon a claim to being the oldest continuously inhabited town in Britain.

At about the same time, two huge banks and ditches cut off a tongue of land between the rivers Thame and Thames to create the site at Dyke Hills, Dorchester. No archaeological excavation has taken place there as, unlike the centre of Abingdon, there is no development threat. This important site is also claimed as a Late Iron Age *oppidum*, and it too continued into the Roman period as a small town although its focus migrated a kilometre northwards to the site of a temporary Roman fort next to the main Calleva–Alcester road. Crop marks reveal an Iron Age riverside settlement which may well predate the digging of the huge ditches, and an unusual quantity of continental fineware indicates a wealthy community. It is possible that its functions and population transferred across the river from Castle Hill to the new location at Dyke Hills.

The creation of two defended settlements beside the Thames, Abingdon and Dyke Hills, and possibly others such as Cassington Big Enclosure, drawing population in from outlying sites, represents a significant change in the social and economic order in this region. It can be presumed that they assumed the roles of local capitals, possibly controlling sub-tribal groupings. Growing river-borne trade may have encouraged consolidation. Alternatively, political instability may have created a need for communal defence. The tribal affiliations of the two communities are unknown; they could even be rival tribal outposts facing each other across a frontier! If the Upper Thames was a buffer zone occupied by independent local groups, these unique sites may have been 'scaled-down' *oppida*, lacking the extensive outworks of their tribal counterparts.

4

The Quiet River

Roman Conquest and Provincial Life

Kingdoms to Colony

During the final century of Britain's independence, the politics and economy of the southern part of the island was bound ever closer to Imperial Rome. Though maintaining the illusion of independence, Rome manipulated and monitored the rival kingdoms by means of alliances, diplomacy, spies and strategic trading policies. While constant rivalry weakened the tribal groupings, an imperially sanctioned status quo kept these noisy neighbours in check. Meanwhile the material benefits of Roman culture were made available among the elite to demonstrate the value of peaceful friendship with Rome. In this way a hundred years passed between Julius Caesar's expeditionary forays in 55 BC and 54 BC and military conquest in AD 43.

Julius Caesar justified his intervention on the grounds that the Gaulish tribes were receiving military aid from their cousins across the Channel. His first expedition in 55 BC was poorly planned. It was already late in the year, and the seasonal weather and strong tides almost caused disaster when a storm destroyed twelve of his transport ships as they were drawn up on the beach. Other damaged ships were quickly made seaworthy in readiness for a withdrawal. After a few days of skirmishing, terms of surrender were agreed, hostages were given and tribute promised. Then Caesar returned to Gaul to attend to greater priorities.

Caesar's second campaign the following year was a much more serious affair. His force quickly advanced to the Thames in order to challenge King Cassivellaunus in his own territory north of the river. Caesar was aware of only one fording point, and he found the Britons massed against him on the opposite bank. They had defended their shore with a palisade of sharpened stakes, with others set into the ford below water level. Despite these preparations, the sheer professionalism of the Roman army gave them the victory and the Britons scattered. The site of this ford is lost, but it has variously been located somewhere between Kingston and London: the Venerable Bede claimed to have seen lead-capped stakes in the river at a place known as Cowley Stakes, just above Walton Bridge, while others dredged from the Thames around Brentford may be medieval or later fish weirs. Caesar then laid siege to Cassivellaunus's stronghold at Wheathampstead and captured it. The Britons' alliance was split and several tribes sued for peace. Once again hostages were taken and annual tribute promised. Then Caesar returned to Gaul before the onset of winter. What had he achieved, apart from personal glory and two chapters in his autobiography? The groundwork for the eventual annexation of these lands had been laid. Britain was no longer an unknown, mysterious place on the edge of the known world. The tribes of south-east Britain were drawn into the ambit of Rome. Alliances and trade links developed, and British rulers increasingly looked to the Empire for protection and support.

An ever closer interest was taken in the succession to the different British tribal kingdoms, as this helped to ensure security on the borders of the Empire. So when Verica, king of the Atrebates, was overthrown around AD 40, he fled to his allies in Rome. At the same time Cunobelin, king of the Catuvellauni, died and his extensive lands appear to have been divided between his sons. It seems that the instability these unauthorised developments created was a trigger in the decision to annex Britain in AD 43.

An account of the campaign was preserved by the historian Cassius Dio;[1] sadly, Tacitus's chapters dealing with these events have been lost. An army of four legions, 40,000 men, was assembled at Boulogne under Aulus Plautius, former governor of Pannonia (a frontier province in the north-west Balkans). Tellingly, Cassius Dio records that the soldiers were initially reluctant to fight 'beyond the boundaries of the known world', but they were soon persuaded. The feuding Britons were 'not ready', and the landing at Richborough on the Kent coast was unopposed. Once again, rivers were used as defensive lines. After several engagements the Britons fell back, first to the River Medway, then to the Thames somewhere towards what was to become London; Cassius Dio locates this stand 'near where the river empties into the ocean and at high tide forms a lake'. Local knowledge once again allowed the Britons to ford the river while the Romans were unable to follow. Plautius commanded his German troops to swim across, while the rest of the force went upstream and found a bridge. Where this bridge was is unclear – the military engineers probably built a pontoon as they had done on the Rhine – but it allowed the Romans to outflank their enemies who then used the low lying marshes to outmanoeuvre them in their turn. The campaign was reaching a stalemate, so Plautius consolidated his position and sent for the Emperor Claudius. Claudius arrived with an extra legion and some elephants (for their shock value), and found Plautius camped on the south bank of the Thames. Naturally the emperor assumed command, then quickly crossed the river, advanced across country and captured *Camulodunum*, capital of the Catuvellauni. This was the catalyst for several tribes to submit, while those who fought on were defeated one by one. In honour of his conquest, Claudius was given the title *Britannicus*. He had been in Britain for only sixteen days.

The fate of the different tribes depended upon their response to the new power. Eleven kings, some presumably leaders of sub-tribes and one who had apparently travelled all the way from Orkney, were quick to make their peace and were duly rewarded. In the first decades of Roman rule, several friendly tribal leaders were retained as client kings with the backing of the Empire. One was Cogidubnus (or Togidubnus) who was granted the title of Imperial Legate and ruled south of the Thames as king of the Atrebates, possibly from the Romanised villa-palace at Fishbourne. Another was Prasutagus who continued as king of the Iceni in East Anglia, in his will bequeathing his lands to his two daughters and the emperor. It was when Nero ignored this provision but instead brought the tribe under direct rule that the bloody Boudiccan revolt was unleashed. A third, Cartimandua, was maintained as queen of the Brigantes, a large northern tribal confederation on the fringe of the province. None of these client kingdoms survived beyond the first generation and by the end of the century all were firmly incorporated into the province of Britannia.

At first Britain was kept firmly under military rule, with four legions garrisoned to consolidate the new power. Military experience was an important part of the training of all imperial civil servants, but in Britain it was of paramount consideration when selecting a governor. Aulus Plautius, conqueror of Britain, was appointed as first governor. Soon after the conquest, a new town was created at Colchester near the former Catuvellaunian capital of *Camulodunum*. This was a colony, legally constituted as a small piece of Rome itself, where military veterans (who received Roman citizenship on retirement) were settled to provide both an example of civil life to the natives and a potentially valuable reserve of loyal ex-soldiers. Colchester may have been intended as the administrative centre of the province, but government quickly relocated elsewhere.

The easy peace and prosperity of the first seventeen years of conquest made the occupying forces complacent. On the death of Prasutagus, king of the Iceni, his territory lost its notional independence and was incorporated into the province, and his people were treated harshly. This brutality sparked a rebellion in the form of the Boudiccan revolt of AD 60, which had been simmering under the surface for many years. The first target of the rebels was Colchester, the Roman colony, which was burned and its residents massacred. The Ninth Legion hurried south from Lincoln to engage the rebels, but was overwhelmed in the field. When news of this reached them, the Second Legion, based in Exeter, refused to march (the acting commander later fell on his sword rather than face disgrace). The rebels marched on London, then St Albans (*Verulamium*). Both towns were razed. The official figure claims 70,000 citizens were slaughtered at the three towns. The governor, C. Suetonius Paullinus, was on campaign with much of his army, crushing the druid stronghold of Anglesey. As soon as news of the revolt reached him, he raced back to defend the province. At a pitched battle along Watling Street near Towcester, a reputed 80,000 British were slain for the loss of only 400 Romans. The revolt was over but the retribution was terrible.

During the conquest the military administration learned a valuable lesson. The Britons' tactics were to use rivers as lines of defence against the invader, counting on local knowledge of fords and currents, just as they had during Caesar's second expedition. Roman commanders saw that the ability to get an army across in good order was essential, as was the need to secure strategic river crossings. Consequently, a number of bridges were built in the province: for example, a late first-century bridge carried Ermin Street across the 10 m wide River Ray at Fencott, north of Oxford. These were the work of the skilled military engineers who also laid out the road network.

Richborough (*Rutupiae*) in Kent was an important naval base and military depot, and a monumental arch symbolised its position as gateway to the province. From there, Watling Street ran westwards beside the Thames before striking north-west across the Midlands. The town at Canterbury (*Durovernum Cantiacorum*), on the site of an existing native settlement, controlled a crossing of the River Stour. Next, the town of Rochester (*Durobrivae*) was established, again on an existing native site, to command the important crossing of the River Medway, and a masonry bridge was built. The road then continued parallel to the Thames as far as modern Southwark, where it met Stane Street, the main road from Chichester (*Noviomagus Regnorum*) on the South Coast. Here a network of low sandy islands and marshy channels reached out into the river. This was the lowest practicable bridging point, and a wooden bridge was built soon after AD 43. Before the end of the century it was renewed in stone, a sign that Rome was here to stay. With two major roads meeting at the bridgehead, huge economic as well as military benefits were generated; and over the bridge the settlement which was to become London (Londinium) quickly sprang up. It seems inconceivable that such a vital crossing point should not be guarded, but to date no sign of a fort has been found to protect the vulnerable southern approach while on the northern bank the small fort at Cripplegate only dates from the following century.

The Roman military seem to have tried to avoid the Thames, perhaps seeing it as a strategic weak link. They built only one other bridge across the river throughout its whole length. That was at the town of Staines (*Pontes*). Elsewhere they must have planned to move troops by ford and ferry, or else relied on their road network, which largely bypassed the river; the main roads were designed first and foremost as lines of military communication.

The administration built a network of forts and roads to control their newly won territory. At first a band of military occupation across the Midlands and South West formed a broad frontier zone behind the line of the Fosse Way. However, the south-east and south-central regions were not heavily militarised. They were occupied by 'friendly' tribes, which, for the first post-conquest generation, continued to be governed by their traditional leaders as client kingdoms. As they were fully absorbed, one by one, into the province, the transition was peaceful. The leading elite and the new urban classes were enjoying unprecedented prosperity, while the mass of rural labourers were certainly no worse off than they had been under their tribal rulers and gradually began to experience a 'trickle down' of benefits. Even the most rural of communities came to realise the potential offered by the market.

As the province stabilised, the military governors followed the standard practice of devolving as much of the civil administration as possible onto the native elite. They adapted the widely used model of the *civitates peregrinae*, self-governing communities of non-citizens. Lists of men of suitable rank to serve on the tribal council and in the various civic offices were compiled. The old tribal elite were enthusiastic as the new system gave them an opportunity to compete for authority and position. From the point of view of the Empire, it encouraged this potentially troublesome class to buy in to the new reality: vested interest is a strong motivation for loyalty.

The tribal areas were constituted as administrative regions (*civitates*), each centred on a tribal capital. Where no suitable town existed, one was created. Though their bounds are not known, these *civitates* were presumably identical with the former tribal areas, and it seems likely the Thames served as a boundary for much of its length. The Cantiaci of Kent were governed from Canterbury (*Durovernum Cantiacorum*), the Atrebates of Berkshire and Hampshire from Silchester (*Calleva Atrebatum*), the Belgae of Hampshire and Wiltshire from Winchester (*Venta*

Belgarum), and the Dobunni of Gloucestershire from Cirencester (*Corinium Dobunnorum*). The huge territory of the Catuvellauni north of the Thames appears to have been divided, re-creating the Trinovantes in the east who had been absorbed by their powerful neighbours a generation earlier. These two divisions were administered from St Albans (*Verulamium*) in Hertfordshire and Colchester (*Camulodunum*) in Essex.

Town and Country

Roman civilisation was essentially an urban civilisation and towns were seen as its embodiment. It is therefore surprising that so few were established along the Thames valley. This may be due largely to the fact that the road network followed direct routes to link the major towns and military installations rather than seeking out the easiest routes; and it was along these that the commerce and official business of empire flowed. The valley of the Thames was largely bypassed. No road wound along the river, giving the region the feel of a backwater. Akeman Street, the main road westwards from London, ran as far as Staines (*Pontes*), where it left the river and headed across the Downs to the *civitas* capital of Silchester and on to Bath. The road north from Silchester to the fort at Alchester (near Bicester) followed part of the Upper Thames, while the road from Alchester to Cirencester cut across the southern flanks of the Cotswolds. Within the framework of the military roads was a mesh of secondary and local roads, ancient trackways that provided the infrastructure for small-scale societies.

Settlement followed the roads, both large and small, springing up to exploit the economic potential of crossroads and river crossings. Few of these roadside settlements achieved the status of a town. Travelling eastwards from London towards the estuary along Watling Street, the road passed through the small towns of *Noviomagus* (Dartford), Rochester and Ospringe before reaching Canterbury, while Springhead (*Vagniacis*) was a major religious centre. The journey was punctuated every few miles by small roadside settlements of varying quality, which catered for the traveller's needs. Travelling west along Akeman Street, a small settlement has been excavated at Brentford where a bridge spanned the River Brent.

The Roman town of Staines was named *Pontes*, highlighting its importance as a bridging point of the Thames – probably the only bridge other than London. The location consisted of a series of low islands among a network of watercourses where the River Colne joins the Thames. This may have created shoals in the main river which recommended it as a crossing point for the Silchester road, perhaps initially as a ford. Excavation has produced no trace of a fort to guard this strategic point, though part of the cheek-piece from a helmet was recovered. Occupation began before AD 65 and the crossing presumably predated this. At first it was a typical roadside settlement; the buildings were mostly of timber with no development behind the street frontage. But the town thrived in the second century, and some impressive buildings were decorated with painted wall-plaster and *tesserae* (simple mosaic tiles) on the floors. A few fragments of window glass reveal the pretentions of some owners. Civic buildings included a temple and a large building of unknown function which may have been a *mansio*, an official imperial posting station. Smithing and iron working, leather working and possibly pottery manufacture were among the local industries. Burials took place along the London road to the east of the town. Perhaps surprisingly, there is no evidence for a riverside quay, suggesting this was not a transhipment point. Unfortunately, its location made the settlement vulnerable to flooding. Attempts were made to reclaim the wet fringes of the main island; the river bank was revetted and a clay bank was built, possibly in an effort to provide some defence against floods. If so, it was unsuccessful, as repeated episodes of flooding sent the community into economic decline in the third century.

Another settlement that probably boasted the status of a town grew up at Dorchester-on-Thames (tentatively identified as *Tamese*). The former *oppidum* at Dyke Hills continued to be occupied into the early Roman period, though around AD 100 the community migrated half a mile to a short-lived military site (beneath the present town). It is believed on the basis of coin evidence that the military site was occupied for no more than thirty years, between around AD 60 and AD 90. Both fort and town were on the main Silchester–Alchester road, which may have overcome the substantial barrier of the River Thames just south of Dorchester by means of a ferry or ford. Its strategic location meant that the town was later chosen as a local administrative centre: an early third-century altar was dedicated by one Marcus Varius Severus, who identified himself as a *beneficiarius consularis*, a customs official who was also responsible for the imperial post.

Though in a different class, the native settlement at Abingdon also displayed the markers of urban life. Occupation at this former *oppidum* continued throughout the Roman period, though excavation has suggested that its fortunes fluctuated. The Thames was probably fordable here. Still in the Upper Thames, major religious centres thrived at Frilford and Woodeaton, while several small roadside settlements sprang up along the Alchester–Cirencester road.

In the far west, Cirencester flourished on the River Churn, a tributary at the headwaters of the Thames. A fort was established not far from the Dobunni *oppidum* of Bagendon within a very few years of the conquest. The native population was attracted by the economic opportunities offered by the fort, establishing a new settlement outside the gate. This settlement was promoted to the dignity of a *civitas* capital, and within two or three decades a new town had been laid out, complete with forum, basilica and amphitheatre. Situated at the junction of two great roads, Ermine Street and the Fosse Way, it prospered. The Churn, which was redirected away from the town centre to form a sort of moat outside the eastern defences, can only have been navigable for the smallest barges. However, colour-coated wares from the Oxford kilns are abundant, perhaps benefiting from water transport. Fragments of sculpted stone, inscriptions and mosaics confirm the existence of grand public and private buildings. After AD 296 Diocletian divided Britain into four provinces, with Cirencester chosen as capital of the new province of Britannia Prima, which administered the South West.

Most of Britain, and most of the Thames valley, was countryside. Life for the vast majority of the population remained bound to the soil and agriculture underpinned the life of the province. Julius Caesar described southern Britain, or at least the parts of Kent he saw, as having a numerous population living in closely spaced farmsteads. This had not changed in the intervening century. Aerial photography has revealed a dense pattern of farmsteads and fields joined by trackways and extending sometimes for miles along the gravels of the river terraces. Very many of these sites have been sampled by excavation, providing evidence for a simple farming lifestyle. At many rural sites this way of life continued into the Roman period without a break. For example, occupation continued at the 'village' at Gravelly Guy, and at the Late Iron Age enclosed farmsteads of Watkins Farm and Old Shifford Farm (all in the Upper Thames). It was not until the mid-second century that this picture of rural stability began to break down as long-established sites were abandoned and new ones created.

This pattern is replicated all along the river. By the Late Iron Age the Middle Thames was densely settled, and occupation at many rural sites spanned the conquest. The area around Reading, including the lower Kennet valley, has been well studied. For example, at Small Mead Farm a system of circular enclosures and curvilinear ditches remained in use into the second century, while at Little Lea Park a pattern of square enclosures contained roundhouses together with evidence for small-scale iron and bronze working. A first-century AD field system and farmstead at Reading Business Park was renewed in the early second century and again a century later. Aerial photography has revealed other, undated, settlements and systems in the immediate area.

Aerial photography and a trial excavation identified a rural settlement at Prior's Pit, Cookham. Here two possible huts, a well, a corn-drying oven, and a system of enclosures and trackways showed occupation between the first and fourth centuries. There is sufficient evidence from Maidenhead to suggest a small occupation on the site of the later town. An enclosed settlement at Cippenham, near Slough, was occupied from at least 50 BC, while an enclosed farmstead measuring about 70 m by 70 m was examined at the Eton Rowing Lake site, Dorney.

A number of farmsteads are known along the River Colne near Staines. Activity around Horton spanned the Late Iron Age to the third century. Not far away, a major project in advance of Heathrow Terminal 5 uncovered an extensive prehistoric landscape.

An earlier field system was remodelled in the Late Iron Age and agricultural activity continued throughout the Roman period. Five rectangular buildings are dated to this later period, and from the third century a number of smaller enclosures and trackways were added to the east of the main settlement, with continuity remaining strong.

Evidence is more difficult to find beneath the Greater London conurbation. However, a number of Roman farmsteads and rural settlements have been identified along the Thames. A first- and second-century corn drier and associated cremation burials at Hurst Park, East Molesley, suggest a farmstead close by. Farmsteads are also known from Hampton Wick and Richmond upon Thames. Activity within a rectangular enclosure inside the earlier Uphall Camp, Ilford, spanned the first to the fourth centuries, though its character is unclear; the excavator suggested communal events such as feasting.

The gravels and other terraces along the river must have carried networks of fields and paddocks, as elsewhere in the valley. Ditches that may have formed part of a field system were seen behind the growing suburb of Southwark, while other field systems were excavated at Launders Lane, Rainham, associated with a barn-like structure with chalk block and flint walls. A Late Iron Age–Roman field system was laid out on the Isle of Sheppey. Along the estuary, the Essex shore has produced notably less evidence for occupation. A rectangular ditched enclosure at Orsett Cock, originating in the later first century BC, continued to be occupied as a farmstead, while an enclosed farmstead at Mucking, complete with a granary and well, burned down in the late second century.

In the rich, agricultural south, the small traditional farmsteads and rural settlements often fell within estates managed from grand villas. Villas represented the high point of rural society. The term 'villa' is used in a number of ways. It conjures up the idea of an elegant country house; and some, such as Lullingstone or Chedworth, certainly lived up to this expectation. At the other extreme, the term is sometimes used as a catch-all for every 'Romanised' residential building in the countryside with stone foundations, a tessellated or mosaic floor, painted wall-plaster or hypocaust tiles. The truth lies somewhere between these positions.

The classic Italian villa was primarily a farm, as were most of the 'Romanised' buildings in the British countryside – the homes of modest farming families. Rarely, and only in the case of wealthy owners, they may have been the centres of large rural estates. Their level of sophistication was closely linked to wealth: size and layout, single or double storied, whether masonry or half timbered, the quality of mosaics and wall paintings, the presence of facilities such as a bath house or garden, all depend on the ability and willingness to invest.

Perhaps 600 villa-like buildings are known along the length of the Thames valley. The Cotswold fringe around Cirencester is known as the 'villa zone' because of the number of fine villas, possibly the country retreats of senior bureaucrats or successful traders from the town, which rose to become a provincial capital. The Upper Thames and north Kent both supported concentrations; elsewhere, the density was lower. A surprising lack of villa-like buildings around the commercial hub of London to match those around Cirencester may be due, at least in part, to modern suburban growth, which limits the chance of discovery.

A villa at Barton Court Farm, just 2 km north-east of the native town of Abingdon, was investigated in 1972–3 by the Oxford Archaeological Unit. Occupation began late in the Iron Age when a ditched enclosure was created, within which a smaller enclosure probably contained the farm buildings. Soon after the conquest, a new enclosure measuring 95 m by 52 m was laid out over the earlier farmstead, subdivided by a ditch. A slight timber building – the villa – roughly 8.5 m by 30 m, had plastered walls, though the lack of broken roof tile indicates thatch. Two settings of six sturdy posts may represent granaries. This complex was in turn abandoned in the later second century and the site lay empty. Sometime in the middle of the following century it was re-planned on a more ambitious scale. A new stone-built villa measuring 10 m by 25 m contained eight rooms (a narrow room may have been a corridor) and a cellar. Even when compared with the local towns, this was an impressive house: tessellated pavements were laid in several rooms – including the cellar – which were decorated with painted wall-plaster, window glass was present, and the roof was tiled. It stood within a ditched enclosure of 41 m by 34 m, surrounded by an outer enclosure of 128 m by 112 m which probably served as a farmyard although few structures were recognised. The sequence of development charts the social rise of an ordinary farm, a process that may have been replicated widely across the region. Its owners – quite possibly more than one family over such a long time span – were willing to invest in order to impress. Despite the superficial upgrading of scale and materials, the function of the site probably remained quite similar, a prosperous working farm perhaps re-presenting itself as the centre of a small agricultural estate. At heart, however, it remained quite a modest affair.

A recent excavation at Claydon Pike, near Lechlade, traced a similar sequence from Late Iron Age farmstead to villa complex. A long-established settlement in Longdoles Field was radically re-ordered in the early second century. A formal gateway opened into a linked pair of large enclosures in which stood two large aisled buildings, at least one of which boasted painted wall-plaster, a tiled roof and a facade incorporating limestone columns. Box hedging and exotic plants such as coriander, celery, carrot and fennel were cultivated in a garden area. Rich finds included jewellery and two seal rings with carved intaglios. A double-ditched enclosure outside the gate may have been a temple. Trackways linked the complex with its fields and paddocks. It has been interpreted as the centre of another emerging estate, possibly reflecting a switch from pastoralism to the creation of extensive hay meadows on the floodplain.

Villas have been excavated throughout the Middle Thames. An example at Gatehampton Farm, Goring, established in the second century, was associated with a field system. A type known as a winged corridor villa in Hapsden Wood, near Henley, was late Roman in date. A villa at Hambledon stood just a few hundred metres back from the north bank of the river. As it was excavated in 1912 its sequence of development is difficult to unpick, but by the fourth century the villa was approached through a large, walled enclosure. Less than a mile away, crop marks reveal a second villa, which may have formed part of the same estate. Villas at Cox Green and Castle Hill are on the edge of modern Maidenhead.

A few villas are known to the north-east of London. In 1715 a floor of coloured *tesserae* was seen during landscaping in Wanstead

Park, and was relocated in the 1960s. A bath house, perhaps associated with a villa, was excavated at Chigwell, while another at Daws Heath, Basildon, is known from aerial photography. Many more are known along the Kentish side of the estuary, including examples at Darenth, Dartford, Gillingham, Gravesend, Milton (near Sittingbourne), Whitstable and Upchurch, many of which boasted painted wall-plaster, *tesserae*, and even window glass. A corridor villa with outbuildings, examined in Cobham Park, was found to have been built a little before AD 100 and abandoned by AD 360. Further likely examples were investigated at Minster on the Isle of Sheppey and Hoo on the Isle of Grain.

London: An Economic Hub

One critical difference between the Late Iron Age and the Roman period was that, almost overnight, Britain became part of an Empire-wide economy in which anything could be bought for a price. Initially the military provided a huge impetus to kick-start production, but a mature, cash-based economy rapidly developed, gradually percolating out from the towns to encompass all of society. London sprang up as the gateway to these endless markets, its burgeoning population quickly becoming a market in its own right. Government follows money, and at least the financial administration of the province was soon transferred to London. This no doubt helped to consolidate the town's commercial predominance, at the same time conferring an informal, semi-official status.

Almost uniquely in the province, the new town of London was not founded as a result of central planning, but instead owed its origin to private traders identifying a commercial opportunity. Prior to the conquest this riverside location was a landscape of fields and farms like any other. It was the building of the first bridge that drew people to this spot and powered its remarkable development. By around AD 50 a settlement had sprung up around the bridgehead to seize the opportunities offered by travellers and the military who were funnelled over this narrow crossing from right across the south-east of Britain. These same entrepreneurs were quick to spot the economic potential of the river, integrating road and water transport. With a tidal range of only around 1.5 m, conditions were relatively easy for the simple vessels and port facilities of the age. In just a few years the foreshore around the bridge was protected by wooden revetments, and areas of hard standing were created to allow the flat-bottomed barges of the day to be drawn up for loading and unloading. Within a decade, timber revetments had been extended along almost the whole river frontage. Shops and workshops, warehouses and private houses jostled for space between the road and river. Southwark began to develop in parallel, though it was never more than a suburb of its mighty neighbour.

Even before the Boudiccan revolt – less than two decades after the conquest – the historian Tacitus could describe London as the chief residence of merchants and the leading centre of trade and commerce in the province.[2] Despite that accolade, the settlement was architecturally undistinguished: it had the character of a frontier town. Activity focused around the road up from the bridgehead to a T-junction, where a left turn took the traveller west towards Silchester and Bath, and a right turn directed them north-east towards Colchester. Shops, workshops and private houses clustered along these roads, and especially that to the west. Dotted among them were circular structures in the native tradition. A range of industrial processes were carried out. These buildings were all basically of timber: no stone-built villas or public buildings have been found at this date. An element of town planning, however, implies a degree of official oversight. The fledgling commercial centre in its strategic location had already begun to attract the interest of the authorities.

As Britain was not a leading manufacturing province, it must be assumed that the bulk of exports were raw materials and perishable goods. Writing before the conquest, Strabo records that the Britons exported grain, cattle, gold, silver, iron, slaves and hunting dogs; and this may have changed little.[3] He noted that they imported luxuries: ivory, amber gems, glass vessels and similar trinkets. The many fragments of amphorae from sites all over Britain indicate that wine and olive oil can be added to this list. An unopened amphora marked in ink '*liquamen* [a fish sauce] shipped from

Antipolis [Antibes, South of France] by Lucius Tettius Africanus'
was found in the silt at Southwark where it may have fallen during
unloading.[4] Imported fine wares testify to a lively trade in pottery,
while quern stones came from the Rhine on the edge of the Empire.

Salt was another valuable commodity. In the Late Iron Age, salt
from the area of Droitwich was traded as far as the Upper Thames,
where its briquetage containers even found their way onto lowly
farmsteads. This trade may have reached an international market
through London. Salt was also made on an industrial scale in the
Essex marshes and into the Thames estuary as far as Canvey Island.
The method involved evaporating seawater in clay tanks, and the
hearths used for drying the salt gave rise to features known locally
as 'red hills'. The earliest sites have been dated to the first century
BC and the industry developed throughout the Roman period.
Trade links may have reached across Britain and the Continent.

The new London that rose from the ashes of AD 60 was radically
different from its spontaneous predecessor. It has all the marks of
a planned town, following an essentially regular grid of streets and
insulae (blocks of buildings). The public buildings which formed
part of a mature civic landscape were nearly all present. Many
of the private buildings which had previously been of wood were
replaced in stone. Expensive coloured marbles were being imported
to give the town a rich texture. Money, both public and private,
was clearly being invested on a large scale. London had a new
confidence.

A forum (market place) and basilica (civic assembly hall) was
erected between AD 70 and 80 at the head of the main road as
it climbed up from the bridge. This was a suitably dominant and
commanding position for the commercial centre of the town. At
a time when many towns had forums of timber, this was solidly
built of ragstone. At the start of the second century the forum and
basilica was replaced on a grander scale. Measuring 166 m by
167 m, five times the size of its predecessor, this was the largest
building of its type in the province and proclaimed the wealth
and importance of London. Another structure designed to impress
visitors was a highly decorated monumental arch over 7.5 m wide,
large portions of which were re-used in the later riverside wall.

On the river frontage between the bridge and the Walbrook was a large complex, which has been identified as the Governor's Palace. Built in the late first century, it was demolished in the third century. A recent re-evaluation has challenged this interpretation, leaving the true site of the governor's London headquarters unidentified – assuming there was one. This leaves the purpose of this substantial structure unknown, though it was surely a public building. Work began in AD 294 on a substantial new complex near the river to the west of the Walbrook. It may have been intended by the usurper Allectus as an administrative centre, but was probably never completed.

A timber amphitheatre was built in the western quarter of the town, just alongside Cripplegate Fort. Dendrochronology suggests a date around AD 74. In the early second century it was rebuilt in stone. Following a period of abandonment, its masonry was finally robbed at the end of the fourth century. Today the curve of the arena wall is marked out in Guildhall Yard. Extensive public baths have been excavated at Huggin Hill. A smaller public bath house was found in Cheapside. Many temples have also been founded, including a Mithraeum, dedicated to the god Mithras.

Following the destruction of AD 60, the wharf facilities were rebuilt in a series of phases, investment initially being concentrated upstream of the bridge. Quays and jetties sprang up from the late first century, and an openwork timber landing stage 35 m long has been dated by dendrochronology to AD 69–91. Work on this scale was probably organised on an official basis and there is evidence of military involvement. The quays were backed by warehouses with streets running down to provide frequent access: for example, a block of six units was constructed to the west of Fish Street Hill after AD 95.

However, climate change had a major impact on this economically vibrant town. The first centuries AD were a period of cooling temperatures and increased rainfall. Globally, the average temperature dropped by about 1 °C, causing the polar icecaps to expand. Consequently, the sea level began to fall and continued to do so throughout the period, reaching perhaps 1.5 m below the present level. Depending upon local conditions, its effects were felt differently around the coast and even up the Thames to the tidal limit. In 1966, the waterlogged remains of two huts were uncovered lying directly on the foreshore in Syon Reach, near Brentford. Others, interpreted as fishing huts, had been found earlier. They date from a period of lowered water level: today their floors stand 70 cm below the mean water level.

During these centuries the river level constantly fell, so that high tide at London in the third century barely exceeded the first-century low-water mark. Depending on slope of foreshore, by the fourth century low water could have been up to 30–40 m from the earliest quay. This had a potentially catastrophic impact on the port facilities, as it became too shallow for vessels to dock, even at high water. As a result, successive new river frontages had to be constructed ever further into the channel simply to maintain an adequate depth of water: for example, at New Fresh Wharf a quay dated AD 235–244 stood 8.25 m in front of the second-century revetment. The transitory nature of these wharfs also dictated that they were built of timber rather than masonry. An unintended consequence was the reclamation of the foreshore.

At its height, the scale of wharf facilities in London was not simply the most developed in the province, but was unequalled in the Roman west. Yet from about AD 250 the wharf seems to have been in decline, and, as if to emphasise this, in AD 270 a riverside wall was erected, separating the town from the river. Trade was no longer the town's raison d'être; perhaps civil service bureaucracy had taken over.

At low-lying Southwark, on the opposite bank, the archaeology around the Roman bridgehead has either long been destroyed or is otherwise inaccessible for study. However, evidence for similar, if far less extensive, work is available. The many channels between the low islands were canalised and revetted. In one channel, an inlet which had been silting up was backfilled and a new waterfront created. Elsewhere, damp land was drained and reclaimed. Then in the late third century, in parallel with developments in London, the wharf facilities appear to have declined and the settlement contracted. As the waterfront ceased to be maintained, flood events increased.

Recent development-led excavation has gone some way to understanding what happened to the important trade. A thriving late Roman settlement has been discovered at Shadwell, on the north bank, over 2 km downriver of London. Previous occupation in this area had been insignificant, but the third century saw an energetic new settlement develop. Several substantial brick and masonry buildings were put up, including a public baths. The peak of Shadwell's boom has been dated to the century between AD 275 and 375, coinciding with the commercial decline of London. It is probably no coincidence that this began at about the same time that the riverside wall was erected at London. The explanation may be that falling river levels had become critical, encouraging entrepreneurs to create a new dock in a more favourable location. Some vessels may have chosen to unload even further downstream on the River Lea, which potentially offered onward river connections as far inland as St Albans and a link with the main Colchester road.

River transport was vital to the prosperity, not just of London, but to the province. The Thames must have been thronged with traffic, both with seagoing craft involved in overseas trade and with barges hauling produce to and from the hinterland. Several vessels of the period have been found buried in the silts of the river. The earliest is the Blackfriars ship, which sank in the mid-second century AD. At around 18.5 m long by 6.1 m wide, and with a hold beneath its plank deck, this ship had seagoing capabilities. When it sank it had been carrying a cargo of Kentish ragstone, building stone from the Maidstone area, but it was probably familiar with the coast of Gaul. A rather different vessel, known as the New Guy's House boat, had been abandoned in a creek near London Bridge in the late second century. This was a shallow, open barge at least 16 m long by 4.25 m wide, well suited for the Thames and its tributaries. Different again was the County Hall ship, found buried in river silts in 1910 during the building of County Hall. Its construction has been dated by dendrochronology to around AD 300. Unlike the other two examples, it was not designed to carry cargo and may have been the personal transport of a wealthy individual or an official. In addition, small river-fishing boats and rowing boats must have been as common as they were in later periods.

Communities and entrepreneurs throughout the length of the Thames valley depended on access to markets and on riverborne trade. By its very nature, much of this trade is invisible to archaeology; the few surviving hints can only represent the tip of the commercial iceberg. Settlements along the river may have maintained small landing facilities for their own needs, though this was not seen at Staines. Traces of occupation have been found beneath Reading; while this may simply represent one or more farmsteads, it has been suggested that Reading could have served as a port for the *civitas* capital of Silchester.

The villa economy of the Upper Thames was predicated on access to distant markets. The estate at Claydon Pike is thought to have specialised in hay production, as may other villa estates with extensive riverside meadows. Hay was a cash crop, essential for the military as well as for the stables of the urban population. The river would again be an ideal means of transport, whether upstream to Cirencester or downstream to London; and hay barges were a common sight as late as the nineteenth century. Another traditional raw material produced in the Cotswolds is wool. Like hay, it is bulky, and might also have been shipped to its buyers. Historically, firewood was an important raw material carried in bulk down the Thames to London from the slopes of the Chilterns, though at this period demand may still have been satisfied nearer at hand.

At the remote roadside settlement of Wantage, in the Vale of the White Horse not far from the Thames, the excavator interpreted a fourth-century stone building as a tower granary. An earlier timber building may also have been a granary. These may be merchants' warehouses where agricultural produce was collected for onward shipment to market. For bulk goods such as grain, the river would offer an obvious transport route. Glass, a luxury product, may also have been made there. If so, it must have been destined for sale in an urban market, and water would be a good way to carry such a fragile material. That the shells of *Ostrea edulis*, the native oyster, have been found far inland in such an out-of-the-way place as Wantage testifies to the extent of the trade network. Were oysters regularly shipped to the upper reaches of the Thames, or were these just a novelty brought back from a visit downriver to London?

Many communities produced at least some of their own everyday wares, but from the early third century the Oxford area became home to a pottery manufacturing industry of national importance.

No urban centre developed at Oxford; the industry was focused to the south of the modern city, around Headington, Cowley and Littlemore, between the Thames and the Dorchester–Alchester road. This afforded access to excellent bulk transport routes, especially towards London, and was one of the key reasons for the choice of location. Suitable clays and grit for *mortaria* (kitchen grinding bowls) were available locally. As it took between 4 cwts and 40 cwts of charcoal to fire a kiln, managed woodlands would be an obvious use for the steep slopes of the Chilterns.

A mixture of fine and coarser wares were manufactured, competing directly with the other major pottery producers nationally. From the mid-third century its fine wares were traded over a wide band across south-central England including London, and by the following century were reaching as far as East Anglia and penetrating into southern Wales. Unfortunately, little is known of the organisation or operation of the industry, though many skilled and unskilled people must have found work. A handful of potters' names are known from their stamps, but whether they were employees or owners is not certain. What is certain is that conditions here created an opportunity for a small number of people to generate wealth and turn a good profit.

The Other River

On a sunny day in spring the Thames can look idyllic. But those who live along its banks or earn their livelihood from its waters know it is a powerful river, unpredictable and capable of sudden, destructive floods. Rivers in Classical mythology carried a sombre association. The great river of the Underworld was the Styx. Coins are found with about 10 per cent of burials in Roman Britain, and are often interpreted as the fare to pay the ferryman, Charon, for the final journey. Rivers also had a long tradition of spiritual association in native British society with roots reaching back at least three millennia.

The site chosen for London was cut by two small rivers, the Walbrook and the Fleet, both tributaries of the Thames. They were tempting conduits for waste disposal and their waterlogged silt has proved a treasure trove for archaeologists. But perhaps the find which has attracted most attention is a collection of over fifty human skulls, most of which came from a short length of the Walbrook. A few other human bones, including jawbones, were found with them, suggesting that they were already 'defleshed' when they were deposited in the river. The vast majority were adult males, though they showed no sign of injury such as would be expected, for example, with execution. The context suggested a date before the second century. This was supported by the radiocarbon dating of a small sample, which fell in the broad range of 100 BC – AD 530.

These were certainly not burials: the law required that burial should take place outside towns. Neither does this conform to any formal Roman religious practice. However, the Empire was a cultural melting pot and evidence is frequently found for the persistence of a diversity of regional traditions, beliefs and superstitions among its subject peoples. So, given the long tradition in Britain of depositing precious objects and disposing of the dead in rivers, could these skulls be offerings to the gods? Do they give a glimpse of the persistence of a cult of the human head among a sector of the native population, related perhaps to that which was seen in the Thames in the later Bronze Age? If so, many similar deposits must remain unrecognised, due in part to the difficulty of dating. For some, at least, the river remained sacred.

Other items may have deliberately been deposited in the river at this time, among them a collection of pewter plates recovered near Shepperton Ranges. Other objects from the same length of the river included pottery and a chisel. These might represent another kind of ritual deposit.

Every town and most smaller settlements had their temples, and wayside shrines would have been a common sight. Two fragments of relief sculpture suggest the presence of a temple or shrine in the small roadside settlement of Gill Mill, near Ducklington, at a crossing point of the River Windrush. An altar to a 'Genius' recovered from the Thames at Bablock Hythe and another to 'Fortuna', ploughed up near Bampton, are further examples.

In addition, several temple sites in the countryside seem to have built upon native beliefs and religious sites. A settlement of some 30 hectares developed around the significant religious complex at Frilford, near Abingdon, with its Romano-Celtic temple and amphitheatre – the term 'Romano-Celtic' recognising a fusion of Classical Roman and native religious belief and practice. This style of building is seen widely across southern England. The temple itself is a square *cella* surrounded by a portico, with three rooms attached to the rear and a fourth on the north-east corner. It stood within a large walled compound known as a *temenos*, and a walled path linked the temple to the *temenos* entrance. What may be a plastered altar base and associated midden were sited inside the entrance, and within the compound to the south of the temple stood a rotunda (a circular building of uncertain function). Outside the gate was a complex of rooms, which may have had a ceremonial use or else been workshops for votive offerings. A form of amphitheatre and other substantial buildings completed the complex. Its obvious and enduring affluence, with votive offerings spanning the first to fourth centuries, argues that worshippers must have been drawn, not just from the surrounding communities, but from a wider catchment. It is not known which divinity was worshipped here, although the site's recent excavators have suggested that the rites involved water.

A rectangular enclosure measuring 45 m by 60 m stands on Lowbury Hill on the Downs south of Blewbury. The enclosure is interpreted as a *temenos* and was originally walled, although the masonry has long since been robbed. Roof tiles suggest that it originally contained at least one building, assumed to be a Romano-Celtic temple. Over 1,000 coins together with other items of copper alloy – brooches, rings, bracelets, etc. – and glass beads are convincingly explained as votive offerings. The coins, jewellery and pottery confirm that the site was in use from the late first century AD, with activity tailing off in the fourth century. Glass vessels, ceramic dishes and animal bones (particularly sheep) suggest ceremonial feasting. Although much smaller than Frilford, this site retained its faithful throughout the Roman period.

Another rural temple site, on Weycock Hill in the Middle Thames, spread over 14 hectares. It consisted of an octagonal temple set within a precinct and a substantial settlement a short distance away, with a cemetery beyond that. Activity is dated between the second and fourth centuries.

Two ivories came from a possible temple excavated in Greenwich Park in 1902. One piece formed part of a scabbard slide; the other was part of a carved plaque decorated with a female bust holding a floral shield over her head. True elephant ivory is rare, making this a potentially significant find.

A major temple complex developed at Springhead (*Vagniacis*) on the Ebbsfleet in Kent. Its location on Watling Street made it a prime site. The cult was centred on the springs, and a small settlement grew up to service the visitors. The building sequence at the sanctuary began around AD 140, though that does not rule out earlier ritual associations for the landscape. A large quantity of metalwork offerings – coins, brooches, part of a lead plaque depicting a dolphin – have been recovered from the Ebbsfleet. Outside the sanctuary complex, twenty-three dogs, a cow, other animal skulls, a human skull and some pottery had been placed in a pit about 4.5 m deep: this also looks like a ritual act.

The Failing Empire

The towns of Roman Britain were initially built without defences, reflecting the peace and stability the province enjoyed. This changed in the later second century when many were surrounded by ramparts of earth. A date of around AD 185 is proposed for the earthen rampart at Dorchester, while at the important *civitas* capital of Silchester defences were erected a decade or two earlier. This development must have been triggered by the unsettled political conditions within the wider Empire. Then, in the early third century, many towns replaced their simple defences with stone walls, and the following century many were upgraded to include towers and bastions to provide platforms for artillery. Yet despite the appearance of insecurity, Britain remained a prosperous province and the fourth century has been described as a golden age. In step with this province-wide pattern, London was encircled by a 3 km-long defensive wall between AD 190 and 220, with the riverside wall added after AD 270.

The final years of the third century were a time of crisis throughout the Empire as ambitious military commanders challenged the power of the emperor. Often frontier defences were weakened as men were drawn off to bolster these claims. In the West, the frontiers of Empire which had been bulwarks for a century or more were threatened by barbarian raiders from Germany and Scandinavia. Their purpose at this date was largely to pillage rather than to conquer. For Britain, the south-eastern coast was exposed and the Thames estuary was a vulnerable route offering direct access to the heart of the province: this became known as the 'Saxon Shore' and strategies were developed to defend it. It was at this date that the riverside wall was put up at London.

One policy pursued elsewhere in the Empire was to settle groups of barbarians inside the boundary in order to provide a buffer. The expectation was that they would join with the regular army to defend their possessions against encroachment. The name 'Saxon Shore' may therefore have referred to a place where Saxons were settled as much as to a coastline they threatened. The other strand of the strategy was organisational. The new office of 'Count of the Saxon Shore' was created before AD 367 to command and co-ordinate the defence of this length of the coast. His authority combined a line of existing and new forts extending from the north Norfolk coast to Portsmouth, with the navy, the *Classis Britannica*.

Richborough was the traditional 'gateway' to the province and had been an important military supply depot since the first century. The fort at Dover had served as the headquarters for the *Classis Britannica*, though a new fort was built alongside the harbour in the third century. An inscription at Reculver, on the north Kent coast and guarding the Thames estuary, suggests a construction date in the early third century. Brancaster and Burgh Castle in Norfolk may date from the middle of the century, while Walton Castle (Felixstowe, Suffolk), Bradwell-on-Sea (Essex), Lympne (Kent), Pevensey (Sussex) and Portchester (in Portsmouth harbour) all originated later in the century. Portchester, the westernmost fort, was already abandoned by AD 370, probably due to the harbour silting up. These forts were built right on the coast, presumably as an integrated unit with a naval harbour; all apart from Brancaster, Dover and Portchester have suffered erosion by the sea in the intervening centuries, while Walton Castle disappeared over the cliff in the eighteenth century.

The end, when it came, was unexpected. In the late fourth and early fifth centuries the Roman Empire was in turmoil from civil war within and barbarian incursions without. In AD 410 the Emperor Honorius turned down an appeal for military help against Saxon raiders, advising the province to look to its own defence – effectively drawing a line under 350 years of imperial rule. Honorius had more pressing concerns as the city of Rome itself was threatened by barbarians and was briefly occupied that same year. With the loss of money to pay the army and the decline of trade with the Continent, Britannia faced political, economic and social collapse. Within a remarkably short time, coinage ceased to circulate, markets collapsed and Roman-style goods ceased to be produced. Administration, now fully in local hands, quickly broke down into small units which were increasingly parochial and self-sufficient in their outlook. The centuries of Rome were over; England was not yet dreamed of – and nature abhors a vacuum.

5

The Harried River

The Struggle for Anglo-Saxon England

Warriors and Princes

In AD 410 when the Empire finally abandoned the old province of Britannia, there was no rejoicing. After 350 years of rule the tribal past was a dim memory, at least in the South. The people had come to regard themselves as Romans, and for 200 years all freeborn Britons had been citizens. So when central authority was withdrawn, local leaders tried to preserve the status quo by establishing their own states along Roman lines and often exploiting the well-established *civitates* structure. One such was Ambrosius Aurelianus, whose parents had 'worn the purple', though precisely where or when he was active remains uncertain.[1] Another petty kingdom, which drew the ire of the monk Gildas in his book *The Ruin of Britain* (compiled around AD 540), was Dumnonia, based on the former *civitas* of the Dumnonii in the South West.[2]

There is some evidence that the earlier policy of using Germanic and Scandinavian mercenaries was continued. Burial continued into the fifth century in two cemeteries associated with the small town of Dorchester. Perhaps this walled town formed a strongpoint for an ambitious noble who set himself up as ruler of a small territory with the support of foreign mercenaries? Elsewhere, Roman military equipment and other Saxon decorative items from a fifth-century cemetery at Shoebury on the northern shore of the estuary may mark the graves of Germanic mercenaries.

In the new states along the east coast, security became an

ever-higher priority as pirate raids increased: Gildas calls them 'greedy wolves, rabid with extreme hunger'.[3] The Anglo-Saxon Chronicle records that as early as AD 443 Vortigern, a ruler in Kent (Gildas calls him a 'tyrant'), invited the Angles to defend his land, granting them the Isle of Thanet.[4] With the clarity of hindsight tinged with prophetic zeal, Gildas spoke of the folly of fighting fire with fire. The first wave arrived in only three boats, landing at Ebbsfleet; but they were followed by a larger force. Almost inevitably, they turned on their employers, and in AD 455 the Angles defeated Vortigern and their leader Hengest seized the kingdom.

This was a dynamic, chaotic time. As the former province fragmented, many small political units emerged around war bands, coalescing, breaking up and reforming. Although these were independent, they acknowledged a hierarchy of more powerful rulers as overlords. This pattern fluctuated with the changing circumstances of the moment, though some strong warrior-leaders managed to impress their will for longer periods: King Aethelberht of Kent, a direct descendant of Hengist (and through him of the god Woden – these genealogies are not always reliable) was recognised as overlord of Britain south of the Humber from AD 560 to 616.

A remarkable document known as the Tribal Hidage lists thirty-three kingdoms and sub-kingdoms in south and central England in the mid-seventh century. It may have been compiled for Wulfhere, King of Mercia (ruled AD 658–675) and overlord of the lands south of the Humber, in order to assess tribute. The size of each unit is given in hides, a hide being 120 acres. And the difference in sizes between units is striking. It begins with Mercia and the East Angles, each at 30,000 hides. Next, the Cantwarena of Kent are given as 15,000 hides; six units measure 7,000 hides; four measure between 5,000–2,000 hides; twenty fall into the range 1,200–1,300 hides. Anomalously, the West Saxons (i.e. Wessex) are given as many as 100,000 hides; perhaps a later figure reflecting a shift in power?

These units were not all political equals or 'sovereign', but formed a nested hierarchy climaxing with 'overlord of the lands south of the Humber'. Many of the smaller units are not known to have had 'kings' but are referred to as 'peoples'; for example the Cilternsaete or people of the Chilterns had 4,000 hides.

The names of several 'people' or kinship groups are preserved in modern place names: the Garinges or 'Gara's people' at Goring, the Readingas or 'Reada's people' at Reading, the Sunningas or 'Sunna's people' at Sonning, while Teddington is 'the hill of Tudda's people'. By the close of the seventh century many of the smaller units had disappeared, absorbed into the larger political units which were consolidating and expanding; their kings and sub-kings had become ealdormen or else their royal lines had died out. Four main Saxon kingdoms emerged from the confusion: East Anglia, Mercia, Northumbria and Wessex.

One outstanding example of territorial growth by a vigorously active 'people' or kinship group was centred on the Upper Thames. By the sixth century the dominant group in the region were the Gewisse, absorbing other kinship groups under their control. By a mixture of conquest, alliance and patronage, they were to become a dominant force in English politics. According to the Anglo-Saxon Chronicle, in AD 560 Caewlin succeeded to the kingdom of Wessex, while in AD 571 Cuthwulf fought the Britons (i.e. native non-Saxon kingdoms) and captured the vills of Limbury, Aylesbury, Benson and Eynsham, the latter two in the Upper Thames. So by this date the writ of the Gweisse royal line extended from the Upper Thames into the future Wessex heartland of Wiltshire. From them came the Wessex royal house.

Another dominant kingdom that emerged at this time was Mercia in the West Midlands. From around AD 630 under their strong king Penda, Mercia pursued a vigorously expansionist policy. The kingdom of the Hwicce, in the Gloucestershire Cotswolds and Severn Valley, formed an alliance with Mercia against Wessex. By AD 661 Penda's son Wulfhere had taken the Upper Thames and was harrying over the Berkshire Downs. The balance of power between these two kingdoms tipped back and forth, though Mercia generally held the upper hand until the ninth century. The great Mercian king Offa (AD 757–96) controlled the Thames to London and extended his authority south of the river into Kent, Surrey and Sussex. For example, in AD 780 Offa's Council met at Brentford, while royal or ecclesiastical councils met at least eleven times at Chelsea between AD 785 and 815. In AD 825 King Ecgberht of Wessex decisively defeated Beornwulf of Mercia at Ellendun. He immediately sent a large army to the east, driving out the Mercian ruler Baldred from Kent and establishing his hold on Essex and on everything south of the Thames.

A number of seventh-century 'princely burials' have been claimed in the Thames valley, marked by prominent earthen mounds. Containing fine, high-status objects, they may represent the final resting places of the last sub-kings. During groundworks at the Bishop of Oxford's palace at Cuddesdon in 1847, two swords, a pair of blue glass bowls, a bronze bucket and a fragment of gilt bronze set with garnets were recovered in association with some skeletons. This was almost certainly a burial within a mound, and the quality of the items provoked the adjective 'princely'. Another rich burial was discovered in 1882 beneath the prominent mound at Taplow.

Both these burials were eclipsed by a remarkable tomb discovered recently at Prittlewell (Southend-on-Sea, Essex). This looks like the burial of a senior member of the East Saxon royal house, though no bone survived in the acid soil. A 4 m square chamber, originally beneath a mound, was lined and roofed with planks. Among more than 100 objects were a gold buckle of Continental design, two tiny crosses of gold foil, a Byzantine silver spoon, bronze hanging bowls, a 'Coptic' copper alloy bowl, a flagon of Eastern Mediterranean type, five wooden drinking vessels with gilded copper alloy or silver rim mounts, two drinking horns, gaming pieces, a wooden lyre, a painted box, a shield, and a folding iron stool. Burial took place in the first half of the seventh century, and the splendid grave goods are second only to the ship burial at Sutton Hoo. Also in Essex, a grave chamber at Broomfield contained, among other items, a sword, spear, knife and shield boss, a buckle plate of gold with cloisonné garnets, a gold and garnet-set pyramid from a scabbard or strap, a pair of glass vessels, a bronze basin, two wooden cups with gilt-bronze rims, two drinking horns, two wooden buckets with iron mounts, and an iron bowl on a stand. A large mass of woollen and linen fabric was identified. Although not as spectacular as the Prittlewell burial, it was nonetheless an outstanding collection.

Several 'palace' sites have also been explored. At this date the art of building in masonry had been forgotten; these were large timber halls forming part of a complex – similar, perhaps, to the Scandinavian royal halls or 'mead halls' described in the epic poem *Beowulf*. Five buildings laid out in an L-shape were seen in 1962 on aerial photographs near Sutton Courtenay in the Upper Thames; the largest measured 25 m by 8 m, another 16 m by 6 m. A contemporary cemetery excavated nearby produced burials accompanied by rich jewellery. A similar series of cropmarks was identified at Long Wittenham, just 4.5 km downriver. They compare well with two excavated sites, at Cowdrey's Down near Basingstoke, and at Chalton, both in Hampshire and dated from the late sixth to the early seventh centuries. Benson was noted later as a large royal estate, so might represent another such Thames site. Were these centres for the Gewisse royal entourage as they moved around their territory, or perhaps, one level down, for leaders of kin groups incorporated by the Gewisse? It has been suggested that the former town of Dorchester, in the heart of this region, may have been a political centre in the seventh century, which would help to explain its choice as the centre for St Birinius's missionary activity. It would not be surprising if the hillfort at Taplow, adjacent to the 'princely' burial mound, was another high-status 'palace' site. There may have been a royal palace at Old Windsor from as early as the eighth century. It continued to be used to the time of Edward the Confessor, and although William the Conqueror built a castle at the nearby New Windsor, the royal court continued to be convened at Old Windsor until 1107.

At different times the Thames may have served as a boundary, first between 'people', then between larger units. However, from their earliest years the Gewisse consolidated their power around the Upper Thames, which flowed through their province. Then, during the Mercian ascendancy the line of the Downs and Chilterns may have proved the more natural frontier. Further east, the river was at different times the boundary between the expanding powers of Mercia and Wessex, while the broad tidal estuary separated the East Angles from the men of Kent until both fell under the control of greater powers. In very different political circumstances, Cnut held an assembly at Oxford in 1018 which, in exchange for tribute of £72,000 plus a further £11,000 from London, set the Thames as the boundary between Danish and Saxon law and custom.

Danish Raids

Two centuries of competition and rivalry between the Saxon kingdoms was suddenly overshadowed as a new scourge from Scandinavia took hold of Britain. In AD 835 the Anglo-Saxon Chronicle reported the first Danish raiders with the ominous words, 'In this year the heathen devastated Sheppey.' Over the next thirty years they repeatedly struck from Cornwall to Northumbria. What began as a localised pirate threat, the raiders interested only in pillaging then disappearing, quickly escalated to engulf the whole country. In the terms of the Chronicle, their 'army' became a 'host', able to strike at will. In AD 851 a force of 350 ships stormed Canterbury and London, routing the Mercian army. Twice, in AD 850 and AD 854, the Danish army wintered in England, at Thanet and Sheppey. The Chronicle appears to show the English trying to continue as far as possible with normal life, but fear must have been rife. Ordinary people could do nothing but farm and hope. The levies were often called out, but the repeated references to great slaughter show that untrained men were no match for the raiders.

A critical change in the nature of the Danish threat came about in AD 865. In the autumn of that year a great army landed in East Anglia, prepared to stay for several years and drain the country. The English alternately fought and made peace – which meant buying off the great army, but only briefly. In AD 870 the great army was back in the field, establishing a fortified base at Reading from which to harry Wessex. The men of Wessex won the first round at Englefield. Four days later King Aethelred and his brother Alfred (later the Great) led the levies to Reading where they lost a bloody battle. In just another four days, the Danish host faced the men of Wessex on the Downs at Ashdown when Alfred took command and won a notable victory, earning a temporary respite.

Following the check at the hands of Alfred, the great army took winter quarters in London in AD 871. The following summer they campaigned in Northumberland. The Danes had changed their plans and were now intending to settle in England; part of the army occupied Yorkshire, while Mercia was partitioned, with half designated as Danish lands. Late in AD 875 the depleted Danish army turned its eyes back towards Wessex. Three years later they occupied Chippenham and had considerable success against King Alfred who withdrew to the Isle of Athelney. After he had rebuilt his strength, he defeated the Danes decisively near Chippenham. As part of the treaty that ended the Danish aggression against Wessex, their leader, King Guthrum, was baptised as a Christian. This treaty defined the Thames as their common boundary for much of its length, though the Upper Thames remained in Mercian hands.

The Thames remained a vulnerable route into the core of Wessex. No sooner was the Danish army nullified than another band of Viking raiders sailed upriver to Fulham, moving on to the Low Countries the following year. Then in AD 885, Rochester was besieged by Vikings until Alfred relieved the town. The following year, in order to strengthen his frontier with East Anglia, Alfred captured and re-fortified London. By the close of the ninth century Wessex had consolidated its control over all the lands south of the Thames and the former East Saxon kingdom. However, intermittent raids against Kent and into the Thames estuary were a constant threat throughout the following century.

Part of Alfred's response to this latest threat was to establish a series of fortified places. The document known as the Burghal Hidage, which dates to between AD 880 and AD 919, is usually understood as a record of the system established by Alfred to defend the frontiers of Wessex against the Vikings. Some of the *burhs* on this list were created by Alfred simply as fortified places, for example Sashes. Others were fully urban and existed before the Viking threat emerged, so the document cannot necessarily be taken as giving a date of foundation. The responsibility for maintaining and manning these forts was laid on the local communities, and the number of hides allocated to this task reflects the size of the defensive circuit at a rate of one person per hide. The section of the list relating to the Thames is given below:

Cricklade: 1,400 hides
Oxford: 1,500 hides
Wallingford: 2,400 hides (where Alfred's defensive circuit survives)
Sashes (an island in the Thames at Cookham): 1,000 hides
Southwark: 1,800 hides

A new Danish menace burst on England in the late tenth century. At first these were hit-and-run raiders, but eventually the whole length of the coast was at their mercy. As the raiders became more organised, the government tried to buy them off with Danegeld, for which a special tax had to be raised. With growing confidence, the raiders boldly sailed up rivers and their army harried widely into the heart of Wessex – they even maintained a storage depot at Reading! Year after year the Anglo-Saxon Chronicle records indiscriminate slaughter from one end of the Thames to the other; the Saxon kings and their people were helpless. Oxford was sacked in 1009, and again in 1010 and 1013. Wallingford, another of Alfred's *burhs*, was burned in 1006. Kent was particularly vulnerable, and in 1012 a huge Danegeld was paid as the price of the army's departure. Before they left, Archbishop Aelfheah (better known as St Alphege) was killed at Greenwich because his personal ransom was not forthcoming.

The wealthy port of London was an obvious target for the raiders; it was also King Aethelred's stronghold. During the siege of 1014 Olaf, King of Norway, attached cables to his ships and pulled down the wooden London Bridge. In 1016 Cnut again besieged London. The ruined bridge would have formed a formidable obstacle to his ships, so he laboriously cut a great channel around the southern bridgehead and hauled his ships to the upstream side. The town itself was surrounded with an earthwork, but the population withstood the siege. King Edmund raised the levies and marched to London, crossing the river at Brentford, and drove off the Danish host. He then pursued the host to Kent where they found shelter on Sheppey. Later that year the citizens of London bought peace and the Danes wintered at London. In November Edmund died (he had been ill throughout the recent campaign), and the following year Cnut became king of the whole realm of England. Cnut's dynasty lasted for only twenty-five years. On the death of his son Harthacnute, Edward (the Confessor), son of the Saxon King Aethelred (the Unready) and brother to Edmund (Ironside), was consecrated king.

Town and Country

For the first 350 years following the withdrawal of Rome, there were no towns in Britain; without their functions for administration and trade they no longer served a purpose. This was a land of rural communities, of farmers and fishermen living in small villages and scattered farms. The landscape was less ordered than it had been previously, with common fields and huge expanses of waste, peppered with the decaying remains of the forgotten Roman way of life. The towns were abandoned and even the techniques of building in stone and brick were forgotten. As buildings began to need repair, they were simply left to collapse. A remarkable eighth-century Anglo-Saxon poem, 'The Ruin', describes the lack of comprehension as a man wanders through an empty town, possibly Bath.[5] The 'stonesmiths' (also, but probably poetically, referred to as 'giants') and their way of life have been dead for generations and their work 'moulders'. It was as if the Roman centuries had never happened.

However, the people were not simply rural hicks. Cultural contacts and trade reached into Europe, and southern British kings made treaties and marriage alliances with their Continental peers. The rich grave goods from a burial such as Sutton Hoo (Suffolk) or the items found in the Staffordshire Hoard demonstrate the existence of highly skilled craftsmen and wealthy and discerning patrons.

Some Roman towns appear to have been partially reoccupied as early as the end of the sixth century, though civic life would have been unrecognisable. In AD 597 Augustine and his mission were granted a plot of land within Canterbury and use of the church of St Martin which was described as being outside the town, though the early Saxon settlement would have been a far cry from the predecessor whose remains it reused. The cathedral at Rochester may also have gathered a settlement around it within the Roman walls. Dorchester may be another rare example, again linked to a religious centre. Several timber halls were built among the ruins during the seventh to ninth centuries, and some sixth-century sunken-floored buildings were also discovered. However, at London the cathedral was built inside the Roman city while the main settlement grew up outside. It was not until Alfred refortified the town that it was reoccupied. Although these were not towns by any Classical measure, their rough appearance belies their importance.

Eynsham was mentioned in AD 571 as being one of four vills taken by Cuthwulf after his victor at Biedcanford: it was clearly an important place – size and grand architecture were no measure. Excavation identified a small group of sixth-century buildings, perhaps those seized by Cuthwulf. A monastic community seems to have been established in the ninth century, and occupation continued beyond the Norman Conquest. A few kilometres to the east, a number of fifth- to seventh-century settlements have been explored on the gravel terrace around Yarnton. Typically consisting of sunken-floored buildings together with a few post-built structures, they are dispersed rather than strongly nucleated settlements with little sign of order or planning. A little further downriver at Barrow Fields, Radley, a fifth- to sixth-century settlement of sunken-floored and post-built structures occupied the open space at the southern end of the Bronze Age barrow cemetery. At the same time, squatters moved into the ruins of the villa complex at Barton Court Farm.

A small quantity of sixth- to seventh-century pottery is the limit of evidence for early–middle Saxon occupation around the crossing point at Staines. Even for the late Saxon period, activity is slight, amounting to just a few pits and ditches on Binbury Island. From at least the eighth century the gravel islands among the braided channels of the Thames at Kingston were settled and farmed. Further downstream at Ham, a rare early Saxon site consisted of one and possibly more sunken-featured buildings. Another early Saxon sunken-featured building was seen at Brentford, where the Museum of London lists seventy-four early Saxon spearheads and other weapons as coming from the river. The quantity and nature of these finds strongly suggest this was more than a small rural settlement. Later, in the eighth century, three important councils were held at Brentford, so a lost high-status site must be assumed. Early Saxon settlements with sunken-featured buildings were examined at Mortlake, close to the river at Hammersmith, and at Tulse Hill where the site was located beside the River Effra, a tributary of the Thames. Excavations in Harmondsworth in advance of development at Heathrow Airport identified evidence for a pattern of fifth- to seventh-century rural settlement. In AD 781 the area was part of a large estate granted by Offa of Mercia to his minister Aeldred.

Rural occupation from the middle Saxon period is less well known. A probable farm stood beside the River Tyburn on the former Treasury site in Whitehall, its timber floor preserved by waterlogging. Another was seen under the National Portrait Gallery, Trafalgar Square, where two personal names, 'Tatberht' on one side and '—dric' on the other, were scratched in runes onto a sheep's vertebra. A post-built structure in Chelsea was dated to the mid-seventh to mid-eighth century, while a hearth, corn drier and possible fence lines at Feltham were seventh-century. At Althorpe Grove, Battersea, a small settlement was established in the late seventh to late eighth century on a former eyot surrounded by marsh and mudflats: in AD 693 land in this area was granted to Barking Abbey.

An apparently extensive and long-term settlement has been investigated at Mucking on the gravel terrace overlooking the Thames in Essex. Excavation distinguished three phases of occupation spanning the fifth to seventh centuries, with the latest datable finds suggesting it was abandoned by AD 685. In total, 203 sunken floored buildings, fifty-three post-built structures and two cemeteries were discovered. Despite appearances, the excavator suggested that this was a small settlement with an average population of less than 100 people, the large number of buildings best being explained as the result of several small farmsteads being rebuilt on new sites each generation. Frankish pottery and items of jewellery point to a link with long-distance trade networks, even at such an apparently ordinary site. The missionary bishop St Cedd preached to the East Saxons, founding several monasteries in Essex including one at Tilbury in AD 653. Even if there was no settlement there already, one would quickly have sprung up.

Many of the towns that line the banks of the Thames are first seen in the later Saxon period, reflecting widespread social and economic developments. Some may have their origins in the slow re-emergence of craft industries and regional trade; others grew around religious foundations; still others were military in purpose. Small rural settlements have been identified on the gravel terraces around Oxford, but there is little evidence for occupation within the urban core before it was created a fortified *burh* by Alfred. However, if St Frideswide's monastery was founded here in the late seventh century, some form of associated settlement seems probable at that date. A stone causeway has been seen by archaeologists on the line of St Aldate's street which may have joined the islands in the river to create a secure crossing; and this appears to have been superseded in the ninth century by a wooden bridge. If so, Alfred chose a well-established settlement and market as the site for his *burh*.

Another of Alfred's circle of strongpoints was Wallingford. This was a greenfield site, though its growth was rapid and it soon acquired a mint. By the late eighth century Cookham emerged as a local centre with a minster, and was probably the site of a *wic* or riverside market. However, when Alfred established a system of strongpoints in the final years of the ninth century to defend Wessex against the Viking threat, he chose to fortify the more defensible island of Sashes half a mile upstream rather than the settlement of Cookham. Old Windsor was the site of a palace of Edward the Confessor, and excavations suggest that the palace and its associated settlement were established by AD 800. Kingston may also have been a royal estate, becoming a powerful political and ecclesiastical centre where a number of Saxon kings were crowned during the tenth century.

Small local trading settlements may have developed along the tidal river, such as at Southwark and Woolwich. Rochester was an ecclesiastical centre and had urban characteristics by this period. Having a bishop, and being on an important crossing point on the Medway, the town was well positioned to develop as a trading centre. When the settlement was besieged by Vikings in AD 885, the townsfolk sheltered behind the old Roman walls until Alfred lifted the siege.

Always a special case, it took archaeologists many years to find the middle Saxon London that was mentioned in historical sources. Ipswich, Southampton (Hamwic) and York were the three other major international ports of middle Saxon England, serving the kingdoms of East Anglia, Wessex and Northumbria respectively. In common with other towns, London was abandoned soon after the Roman withdrawal. Activity moved outside the walls to the west, and by the mid-seventh century it was confined to a small area beside a Roman road, roughly the line of The Strand, which may have been a riverside marketplace. This was the port of Lundenwic, a name first seen in the AD 680s – the ending 'wic' referring to a riverside trading point. However, its importance far outweighed its physical presence. Despite its simple facilities, it was a major centre for seaborne and Continental trade. Bede (writing in the AD 730s) described it as 'a mart of many nations';[6] archaeological and documentary evidence suggests that its strongest links were with Francia and Frisia (the Low Countries). To the landlocked kingdom of Mercia, Lundenwic represented an essential commercial link, while King Offa (AD 757–96) was particularly concerned to promote trade, making commercial treaties with the great Charlemagne.

As early as the AD 670s London's character as a port was mentioned incidentally in the text of a Chertsey charter. A late seventh-century Kentish law code of the kings Hlothhere and Eadric refers to a royal official, the *wic-gerefa*, based in London, who collected tolls on vessels passing through Kentish waters.

The port facilities combined hard standing with a simple embankment, and archaeology has revealed a piecemeal variety of construction methods rather than one single scheme. Excavations at York Buildings found a plank-and-stake structure dated by dendrochronology to AD 679. Brushwood had been laid behind this to form an embankment 17 m wide. Worked wood from a neighbouring site suggests this embankment – probably for unloading boats – could have extended for over 150 m along the foreshore. Observations during piling at 14 Buckingham Street identified late seventh- to mid-ninth-century foreshore deposits and possibly part of the waterfront embankment. A range of crafts and industries included metalworking and smithing, textile manufacture, antler, bone and horn working, tanning and leather working, comb making, glassmaking and woodworking, and a mint was established.

Over the next 100 years the settlement grew considerably to cover an area of perhaps 60 hectares extending from Trafalgar Square to Aldwych. Any estimate of population must inevitably make a lot of assumptions, but for the mid-eighth century an estimate of 5,000 to 10,000 is plausible, compared with only 2,000 to 3,000 for contemporary Hamwic (Southampton). This compares with around 25,000 to 30,000 for Roman London at its peak in the early second century. The decayed, almost certainly collapsed, London Bridge was clearly not necessary to Lundenwic's success: it was probably only rebuilt as part of Alfred's re-founding of the town in the late ninth century. Travellers may have preferred to cross directly opposite the *wic* where the river was probably fordable, though rising river levels would have made it increasingly treacherous.

Although the trading settlement of Lundenwic focused along The Strand, the Roman town retained a symbolic value and was not entirely deserted. The East Saxon King Raedwald founded the cathedral church of St Paul the Apostle in AD 604, soon after his conversion, probably on the site of the present St Paul's. That first church may well have been wooden, though it could equally have been formed out of the ruins of a major Roman building. A bishop's house probably stood nearby, and there are also references to a monastery and a king's hall. At the least, then, the walled area may have served ecclesiastical and administrative functions.

The population of Lundenwic may have been encouraged to retreat behind the relative security of the derelict Roman walls in the face of renewed Danish raids in the mid-ninth century. The archaeological evidence points to a contraction in activity at Lundenwic at this time, though not its abandonment: the facilities for beaching ships may have been too valuable to lose. A clear change in London's fortunes followed Alfred's capture and re-fortification of the walled town in AD 886. As part of his re-founding, a harbour was created at Queenhithe, initially named Ethelred's hithe after Alfred's vice-regent in London. Land on either side of Bread Street Hill, just behind Queenhithe, was granted to the Archbishop of Canterbury and the Bishop of Worcester respectively, entitling them to hold markets and moor ships. The charter mentions a trading shore – *ripa emptoralis* – implying that trading was direct from vessels beached on foreshore. Activity of this sort would require next to no facilities.

The bridge was rebuilt at this time. The old road would have led down to the river bank on either shore, and the ruined brick or masonry piers of the late Roman bridge may still have been visible above the water. Consequently, the new bridge most probably followed the course of its predecessor, perhaps just adding a new timber superstructure. To an astute tactician such as Alfred, a bridge had military as well as a commercial value: it could be defended, preventing the enemy's ships from sailing upriver.

Alfred's harbour at Queenhithe was on the upriver side of the bridge, making it less convenient for larger seagoing vessels, but by the late tenth century riverside facilities were being developed elsewhere along the London waterfront. A haven at Billingsgate is first mentioned in a law code dated around 1000. A little upriver, a rubble embankment was heaped against the surviving Roman timbers which still protruded from the riverbed. To the west of this, a jetty and landing stage measuring 13 m by 7.5 m wide was built out over the river on timber posts. The shallow vessels of the time would have rested on the hard standing around the jetty which facilitated the handling of cargoes. Access must have been made through the Roman wall at this point, either a breach or a formal opening; the medieval alley of Rothersgate later perpetuated this line. Soon the waterfront between Billingsgate and the bridge was embanked to provide wharfage, while German and French merchants were granted special rights at Dowgate, perhaps another trading shore.

London's imports included glassware, lava querns from the Rhineland and pottery from Northern France and the Rhine. Yet despite its international reputation, much of its trade at this period was upriver. As a marker of this, London's pottery in the late ninth and tenth centuries was mostly produced in Oxfordshire, while imported wares represented about 10 per cent by weight. As a measure of the importance of this trade, cuts or canals were made to bypass difficult sections. Around 1052, at the request of the men of Oxford, Abingdon Abbey dug a navigation channel known as Swift Ditch to avoid the loop past the town. The abbey collected tolls on this quicker route, which incidentally created Andersey Island.

Many riverside settlements may have supported their local

wics; these would leave little trace in the archaeological record however – some hard standing, a few temporary stalls and little else. One more significant place may be Dorney, where its situation on the border between Mercia and Wessex may have offered additional commercial possibilities. A long-running programme of excavation allowed a large area to be studied. Activity spanned the period from AD 700 to 900, and finds consisted largely of pits and industrial waste – smithing, copper alloy, textiles, carpentry. Imported material included quernstones of Niedermendig lava from the Rhine, glass and pottery – Ipswich ware (which may represent containers for other produce), Tating ware and North French wares – though the excavators note that imported ware made up only 3 per cent of the total compared with nearer 10 per cent in Lundenwic.

A number of smaller and possibly less regulated *wics* which linked into the wider trading network of north-west Europe may have developed around the Thames estuary, often associated with minsters or monastic sites. These could include Tilbury, Minster-in-Sheppey and Reculver. Beyond the estuary, Richborough, Fordwich and Sandwich may also have tapped this trade.

The range and type of vessel used on the Thames and its tributaries was considerable. Seagoing cargo ships combining sails and oars were capable of navigating from the stormy Norwegian waters to the Mediterranean. At the bottom of the scale, a number of traditional log boats have been recorded, a few of which have been dated to the Saxon centuries.

Fragments of several late Saxon vessels have been found in the estuary. A scatter of timbers at New Fresh Wharf in the City were part of a clinker-built boat. This seagoing, shallow-drafted, open rowing boat was of a style known from the southern Baltic, and dendrochronology places its construction around AD 920–955. It lay on the Saxon foreshore, presumably where it was abandoned. Another seagoing vessel of similar date was discovered in the Graveney Marshes during a drainage scheme. Also clinker-built and with a mast, it was 14 m long by 3.9 m wide and could carry a cargo of 7 tons. Timbers from other boats were reused in the waterfront embankment at Billingsgate.

The Thames was a valuable economic resource for the

communities along its bank in other ways. Early and middle Saxon fish traps have been recorded at Putney, Barn Elms Chelsea, Isleworth and Shepperton. Others are known from the Blackwater Estuary in Essex and elsewhere. These are ephemeral structures and must have been a common sight along the river. They consist of V-shaped settings of stakes woven with wattle work, funnelling the fish into a net. On the non-tidal river, fishermen would wade or perhaps row out to check their catch. A small excavation in the basement of a building in Earlham Street, Westminster, located the former channel of the 'Cock and Pye Ditch', one of several small streams which flowed into the Thames. A scatter of timber stakes at the base of the alluvium that covered the stream bed were interpreted as a middle Saxon fish or eel trap which had collapsed.

Religious Melting Pot

In the late Roman period the Empire was a melting pot of cultures and religions, and Britain was no different. Although Christianity was at certain times the official religion, the old Roman gods and their temple worship were never abandoned, while it is unclear how far either of those systems had penetrated the rural population (known as *pagani*, rustics). In the years of upheaval that followed, both Christianity and the Classical gods were forgotten, while the conquering Saxons brought their own beliefs which owed nothing to either tradition.

Christianity clung on in the far west, and Irish missionaries and holy men carried it back to Wales and the western Scottish seaboard. For the south of England, the key was a dynastic marriage between Aethelberht, King of Kent and overlord of the lands south of the Humber, and a Merovingian princess, Ingoberga, daughter of Charibert. She was a Christian. In AD 596 Pope Gregory sent a monk, Augustine, with several of his brethren, to preach the faith to the English. To their evident surprise they were favourably received by the king who gave them accommodation in Canterbury. The queen worshipped in a church outside the town dedicated to St Martin, and the monks made it the centre of their mission. The king himself was converted, followed by his people in their thousands. Augustine was consecrated the first bishop. His progress can be measured by the fact that, seven years later, a second see was created in the Kentish lands and Justus was made first Bishop of Rochester. Mellitus was sent to preach to the East Saxons. No doubt under Aethelberht's influence, Raedwald, king of the East Saxons, converted and Mellitus was made Bishop of London. The two gold foil crosses in the tomb at Prittlewell may be a tangible result of this decision. The course of the new faith was not straightforward, however. Raedwald's successor drove Mellitus from London, while Aethelberht's son temporarily reverted to his heathen traditions, taking his people with him, though Bishop Laurentius of Canterbury remained firm. In the mid-seventh century Cedd, brother of St Chad, led a successful mission to re-convert the East Saxons. Following the death of King Penda in AD 655, the Mercians also received the Christian faith. Religion and politics were linked, as the English kings began to covet acceptance from their Continental peers.

Bede, in his *Ecclesiastical History of the English Nation*, records with relish the conversion of the Gewisse. Birinius, an Italian bishop, was sent on a missionary expedition to Britain by Pope Honorius. He presumably travelled up the Thames from the Christian kingdom of Kent, and on reaching the people of the Gewisse he found they were pagans. In AD 635 he converted Cynegils, the king. Oswald, the Christian King of Northumbria and Overlord of Britain, stood as godfather at Cynegils' baptism, using the occasion to make an alliance, cemented by marrying his daughter to Cynegils. At this period, the conversion of a ruler was usually followed by the mass conversion of his people. Birinius was granted land in Dorchester to establish his episcopal see under the patronage of both kings. This soon became an unstable frontier zone. As the rising power of Mercia was increasingly felt in the region in the AD 660s, the Gewissian bishopric re-located to Winchester; and Dorchester was briefly a Mercian see in the AD 670s before transferring to Lichfield and then Leicester.

During the late seventh to early eighth centuries a number of minsters (a mother church with a religious community) were established along the Thames valley. At Oxford, the minster church founded for a community of religious women at the request of

St Frideswide may date from the AD 690s. Eadfrith son of Iddi founded a minster at Bradfield around AD 670. A minster at Bermondsey dated from the first decade of the eighth century. Other early minsters are known or suggested from Abingdon, Charlbury and Thame, and minsters continued to be established over the next 400 years. These minsters were founded by Mercian royalty and their sub-kings, confirming their political dominance in the region; for example, the foundation by Frithuwold, a Mercian sub-king, at Chertsey in the AD 670s was confirmed by Wulfhere, King of the Mercians.

Several minsters were founded in north Kent in the seventh century. One was established within the abandoned Roman fort at Reculver. Another at Hoo was founded around AD 686 by Caedwalla, a West Saxon. Others were at Minster-in-Sheppey and possibly Milton (a royal estate). On the Essex shore, minsters were founded at Tilbury, Benfleet and Upminster, and at Waltham Abbey perhaps as early as the sixth century; King Harold was buried at the latter church after the Battle of Hastings. In AD 666 Erkenwald (later Bishop of London) founded a monastery at Barking for his sister, Aethelburga; it was destroyed by the Danes in AD 870 but re-founded around AD 930.

Hints of an older tradition occasionally emerge from the waters of the Thames. A number of Viking-age and late Saxon swords, knives and spearheads have been recovered from the river: John Blair counted ten swords, eight knives and thirty spears from the stretch between Oxford and Reading. A large concentration of mostly early Saxon weaponry came from the river at Brentford. While these finds could be the result of casual loss or a skirmish, their sheer quantity makes deliberate deposition a more plausible interpretation, evidence of either persisting or new beliefs about offerings to the gods.

The Creation of England

For 600 years the country suffered periodic insecurity, being fought over by competing internal rulers and by successive raiders and invaders. When Alfred's son Edward the Elder succeeded to the Crown of Wessex in AD 899, all the lands south of the Thames belonged to Wessex, while the Midlands were divided between English Mercia and several Danish military leaders. It had been a reign of constant military campaigning, but by the time of Edward's death in AD 924 his rule was recognised both by English Mercia and by the Danish lands south of the Humber. His son, Athelstan, consolidated his position as King of English Mercia as well as Wessex. After the hiccup of Cnut's dynasty, the Wessex line resumed with Edward the Confessor and a confident Saxon England began to flower, only to collide with the ambitious Norman, William, and be re-cast yet again.

6

The Meandering River

The Creation of England and the Middle Ages

Within these Walls

The England that William the Conqueror claimed was already a well-ordered place. William's great tax return, Domesday Book, preserves an invaluable snapshot of the country soon after the Conquest. Most of the great estates had already been transferred to loyal Norman nobles and knights, but the compilers of Domesday Book frequently record who previously owned the land and under what terms. Vast acreages were also owned by the king, just as they had been under Edward the Confessor. At this period the theory, at least, stated that all land was owned by the king; the great nobles were not technically landowners in their own right but his tenants, each with their sub-tenants, and so on down the scale. This, together with the associated duties, was the backbone of the feudal system under which England was to be ruled for many centuries.

William's followers built castles to help maintain their fragile grip over their new lands and their subject people. This first generation of fortifications was constructed of earth and timber, defences which could be thrown up quickly. Only as the situation stabilised could landowners afford to rebuild in stone, and not all felt it necessary. Most of the largest castles were royal. William himself built castles along the Thames; these included the White Tower of the Tower of London, Windsor Castle and within the north-eastern corner of the Saxon defences of Wallingford. The latter, today just a country town, was an important crossing point on the river and one that William himself had used in 1066 as he approached London.

Three of the strongest castles along the Thames were not always royal fortifications. The stark Norman keep of Rochester Castle is an imposing landmark, defending an important crossing of the Medway. Originally an earthen motte was squeezed into the corner of the Roman walled town. The work of strengthening the castle in stone was begun by Bishop Gundulf, and the present formidable keep was erected early in the twelfth century after his death. For a time the fortress belonged to the Archbishops of Canterbury before King John took it back into royal hands. Baynard's Castle was erected on the bank of the Thames at the western side of the City of London. Unlike the White Tower, it was not a royal castle but was built by the powerful Baignard family. It must have been uncomfortable for the Crown to share the City with a private castle, so Henry I confiscated it, after which it remained a royal residence until the fire of London of 1666. Oxford Castle stood at the western edge of the town wall, which originated in the Saxon period. Robert d'Oilly built the surviving 64-foot-high motte in 1071, topped with a stone keep. This was followed over the next few years by a curtain wall with seven defensive towers, including St George's Tower, which still stands. In the eighteenth century the site was taken over for Oxford Gaol, itself now closed.

Many, perhaps most, castles were simply fortified residences, the centres of quite modest estates. Many of the small, earthen motte and bailey castles thrown up in haste remained in use for a century or more. As the Norman lords became English, new landowners and social climbers often sought royal permission to crenellate or fortify their manor houses. For example, Nicholas de la Beche, a royal official, was granted a licence to crenellate at Aldworth in 1338, while in 1346 Sir John de Grey was licensed to crenellate his house at Rotherfield Greys. The objective for such people was usually more to do with domestic security and status than any real provision for warfare.

Between 1135 and 1153 England was wracked by a civil war known as the Anarchy. On the death of Henry I (younger son of William the Conqueror), his nephew Stephen of Blois and daughter Matilda struggled for the English throne. Stephen rushed to

London and was crowned in December 1135, while Matilda, who was married to the Count of Anjou, was busy directing a military campaign in her French lands. In 1139 Matilda landed in the South West, where her main supporter was Robert, Earl of Gloucester, her half-brother, and quickly consolidated a support base in the region. The war touched most parts of the kingdom as well as Stephen's lands across the Channel, proceeding mostly via a series of skirmishes, sieges and diplomatic manoeuvring. London was one of the key prizes, and that was securely held by Stephen.

One of the main fronts was along the Upper Thames where Matilda's faction held the strategically important castles of Wallingford and Oxford. Other castles (or strongpoints) were quickly thrown up at strategic points; these hastily constructed fortifications are known as adulterine castles, and most were demolished under the terms of the treaty that ended the conflict. In the Upper Thames, Stephen captured adulterine castles at Cirencester, Bampton and Faringdon. His cause seemed lost when he himself was captured in 1141 at the Battle of Lincoln and imprisoned in Bristol Castle. Matilda sought the blessing of the Church before progressing to London to make plans for her coronation. Then, on 24 June, the citizens rose up and drove her out. Matilda withdrew to Winchester, where Stephen's supporters achieved an emphatic victory, capturing Robert of Gloucester. This levelled the playing field, and the two chief prisoners were exchanged. The war was stumbling into stalemate.

The following year Matilda was trapped in the strong castle at Oxford. The siege dragged on until, just before Christmas, she managed to slip away by foot across the frozen river to Wallingford Castle and on to Devizes. Wallingford was sieged on several occasions but Stephen never managed to take it. In the summer of 1153 the two armies faced each other across the Thames at Wallingford, but the outcome on that occasion was a negotiated truce rather than a decisive battle. Enthusiasm for the war was declining. Robert of Gloucester's death in 1147 had left Matilda without her right-hand supporter, and she returned to France. The whole complexion altered with the death of Stephen's eldest son, Eustace, in 1153: it became clear that Henry, Matilda's son, would be the next king. Conflict drew to an end with the Treaty of Winchester, which recognised Henry (later Henry II) as heir to the English throne.

National defence continued to be an issue. The east coast and the estuary remained exposed to enemy raids, just as they had been throughout the Roman and Saxon periods. Whenever England was at war, the enemy could strike swiftly and depart before opposition could be gathered. Gravesend had been enclosed within a wall in the Saxon period, though it appears not to have helped in 1380 when the town was plundered by the French and many townsfolk were taken captive. Lord Cobham fortified Cooling Castle on the Isle of Grain in the late fourteenth century, presumably in response to the French threat. A castle was built at Hadleigh, Essex, in the 1230s by Hubert de Burgh, Earl of Kent and justiciar to King John. When he fell from favour the castle returned to the Crown, until Edward III re-fortified it as part of his coastal defence. Edward III's castle at Queenborough was also a strongpoint against the French.

The imposing Norman castle within the Roman walled town of Rochester at the mouth of the Medway was upgraded in stone over the following century. The town walls were strengthened after the castle was besieged and taken by King John in 1215, and were strengthened again in the mid-fourteenth century in anticipation of a French invasion. This was the period of the Hundred Years' War. In 1338–9 a palisade was even erected along the London river frontage as defence against possible French attack, though the defeat of the French fleet at the Battle of Sluys in 1340 removed any immediate danger.

No serious attempt at invasion materialised on this occasion, though the fear was genuine and the impact of hit-and-run raids was catastrophic for local communities. Very visible investment in defensive measures by the king must have generated some confidence among the local population. Despite this, in a display of self-help the hamlet of East Tilbury received royal approval in 1402 to erect protection against sea raiders.

On several occasions the Thames and London Bridge combined, moat-like, to defend the capital against rebel forces. On 11 December 1263 Henry III's supporters prevented Simon de Montfort from entering the City by defending the bridge. The London citizens made a different decision in 1381 during the

Peasants' Revolt, allowing Wat Tyler's followers to enter the City unopposed. Londoners were less supportive during Jack Cade's rebellion of 1450 which concerned only local grievances. When Cade led a force of 5,000 Kentish men to London, the citizens failed to raise the drawbridge in time. The king had fled, so the rebels beheaded several royal officials before turning their attention to looting. The following day at the Battle of London Bridge the rebels suffered a heavy defeat at the hands of the outraged townsfolk and were forced to retreat. London Bridge again played its part in 1471, during the War of the Roses. Thomas Fauconberg commanded an army in support of the Lancastrian claimant Henry VI. On 12 May he reached Southwark and demanded passage through the City. When the bridge was closed against him, his force crossed downstream and approached Aldgate, burning the eastern suburbs, but the citizens drove them off.

Royal Favour

Royal power has centred along the Thames since the medieval period. London was the capital, but a monarch could not afford to stay in one place. It was by moving around the country that the king remained in touch with the nation. He was accompanied on his travels by the whole apparatus of government, a huge entourage of court officials and administrators. The monarch owned manors and estates all over the country. Some properties were designed for court use; others were intended for pleasure, for example as hunting lodges or retreats from the pressure of court life. On other occasions it was necessary to leave London to safeguard the monarch's health, to avoid times of plague or other epidemics. The banks of the Thames were a favoured location, providing both easy access to London and a pleasant setting. Over the centuries, numerous 'palaces', not all as grand as the term implies, passed in and out of favour.

Edward the Confessor maintained a palace at Westminster as a symbolic centre of power. He also had a palace at Old Windsor and enjoyed his manor at Havering-atte-Bower, dying there in 1066. William the Conqueror was quick to exploit the symbolism of Westminster, becoming the first monarch to be crowned in Edward's newly built Westminster Abbey and holding the secular coronation celebrations in the adjoining Palace, emphasising the continuity of a rightful heir rather than the disjuncture of a conqueror. He was aware, however, that his hold on his new kingdom was tenuous, so he built castle-palaces at the Tower of London and Windsor.

Edward III maintained a palace (or manor) at Rotherhithe on the Surrey bank of the river opposite London. At this date the area was still fairly rural, a quiet retreat within sight of the capital. The palace included a royal wharf as well as gardens. Edward granted the royal manor at Kennington to his son, the Black Prince, who remodelled the house, adding among other things a great hall measuring 82 feet by 50 feet with a vaulted undercroft. It was later demolished by Henry VIII to provide materials for his building project at Whitehall. Edward III was a regular visitor to his manor at Gravesend, in the estuary. He left both this and his Rotherhithe manor to the Cistercian Abbey of St Mary Graces, East Smithfield, which he had founded in 1350. He was also responsible for building Queenborough Castle to an advanced circular design.

Edward I held court at his manor of Sheen, on the bank of the Thames, which became a favoured residence of Richard II. It was rebuilt by Henry VII and renamed Richmond Palace after his title of Earl of Richmond (in Yorkshire).

Given to Edward II in 1305 by the Bishop of Durham, Eltham Palace in Kent was another favoured royal residence within reach of the capital. Henry IV entertained the Byzantine Emperor Manuel II Palaiologos at Eltham over the Christmas and New Year of 1400–01. The Tudors often chose Eltham for their Christmas celebrations, and it was here in 1526 Henry VIII and his court spent the sombre 'Still Christmas' to escape the plague which was then raging in London. With the rebuilding of Greenwich Palace, Eltham became little more than a hunting estate, and Charles II finally leased the manor to Sir John Shaw who had provided financial assistance while he was in exile.

Henry I established Beaumont Palace outside the north gate of the city of Oxford as a convenient staging post on the journey to his favoured manor of Woodstock. The future kings Richard the Lionheart and his brother John were both born at Beaumont Palace. It fell out of favour, and in 1390 Edward II gave it to the Carmelite friars in fulfilment of a vow made at the Battle of Bannockburn. Woodstock had a different story. It had been a royal manor since Saxon times, and continued to be popular as a hunting lodge with several monarchs. Henry I may have kept a menagerie in the park, but it is perhaps better known as the scene of King Henry II's courtship of Rosamund Clifford ('Fair Rosamund'), his mistress. After bearing him at least two children, she retired to the convent at Godstow near Oxford in 1176 shortly before her death. The ruins of the manor house were finally cleared for the construction of Blenheim Palace, gift of the nation to the 1st Duke of Marlborough, in the early eighteenth century.

Greenwich was already a royal manor when Humphrey, Duke of Gloucester and brother to Henry V, built a great house beside the river in 1426. Duke Humphrey was a notable collector of books, and his library was donated to the Bodleian Library at Oxford. It was a favourite residence. Henry VII rebuilt the palace, naming it Placentia – pleasant place. Elizabeth of York, Henry VII's future wife, was born there, as were Henry VIII and his two daughters Mary and Elizabeth. This palace stood neglected until the late seventeenth century, when it was demolished as part of the scheme for the Royal Naval Hospital.

From the late eleventh and early twelfth centuries, the rising wealth and influence of London and the increasing focus of the royal administration on Westminster Palace led to nobles and bishops feeling the need for a residence close to the seat of power. The Archbishop of Canterbury has Lambeth Palace, while his colleague the Archbishop of York maintained York Place (later Whitehall). The Bishops of Durham, Norwich, Winchester, Bath and Wells, Lincoln, Salisbury, Ely, Rochester and Carlisle all had townhouses in London or on the South Bank. Cardinal Wolsey's princely palace at Hampton Court was in this tradition. The secular nobility also maintained townhouses for the same reason.

Conflicts of Interest

The Thames was a significant source of revenue for the Crown, as ever more ingenious charges were levied for using the river.

When Richard the Lionheart was desperate to fund his Crusade, he identified the Thames as a saleable asset. In 1197 the City administration bought the rights and responsibilities in the tidal portion of the Thames (apart from customs duties) for the huge sum of 1,500 marks, an indication of its vast commercial potential. This investment was amply repaid over the next 660 years, until their rights were handed over to the Thames Conservancy in 1857. Their writ ran from the London Stone at Staines, erected in 1285 to mark the limit of the tidal reach, to the Crow Stone on the foreshore at Chalkwell, west of Southend and opposite Yantlet Creek.

Upriver of Staines, the question of jurisdiction seems to have been less clear. Authority was fragmented, divided between the larger landowners each with vested interests, while people with properties on the bank went largely unchecked. Different usages conflicted and decisions made by central government, such as the frequent order to remove weirs, were seldom carried though with any vigour.

King John has often been caricatured as 'Bad King John', though recent historians suggest he was an able administrator and military leader marred by negative character traits. When a political dispute with Pope Innocent III over the choice of the Archbishop of Canterbury got out of hand, England was excommunicated. Then 1214 saw a disastrous military campaign lose much of England's French possessions. These humiliating episodes damaged John's reputation, but it was his 'interpersonal skills' that provoked rebellion: his dealings with his powerful nobles had been disrespectful. A rebel alliance seized London and John quickly agreed to come to terms. The two sides met on an island in the Thames near Windsor on 15 June 1215, where the peace agreement later known as Magna Carta was signed. Runnymede may have been chosen as a neutral location, with the river minimising the possibility of traps being set by either side.

In Magna Carta, John agreed to certain clauses to limit his powers: his will was not arbitrary, but governed by law. This document has often been proclaimed as the foundation of British constitutional freedom, though in the conditions of the age many of its clauses were never seriously enforced. A number of clauses dealt with specific grievances. Several addressed matters of trade and the River Thames, and were probably put forward by the Mayor of London, William Hardell. Their inclusion is a measure of how important trade had become to the national economy, and his very presence, the odd man out in that noble company, is a sure indication of the rising power of London.[1]

Clause 13 states that the City of London should enjoy all its ancient liberties and free customs by land and by water, incidentally extending that provision to all towns.

Clause 33 declares that all fish weirs should be removed from the Thames and Medway, and from rivers throughout England. This reflected the conflict between river-borne trade and the economic rights of riverside communities and landowners, a conflict that ran into the nineteenth century.

Clauses 35 and 41 express commercial concerns. The first established a set of standard measures throughout the country, while the second protected merchants engaged in international trade.

For centuries the Thames had been a battleground of conflicting interests – the river as one of the main highways of the nation versus the local concerns of the communities and landowners along its banks. The removal of fish weirs was a concern as early as the Magna Carta – though this clause remained something of a dead letter. A fish weir was a structure, usually of timber, built either wholly or partially across the river in order to funnel fish towards a net. Weirs were therefore an obstruction to shipping. The issue dragged on unresolved. The Lord Mayor of London, 200 years later, was still ordering the destruction of every weir below Staines, that is, within that part of the Thames under the jurisdiction of the Corporation of London; needless to say, he achieved little if anything.

Watermills also disrupted the river. Watermills were frequently mentioned in Domesday Book – windmills were not introduced to Britain until the twelfth century – and many more were constructed as the Middle Ages progressed. These, too, often incorporated a weir, in this case to create a head of water which flowed along a leat to power the mill before being returned to the river lower down. These weirs frequently dammed the river to make a pool, and the water level upstream could be significantly higher than that downstream. To allow vessels to pass, a flash lock was created. These were very basic pieces of hydraulic engineering: a number of boards or paddles could be removed from a gap. Once the water had rushed through and the levels equalised, a vessel could get through – though it was always hard work to haul it against the flow. Flash locks could be dangerous, however, and also slowed down river traffic as it was necessary to wait at each one. The lock keepers tended to charge high tolls for this inconvenience, causing further friction between the opposing interests.

A combination of poor maintenance and weirs made the upper reaches increasingly difficult for navigation, and this reached a crisis during the later thirteenth century. Henley reaped the benefits. There were only five locks from London to Henley, but twenty between Henley and Oxford: these were flash locks not pound locks, making travel slow and potentially dangerous. As a measure of these difficulties, in 1295 it cost 2*d* to ship a quarter of grain 68 miles from London to Henley, but a further 3*d* to carry it the extra 10 miles to Reading. Commercial use of the river above Henley dwindled as many merchants came to regard that town as the highest navigable point, continuing to Oxford and elsewhere by road.

Commercial River

The wealth of England throughout the Middle Ages depended primarily upon the wool trade. The quality of English fleeces meant that they were sought from Italy to the Baltic. Raw wool dominated the export trade into the early fourteenth century, and heavy taxes helped fill the public coffers. Then, due in part to political changes affecting the Flemish textile industry, finished cloth replaced wool as the major export. The Cotswolds was a leading wool-producing region, and towns along the Thames such as Reading developed as textile manufacturing centres. The river was a vital component in this trade: it remained a major artery reaching into the heart of southern England, while London remained England's premier international trading port. Yet the Thames was generally shallower and wider than today, meandering and braided into several channels separated by islands and shifting sandbanks, making navigation treacherous. Despite this, the economics of water transport for bulky or fragile goods was irrefutable: for example, in the late thirteenth century transporting grain to London could be twelve to eighteen times more expensive by road than by water.

Apart from its role as a port, London offered a growing market for food, fuel and manufactured goods, and many towns upriver developed their waterfronts to tap this trade. A wharf is recorded at Abingdon before the river became impassable. The foundations of a massive wall which were seen in the 1970s near the bridge but outside the monastic precinct may have formed part of that wharf, and were dated to the twelfth century on the basis of pottery recovered. At Reading, consolidation of the waterfront along the River Kennet in the late twelfth to early thirteenth centuries may have been associated with the founding of the abbey. At first an artificial 'hard' was laid for beaching barges, but a wharf was soon created with possible warehouses behind. Documentary sources mention the problems for shipping caused by the irregular seasonal flow. A lock owned by the abbey between the Kennet and Thames, for which the abbey charged a toll in the fifteenth century, may have been an attempt to manage the flow. However, as the abbey owned several mills and a fishery at the Dissolution, it is possible the lock related to these. The abbey did not have a monopoly on waterborne trade. A town wharf is also attested in fifteenth century records, and money was spent on repairs in 1464 and 1481. At Kingston, what may have begun as an exercise in strengthening the river defences developed in the fourteenth and fifteenth centuries into the creation of quays together with industrial activity on the reclaimed riverside. A borough charter of 1441 established market rights, and the town prospered. Not every settlement appears to have chosen to develop its riverfront. For example, at Windsor the timber revetments around the northern end of the bridge were too lightweight for serious wharfage so were presumably intended simply to consolidate the bank.

Many lords saw the financial possibilities of establishing their own market centre, so in the eleventh to thirteenth centuries there was a rush to lay out planned towns, each with a market charter; though many failed to deliver. Henley fitted this pattern of speculative development. In the Saxon period this section of the Thames had formed part of the royal estate of Benson, so the town may have been a royal foundation. Its urban core was laid out sometime in the late twelfth century based on a series of standardised long plots 1½ perches wide (a perch was 16½ feet), fronting the roads. King Stephen issued a charter here in 1145, suggesting the town may have started to take shape – though he could have held court at an earlier royal estate centre of which there is no record. With the benefit of river trade, Henley seems quickly to have found economic success. A stone bridge improved the town's position as a transhipment point. It was granted an annual fair around 1200, and by the 1260s it had a guild of merchants. London merchants dominated the corn trade at Henley in the mid-fourteenth century, while 100 years later wool was the valued commodity. Even so, with a population of 1,000–1,500 by 1300, it was only 1 per cent the size of London.

River quays were generally good investments. The Priory of the Holy Trinity, Aldgate, owned a quay over the river at Woolwich, while the Priory of St Mary Overy, Southwark, bought a wharf at Glass Yard in 1442. A ferry was certainly crossing the Thames there by the fourteenth century. Other religious houses owned riverside facilities for their own domestic use. A thirteenth-century masonry dock was excavated upriver at the Augustinian Abbey of Osney, just outside Oxford. The abbey, which stood on the islands within the braided channel of the Thames, also powered a corn mill. Waltham Abbey on the River Lea had its own dock, with large barns to provide warehousing.

London had been the country's leading town since it first grew up under Roman rule, punctuated only by a blip in the Dark Ages when activity relocated a short distance to a trading beach on The Strand. Throughout the medieval period the City was governed by a powerful body named the Corporation of London, composed of leading citizens who were all tradesmen or craftsmen. Its origins are lost, but around 1067 William the Conqueror granted a charter confirming its assumed rights and privileges. Clause 13 of Magna Carta reaffirmed these rights. In need of money, King John made the Mayor of London into one of the first elected offices. Guilds developed to regulate particular trades, and hence acquired a significant role in civic life: they subsequently became the oldest of the livery companies. Consequently, London quickly developed into a sophisticated and self-governing town, as well as being a motor generating the nation's wealth.

The main market for London at the time of the Norman Conquest was at Cheapside. During the twelfth century other markets sprang up. Leadenhall Market was added in the thirteenth century. Smithfield specialised in livestock, while Billingsgate developed as a specialist fish market behind the dock. One of the mainstays for these markets was the provision of fresh food for the growing London population. Wholesale markets for non-food goods included Blackwell Hall, Basinghall Street, which became the centre of the woollen cloth trade.

Many of the streets were lined with shops, and these often included a craftsman's workshop to the rear, with goods made and sold on the same site. Industry was small-scale. Kilns for metalworking and pottery have been found on many sites across the City, and the waste from leather, bone and other materials is often recovered. A number of watermills ground grain. The Abbey of Westminster canalised the Tyburn in the thirteenth century to create a tide mill; the following century the site of the former royal manor house of The Rosary in Southwark included two watermills. Windmills were first introduced to Europe in the twelfth century, and one may have been built at Clerkenwell as early as 1134. Several are clearly attested in Middlesex over the next 100 years and others may be unrecorded or unrecognised. Certainly, many mills would have been essential in and around the town to satisfy the daily needs of the population.

As early as the Venerable Bede's time in the eighth century, London was established as an international trading focus. By the Middle Ages it was one of the major ports of north-west Europe. Chief among its exports were woollen cloth and raw wool. Imports included timber, furs and fish from Scandinavia, high quality cloth from Flanders, wine from south-west France, wine and olive oil from Spain, and luxury goods such as silk, spices, sweet wine and glass from Italy. Merchants from Rouen and Cologne were based at Dowgate. A masonry building interpreted as the guildhall for the merchants of Cologne was excavated at the Steelyard, now beneath Cannon Street Station, and this developed into a centre for all German merchants. The Baltic Hanse and merchants from the Low Countries and France all traded regularly with London.

By the time of the Norman Conquest there were several berthing places on the London waterfront where customs dues were collected, including Alfred's dock at Queenhithe, the 'common quays' at Billingsgate, the small inlet of St Botolph Wharf, and possible beach markets at Dowgate and Vintry. The waterfront continued to develop, so that by the fourteenth century timber and stone quays made up a significant length. The stone-built St Olave's dock originated in the thirteenth century, with access via a lane off Tooley Street: by the sixteenth century this was a substantial dock over 32 m long by 6 m wide. A stone warehouse with a cellar was built after 1350 on reclaimed land, together with other similar buildings. Further west, documentary sources mention quays and wharves from as early as the twelfth century, often associated with riverside tenements. The mouth of the Fleet was also a navigable inlet.

In the later decades of the thirteenth century the river frontage running west from the Tower of London consisted of a gravel foreshore. The southern curtain wall of the Tower originally stood directly on this gravel, lapped by the river. Edward I ordered the moat around the Tower to be extended along its southern side, possibly so that it would remain wet at all states of the tide. As part of this exercise, Tower Wharf was created. This may have triggered reclamation along this length of the foreshore, and during the fourteenth century several quays and shipyards developed to the south of Thames Street as far as the Custom House. The Custom House itself was established in a rented property at the Wool Quay, probably from its inception in 1275. A well-built timber drain ran from here towards the river. The excavator mused, 'It is an interesting thought that the most famous controller of Customs, Geoffrey Chaucer, may have used this latrine'![2] Following the Fire of London, the Custom House was rebuilt on the same plot by Christopher Wren. The present building was erected on the neighbouring site in 1814 to designs by David Laing. Due to structural problems, it had to be remodelled just a few years later by Sir Robert Smirke, who took the opportunity to make the building fireproof using the innovative new technology of structural ironwork. The Wool Quay is first mentioned in documents in 1295, by which date it was already associated with the wool trade. Stone Wharf was immediately to its east. A cross-braced timber revetment was built on the foreshore and back-filled with refuse to form a wharf, while a jetty projected into the river. A second revetment was soon built in front of the first.

Excavation at Trig Lane demonstrated that the City riverfront should not be thought of as a single, unbroken wharf. It also illustrated the extent to which the upkeep and extension of the waterfront was the responsibility of individual occupiers. Three adjacent tenements were owned in 1291 by John de London, who leased them to tenants. Only two of the properties shared a common revetment, with the third lagging behind. A similar situation was seen in 1350. By 1430 all three tenements were owned by William Stokke, but each had its own revetment and river stair. The occupants were either fishmongers or dyers, trades requiring plentiful access to water. Small boats could be moored to their river stairs, but loading and unloading cargoes was not a factor for these men. The main motivation for investing was to maintain a sound river frontage, with a new revetment being placed in front of an old, rotting one. Reclamation may have been a secondary consideration, but the need to keep up with one's neighbours to avoid the formation of inlets where refuse could accumulate was equally significant. In the mid-fifteenth century a single stone waterfront and river stair was created behind these tenements, bringing the cycle to a halt. A similar pattern would probably be found wherever a formal wharf was not established.

Ship building and repair were two related riverside crafts, and vessels must have been built along the Thames since time immemorial. Edward II ordered twenty-six English towns to share in building twenty galleys in 1294, including Newcastle, York, Dunwich, Ipswich, Southampton, Lyme and London. From at least the fourteenth century, Deptford, Rotherhithe and Shadwell were major ship building and repair centres, and shipyards also developed on the foreshore in the eastern part of the City. St Mary Overy's wharf in Southwark apparently diversified into small-scale shipbuilding and repair.

At least twenty-eight named types of boat plied the Thames in the medieval period. The main medieval trading vessel known as a 'cog' was found widely across Northern Europe by 1200 and they are commonly recorded in fourteenth-century documents. They were slow cargo vessels, with a single mast, flat-bottomed, and a length-to-width ratio of 2:1.

Very few vessels of the period have survived. Parts of a flat-bottomed barge perhaps 3.5 m by 9.75 m in size were reused in the medieval waterfront at the Custom House. It had been built locally around 1160–90 and was designed for work in the river. Fragments of numerous barges have been found among the timbers of the waterfront revetments; recycling was clearly the expected fate of old boats. Another boat lay on the bed of the Thames near Blackfriars where it had sunk. Built about 1380–1415 and measuring 4.3 m by 14.6 m, it was a flat-bottomed, masted vessel and could carry a cargo of an estimated 7.5 tonnes. It may have sunk following a collision with a similar vessel carrying a cargo of Kentish ragstone which lay at right-angles to it. These barges were clearly able to work as far as the estuary and could manage significant loads, but they were not seagoing vessels.

River Crossings

Ford and ferries provided the vital cross-river link as they had always done, whether carrying long-distance travellers over the barrier of the Thames or opening up the hinterland of a local market. There were many fords upstream of London, as the river was shallower and wider than today, though Wallingford was the lowest ford that was passable year-round. Most towns and villages operated at least one ferry, as did monastic houses on the river bank. The lowest ferry ran between Higham and East Tilbury. It has been estimated that between Kew and Cricklade there was an average of one ferry per kilometre. These were privately owned commercial ventures and charged a fare.

In London, the profession of the waterman sprang up in response to the need to cross the river, and that of the lighterman to load and unload shipping mid-stream. Rather like water taxis, they largely replaced the need for designated ferry crossings. They developed a reputation for dishonesty and a rough way of life; eventually their business was regulated to protect customers and the Company of Watermen was incorporated by Act of Parliament in 1555. After that, only licensed watermen were allowed to ply their trade between Windsor and Gravesend. Members wore a large badge to show they were qualified, and a seven-year apprenticeship was designed to prevent fatalities on the river.

One of the clauses of Magna Carta protected towns and individuals from being forced to build bridges over rivers unless required to do so by ancient custom and law. However, many towns saw the commercial advantage of building a bridge. The tolls for passing over or under the bridge would also provide an income. By the time of the Norman Conquest, London Bridge, Wallingford bridge and Radcot bridge (the latter two on the Upper Thames) were the only bridges on the river. When William the Conqueror marched from Hastings to London to claim the kingdom, he took his army on a long detour in order to cross at Wallingford rather than risk London Bridge being held against him. London Bridge was destroyed several times, by extreme weather and by fire, each time being rebuilt in timber. It was Henry II who took the decision to rebuild in more durable stone. This was part of his penance for the murder of Archbishop Thomas à Becket, so the bridge was to include a chapel dedicated to the martyr. The work was undertaken by Peter of Colechurch, Warden of the Brethren of the Bridge, a religious order of bridge keepers. Beginning in 1176, it took thirty-three years to complete. The bridge was about 900 feet long and 26 feet wide, carried on nineteen arches. A drawbridge in place of the central arch could be raised to allow masted ships to pass; the drawbridge and southern gatehouse meant the bridge could be defended. To offset the cost, building plots were sold on the bridge and tolls were charged. By the end of the Middle Ages there were around 200 buildings on the bridge, overhanging to turn the roadway into a dark tunnel: it was said that neighbours could shake hands across the gap.

Upriver, the first town to invest in a bridge was Caversham, where a timber bridge was built sometime in the late twelfth to early thirteenth century. It included a chapel to St Anne where travellers could pray for a safe journey. Timber bridges quickly followed at Windsor (1172), Staines (by 1222), Marlow (by 1227), Kingston (early thirteenth century) and Maidenhead (about 1280). A short-lived bridge at Shillingford is attested in 1301. Henley Bridge (1232) was unusual in having masonry piers from the outset. Stone was a more common material for bridge-building on the Upper Thames, perhaps because the river was narrower. Stone bridges are known from Osney and Godstow, both the sites of religious houses near Oxford. A timber structure at St John's Bridge, Lechlade, was destroyed by floods in 1203 and rebuilt in stone. King John contributed 50 marks towards the cost, and a few years later the Priory of St John was founded with specific duties in respect of the bridge. New Bridge (Oxon), also of stone, dates from the thirteenth century. A licence to build a wooden bridge at Chertsey was granted by Henry IV in 1410. Two masonry bridges and a causeway across the braided river and low-lying Andersey Island at Abingdon were built in 1416–22. The new crossing would often replace a ferry. This burst of bridge-building was a sign of the economic success that the country was experiencing and in which the riverside towns shared. Unprecedented wealth was being generated and no-one wanted to miss out. Sometimes the funding came from the new town authorities, while elsewhere monastic landowners made the investment, though a return by way of tolls was usually expected.

Other bridges crossed tributary streams, such as Clattering Bridge over the Hogsmill at Kingston or the timber bridge over the Brent at Brentford. Maud, Queen of Henry I, commissioned a gravel causeway at Old Ford, and stone bridges over the River Lea at Bow and the Channelsea River at Stratford, to the east of London. These crossings could be just as important to long distance trade and the local economy as bridges over the Thames itself.

Bridges, and especially timber bridges, required constant maintenance and expenditure. Damage from barges passing underneath was also routine. Money from tolls and donations at bridge chapels might go some way towards defraying these costs. An account of the admission of Richard Ludlow to the hermitage on Maidenhead Bridge in October 1423 is preserved in the Episcopal Register of John Chandler, Bishop of Salisbury.

It appears there was both a hermitage, which had recently been rebuilt, and a bridge chapel with its own chaplain. The role of bridge hermit was clearly set out, combining religious and civic duties. In his profession, Ludlow undertook that any money he collected from travellers, once his minimal needs had been met, would be used to repair the bridge and the common roads of the town. Arrangements of this sort were a quite usual way of managing maintenance. Even so, there was often disagreement over who was responsible for repairs. For example, in Edward VI's reign a commission found that responsibility for the repair of Lechlade Bridge had been transferred to the Dean of Wallingford together with the assets of a chantry conveyed by Henry VII. Henry III gave an oak as a gift in kind towards the repair of Marlow Bridge, though more usually the monarch granted pontage (the right to levy a bridge tax) for a specified number of years to help towards the cost.

Religious River

The England of the Middle Ages was an unquestioningly religious country, and the Catholic Church came to dominate every aspect of society. The Thames valley was no exception. Religious houses were typically granted property at the time of their foundation and continued to receive gifts throughout their histories, making them collectively and often individually into great landowners. At the time of the Dissolution they owned roughly 25 per cent of land in England, much of which was leased out to tenants.

Domesday Book records a number of Thames-side abbeys as landowners, both great and small. For example, Abingdon Abbey had extensive estates in Berkshire and Oxfordshire, much of it along the river. As the Middle Ages progressed, religious houses multiplied across the region, many having river access. They were of all types and conditions – the whole gamut of orders, purposes, wealth, size; some independent, others attached to a mother house. Among the largest and most powerful were Reading Abbey, Syon Abbey, Sheen Abbey, Waltham Abbey, Barking Abbey and of course Westminster Abbey. London, being by far the largest town in the realm, was a magnet for religious institutions of every type. Some were the chief English houses of their order, necessarily located near the seat of power; others were simple monasteries or institutions seeking to serve a community. The larger houses tended to be located just outside the town walls because of their requirement for a block of land. In due course, every settlement and community found itself within a short distance of one or more religious houses, and their pervasive presence helped to define the character of the nation.

The heads of only two dozen religious houses in England were honoured with the status of 'mitred abbot'; three of these were in the Thames valley, the abbeys of Westminster Reading and Abingdon. In about AD 960 St Dunstan, then Bishop of London, settled a group of Benedictine monks beside the Thames at Westminster on a marshy area called Thorney Island surrounded by tributaries of the Tyburn stream. Edward the Confessor rebuilt the abbey, which was consecrated on 28 December 1065. Westminster Abbey quickly became one of the foremost religious houses in England. It saw the coronation of William the Conqueror a year later, and has been the setting for every subsequent coronation. As royal and political power aggregated in Westminster, the abbey became the natural venue for national events and its prestige grew. Abingdon Abbey was also Benedictine. Reading Abbey, founded in 1121 as a Cluniac house by Henry I, later joined the Benedictine order. The monks and their tenants were granted immunity from all customs, tolls and port-dues throughout the kingdom, as well as various property and jurisdiction over the town of Reading. By another charter Henry granted a fair on the festival of St Laurence and on the three following days. These were valuable concessions, particularly for a monastery adjacent to the Thames waterway.

The wool and cloth trade made Oxford prosperous in the late twelfth century and by 1227 it paid a larger tallage (property tax) contribution than any town in the realm apart from York and London. Oxford also attracted the religious orders in large numbers. St Frideswide's eighth-century nunnery had presumably withered away by the time the Augustinian Priory was refounded in 1122: its chapel is the modern cathedral. Osney Abbey was also a twelfth-century Augustinian foundation, while Godstow Priory was a Benedictine nunnery of similar date. The following century the Franciscan, Dominican, Carmelite, Austin and Trinitarian friars moved into the town. These were preaching orders, attracted by the town's reputation for learning which developed in the twelfth century, with seventy masters teaching by the end of the century. Some of their houses have transformed into today's colleges, other colleges were established as secular institutions; but it is not known why Oxford was chosen as a national centre of teaching.

Black Death

The Black Death, first recorded at Stepney in London in 1348, killed one-third of the population of England. London was heavily hit due to its overcrowded conditions and, ironically, its trading contacts, but no settlement was left untouched. One unexpected consequence was the loosening of the bonds of feudalism which tied ordinary people to the land, making it easier for ambitious or restless individuals to seek a new life in the towns. In the years after that first epidemic, accounts speak of large tracts of agricultural land left fallow and untended. That may have been less true of the fertile lands of the Thames valley than it was on the surrounding uplands or the marshy areas of the estuary. Even so, the sheer unimaginable quantity of sudden death had a lasting impact on those who lived through the horror, and for generations to come. It was a trigger that helped to change the nation, though both the economy and the collective psyche were slow to recover.

7

The Broken River

From the Tudors to the Great Fire of London

Long-Term Underinvestment

The Tudor dynasty ushered in a new era of confidence for England: the nation state and the world stage beckoned. With the Stuarts, England became Britain, but the nation descended into civil war and experimental politics, from which it was emerging as the century and dynasty changed. Foreign wars, civil war and the disastrous Fire of London combined to stifle commerce and drain the nation's wealth. Civil infrastructure, such as the Thames, was left without investment, and no new bridges were built along the river.

Since the days of barbarian raiders ravaging the east coast of the Roman province, if not earlier, the beckoning Thames estuary has been exposed to invaders. Despite the many hard lessons, little serious preparation was ever made. Government policy regarding the defence of the Thames, and ultimately of London and the heart of the kingdom, followed a pattern of 'boom and bust', 'knee-jerk response' and the withdrawal of funding.

Henry VII had seized the throne in 1485 following a protracted civil war. His son, Henry VIII, who succeeded to the throne in 1509, was acutely aware of the need to produce a male heir to secure the succession. His political marriage with Catherine of Aragon had been made to hold the balance of power in Europe and cement an alliance with Ferdinand and Isabella of Spain. The complication was that Catherine had previously been married to Henry's elder brother Arthur who had died after a year aged only fifteen, but a papal dispensation for this irregular marriage was secured. However, as the years went by, Henry and Catherine's inability to produce a son came to dominate national policy, leading ultimately to Henry's formal break with the Catholic Church in 1534. This left England alone in Europe; and Henry had personally slighted the most powerful ruler in the world, Charles V, Holy Roman Emperor, by divorcing his aunt Catherine.

The year 1538 looked like the time of reckoning for Henry and England. He was excommunicated by Pope Paul III, a sanction which marked the end of diplomacy. When the squabbling superpowers of France and the Holy Roman Empire signed a truce, an invasion to return England to the fold of the Catholic Church seemed inevitable. Henry immediately began preparations. Money and resources were found to build a series of forts and other defences along the Channel coast (especially around the vital harbours of the Solent and Portsmouth), the Kent coast and the Thames estuary. These were a new breed of fortification designed for artillery. They tended to be small and compact, with thick walls, gun ports, semi-circular bastions to provide gun platforms, and surrounded by moats. In some places, neighbouring forts were linked by a series of earthworks. Between 1539 and 1542, thirty separate fortifications were built, including ten castles. In response to renewed war with France in the 1540s, the scheme was bolstered with the addition of further fortifications.

Five blockhouses were built to defend the Thames estuary, each with twenty-five to thirty cannon. The Milton blockhouse had thirty cannon as well as handguns and other weapons, and its guns were able to cross their fire with those at West Tilbury, preventing vessels from sailing upriver. A second blockhouse further downriver at East Tilbury crossed fire with its partner at Higham on the Kent shore. The dockyard at Gravesend was defended with a further blockhouse. The two Tilbury blockhouses each cost around £500 to build, while the three on the southern shore were around £1,000. Although they were formidable offensive positions against shipping, their weakness was in defence from a land-based assault.

The regular garrisons at these fortifications were small, responsible for keeping the fort and its equipment in readiness. In time of crisis their numbers were to be augmented from the local militia. However, the immediate threat quickly passed and England's diplomatic relationships with her European peers stabilised. The scheme was expensive to maintain, so in 1553 the Thames blockhouses were decommissioned, though most were hurriedly modified and reused in response to later dangers. After Henry's initiative, work on the estuary and dockyard defences was carried forward piecemeal, with no government having the will to see though an integrated system.

Relations with Spain were always strained, and the estuary was within easy striking distance of the Spanish-controlled ports in the Low Countries. Despite its vulnerability to assault, the Lower Thames was rapidly becoming a key naval installation. The upper reaches of the Medway below Rochester Bridge were used increasingly to lay-up the navy when out of commission. This developed into Chatham dockyard. To protect these defenceless ships, Elizabeth I ordered a new battery to be built. Land was bought in 1559, and work progressed slowly. The resulting battery, Upnor Castle, on the north bank, was very different in design to her father's solid castles. Although a triangular gun platform projected towards the river, the main building behind was not squat and circular but foursquare. Towards the end of Elizabeth's reign, Upnor was enlarged and strengthened. Another fort was built at Swaleness and a blockhouse at Sheerness. A chain could also be stretched across the Medway as a further defence, and a system of warning beacons was established along the estuary. As a measure of desperation, Edward III's old castle at Queenborough was also pressed into service. By this date it was already militarily outdated, and was finally demolished after 1650.

The victualling yard on Tower Hill, established on the former site of the Abbey of St Mary Graces and reusing some of the surviving abbey buildings, was the principal Royal Naval victualling establishment from 1560 until 1785. Unsurprisingly, it is regularly mentioned in Pepys's diary. Following its closure, the site was taken over by the Royal Mint.

As England and Spain postured, Queen Elizabeth's advisors were all too aware that the Thames offered Philip a route to strike at the heart of the nation. When the much-anticipated war broke out in 1585, an inspection found that, once again,

Top: 1. The official source of the Thames is the slight hollow in front of the dead tree. The stone was placed by the Thames Conservancy to mark the spot, while the signpost indicates the Thames Path National Trail and records that a would-be walker must cover 184 miles or 242 kilometres before they reach the trail's end at the Thames Barrier. (© Andrew Sargent)

Middle: 2. Water gushes from a fountain head at Thames Head. Today the structure is long gone and water only flows occasionally. The mast visible over the wall is a reminder that the Thames & Severn Canal had been opened just five years previously. Pumping to maintain this high section of the canal contributed to the lowering of the local water table. (Aquatint by J. C. Stadler after a drawing by Joseph Farington, published in Combe, W., *An History of the River Thames*, London: J. & J. Boydell, 1794 & 1796)

Bottom: 3. The source is not always dry. This photograph was taken on Millennium morning, 1 January 2000. Water was bubbling up to form a pool, from which a stream flowed across the meadows to Lyd Well, often the effective starting point of the river. (© Carol Butler)

Above: **4.** The Thames & Severn Canal joined the Thames just above Lechlade. The lock gates by the bridge formed the entrance to the canal. The unusual drum-shaped building was the lock keeper's cottage, and is still standing. (From Combe, *An History of the River Thames*)

Left: **5.** Old Father Thames was cast in concrete by Rafaelle Monti in 1854 as part of a set to decorate one of the huge garden fountains at the Crystal Palace in its new Sydenham home. The statue stood at the Thames Head for several years before being moved to Lechlade lock. The bales and barrels signify commerce. The shovel and red flowers are a modern addition. (© Andrew

6. This pill box on a peaceful section of the Thames near Lechlade was part of the GHQ stop line during the Second World War, Britain's last line of defence against invasion. (© Andrew Sargent)

7. The 'dreaming spires of Oxford' seen from Boars Hill, near the spot where the poet Matthew Arnold reputedly found his inspiration. The River Thames lies between the camera and the City. (© Andrew Sargent)

8. As a riverside town, Abingdon was heavily engaged in the river trade from an early date. This section of the Thames frontage is known as St Helen's Wharf, taking its name from the neighbouring thirteenth-century church. Today, pleasure craft are moored where barges once unloaded. (© Andrew Sargent)

9. Looking north from the Late Bronze Age enclosure and Early Iron Age hillfort on Wittenham Clumps, 6,000 years of England's history are laid out before you. The Late Iron Age site of Dyke Hills lies in the field between the photographer and the town. Surrounded on three sides by the rivers Thames and Thame, a huge bank and ditch completes the circuit. Half a mile to the north, a first-century AD Roman fort was succeeded by a Roman town and Saxon settlement. The missionary bishop St Birinius founded a church and monastic site in AD 634, which was replaced by a medieval abbey; only the church with its long red roof survives. Just to the north of the eighteenth- and nineteenth-century town of Dorchester-on-Thames (and not visible in this photograph), gravel workings uncovered a complex of Neolithic and Bronze Age sites in use from 3700 BC to 1200 BC. (© Andrew Sargent)

10. The ancient Thames carved out the Goring Gap, a narrow passage through the chalk of the Downs. The prehistoric tracks known as the Ridgeway and Icknield Way meet the river here, and the Romans built a ford at this important crossing. The twin towns of Goring and Streatley, which face each other across the river, have been linked by a bridge since 1837. (© Andrew Sargent)

11. This was where William the Conqueror crossed the Thames in 1066 on his march to London to claim the kingdom. The large Norman motte of Wallingford Castle was thrown up in the corner of Alfred's burgh to command the river and the important crossing point. It saw action during the Anarchy (AD 1135–53) when it was a key stronghold of the Empress Matilda. (© Andrew Sargent)

12. Henley Regatta was a popular social and sporting occasion by the turn of the twentieth century. It was said that there were sometimes so many boats on the river during the regatta that it was possible to walk across. It looks almost possible to believe it! The barges moored on the right served as private grandstands. (Photograph: Henry Taunt, reference no. HT13443. Reproduced by permission of Oxfordshire County Council – Oxfordshire History Centre)

13. Henry Taunt, photographer of the Thames, meets Jerome K. Jerome's *Three Men in a Boat*. This photograph may have been taken while Taunt, seated in the centre, was researching for his *New Map of the Thames*. A canvas awning has been rigged over the boat to create a tent. Meanwhile, Taunt and his assistants eat their informal supper. (Photograph: Henry Taunt, reference no. HT14014. Reproduced by permission of Oxfordshire County Council – Oxfordshire History Centre)

14. Between Cookham and Maidenhead, the north bank of the river is a steep escarpment cloaked with a romantic wood. The grand Cliveden House commands a spectacular panoramic view from the top of the slope; the eighteenth-century Octagon Temple, one of its ornamental buildings, is perched right on the edge of the garden terrace. (© Andrew Sargent)

15. Eel fishing was traditionally an important source of income along the Thames. These five eel bucks of woven willow mounted on a frame near Caversham were photographed in 1870. They were lowered into the river to catch eels and raised to empty them. A platform provided access for the fisherman. (Photograph: Henry Taunt, reference no. HT01342. Reproduced by permission of Oxfordshire County Council – Oxfordshire History Centre)

16. In 1215 King John signed Magna Carta on an island at Runnymede. A memorial to this event, which is often seen as foundational to human rights legislation, was erected in 1957 by the American Bar Association. This view looks from the memorial towards the wooded Magna Carta Island where the signing is traditionally believed to have taken place. (© Andrew Sargent)

17. The Normans built a compact and functional castle at Windsor. During the medieval and later centuries it grew into a grand and extensive royal palace, which even today dominates the surrounding landscape. (© Andrew Sargent)

18. This drawing gives an idea of life on the river at Windsor at the end of the eighteenth century. Overshadowed by the imposing mass of the castle, masted barges negotiate the awkward spans of the wooden bridge, while a boat builder works on the bank. (From Combe, *An History of the River Thames*)

19. David Garrick, a successful actor and impresario, bought a house by the Thames at Hampton in 1754. He was painted on several occasions by Johann Zoffany, a German artist who also enjoyed royal patronage. One painting shows him entertaining friends on the lawn. Another depicts him outside the Temple to Shakespeare (the garden building to the left) with his wife. (From Combe, *An History of the River Thames*)

20. Cardinal Wolsey built Hampton Court as a palace fit for a cardinal-archbishop. Following his fall from power in 1529, it was seized by Henry VIII. It remained a favourite royal residence until George III decided not to live there in the later eighteenth century. (© Andrew Sargent)

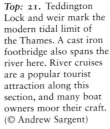

Top: **21.** Teddington Lock and weir mark the modern tidal limit of the Thames. A cast iron footbridge also spans the river here. River cruises are a popular tourist attraction along this section, and many boat owners moor their craft. (© Andrew Sargent)

Middle: **22.** Looking towards Richmond Hill from Twickenham, the rural landscape is reminiscent of carefully designed parkland, more natural than Nature. Since the eighteenth century the view from Richmond Hill has been recognised as one of the most beautiful in southern England. (Combe, *An History of the River Thames*)

Bottom: **23.** This drawing shows how wide the Thames was before it was embanked. Lambeth Palace, on the far bank, is the London home of the Archbishop of Canterbury. At this date it was still a fairly rural location on the edge of the growing capital, though the distant Westminster Bridge, opened in 1750, was beginning to promote development on the South Bank. (From Combe, *An History of the River Thames*)

24. John Norden's view of London Bridge shows the substantial houses which lined the roadway. In 1599 Thomas Platter wrote that it contained 'many tall handsome merchant dwellings and expensive shops, where all manner of wares are for sale, resembling a long street'. The buildings were removed in the 1750s to improve traffic flow. The ancient structure was replaced with a new bridge in 1831, which was itself replaced in 1973. (© Jonathan Reeve JR 1062b10prelims 16001650)

25. This extract from Claes Visscher's *Panorama of London* of 1616 gives a good impression of the difference in scale between St Paul's Cathedral, towering over the medieval City, and the huddle of domestic and commercial buildings leading down to the river at Queenhithe and Three Cranes Wharf. All this was swept away in the Great Fire of 1666. The Bankside and second Globe theatres stand in the foreground on the Southwark bank. (© Jonathan Reeve JR1076b3fp166 16001650)

26. This dramatic picture gives an impression of the extent and fury of the Fire of London as it raged from Sunday 2 September to Wednesday 5 September 1666. Remarkably, the reported death toll was in single figures, but 465¾ acres of the capital, including its dockside facilities, were destroyed and over 65,000 townsfolk were left homeless. (© Jonathan Reeve JR446b8fp108 16501700)

THE "SILENT HIGHWAY"-MAN.
"YOUR *MONEY* OR YOUR *LIFE!*"

27. Published in 1858, the year of the 'Great Stink', this cartoon captures popular concern at the state of the river. Cholera epidemics in 1832, 1849 and 1854 had already been traced to problems with London's water supply, and the government was feeling pressure to act in order to safeguard public health. (*Punch*, 10 July 1858)

Right: **28.** The French artist Gustave Doré captured the dark side of London street life in the late Victorian period. This illustration shows the labour-intensive, heavy and dangerous nature of dock work as bales of goods are loaded onto carts from warehouses. (Doré, G. and W. B. Jerrold, *London: A Pilgrimage*, first published London: Grant & Co., 1872)

Below: **29.** On the eve of the Industrial Revolution, Naval shipbuilding was the largest industry in Britain. This drawing looks east from the Naval shipyard at Deptford towards the Naval Hospital at Greenwich. (From Combe, *An History of the River Thames*)

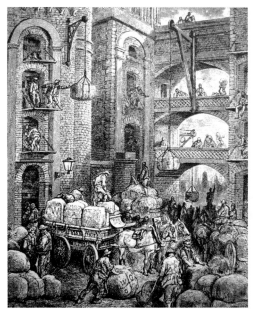

30. Built in the thirteenth century as a private castle, Hadleigh became part of the makeshift jigsaw of coastal defences against the threat of invasion by the French. *Hadleigh Castle, The Mouth of the Thames – Morning after a Stormy Night*, painted by John Constable in 1829, captures the atmosphere of the estuary where the elements meet. (Yale Center for British Art)

31. In the seventh century a Saxon church was built within the protective walls of the Roman fort of Reculver (*Regulbium*) on the north Kent coast. Half of the fort has since been washed away by the sea. In 1805 the church was demolished, though fortunately the distinctive Norman towers were left standing as a landmark for shipping. (Photograph: Peter Watson, 2009)

32. Three Maunsell Forts, heavily fortified anti-aircraft towers, were built in 1942 to protect the Thames estuary and ultimately London itself. Concrete rafts were floated out and sunk to provide a solid foundation. The fort on Shivering Sands, pictured here, was furthest out to sea of the three. (© David Lee)

the Thames blockhouses were ill-prepared, with few guns and rotten gun carriages. Refurbishment was urgently set in motion, and by the time the Armada sailed in 1588 the Thames defences had been bolstered. Henry's old artillery fort at West Tilbury was strengthened in line with the latest military thinking by the addition of a star-shaped rampart, and landward defences were thrown around Gravesend. The river could be closed with an 800-yard-long moveable boom. Elizabeth delivered her famous morale-boosting speech to a field army 23,000 strong which was encamped on the heights above Tilbury in case of a Spanish landing. These preparations, especially the standing army, were a drain on the public purse. Funds quickly dried up once war with Spain ended in 1604 and the forts and blockhouses decayed. During the Civil War they were given a brief new life by Parliament to control shipping on the approach to London.

Civil War on the Thames

King Charles I's philosophy of government, coupled with his stubborn nature, set him on an almost inevitable collision course with the rising power of Parliament. He believed in the 'Divine Right of Kings', and when he found himself at loggerheads with the people's representatives he simply chose not to summon Parliament for eleven years. Finally, driven by lack of funds, he recalled Parliament in 1640, only to dissolve it within a few weeks. Charles was forced to summon another Parliament in November of that year, which proceeded to wring concession from the king in exchange for taxes. Exasperated, in January 1642 Charles attempted to arrest five members of the House of Commons, raising the spectre of civil war.

From 1642, Parliament was firmly based in London while King Charles took Oxford for his headquarters, making the Thames Valley one of the key axes of the Civil War. Both armies crossed and re-crossed the region, securing towns and harrying one another; for example, the important town of Reading was besieged and changed hands. After an initial period of Royalist ascendancy, the net began to close in around the king at Oxford.

The Thames was essential to Parliament for provisioning London, while the king needed to supply Oxford. Normal commercial use of the river by the non-combatant towns along its bank must virtually have ceased: in April 1644 barges from Henley were seized and taken to Reading. In 1643 the (Parliamentarian) Committee for the Safety of the Kingdom instructed the Lord Mayor of London 'to consider of some speedy way for guarding the river Thames' to prevent provisions from being smuggled upriver to the Royalist garrisons at Reading and Oxford.[1]

Henley may have been typical of communities along the river, aware of the national struggle going on around them while they tried to continue with business as normal. Non-combatants were simply in the way. As early as August 1642 the town corporation was concerned at the 'great peril' caused by armed bands passing back and forth through the area, while January 1643 saw a skirmish in the streets. Some of the larger houses in the district were fortified. Phyllis Court, on the northern edge of the town, was garrisoned for Parliament from 1644: a drawing shows an earth rampart with a moat and drawbridge surrounding the old house. Earlier, in 1642 and 1643, Prince Rupert intermittently stationed troops there, though there seems little evidence that the town itself was ever fortified. A few miles downstream, the house of Greenlands (near Hambleden, Bucks.) was garrisoned for the king in 1644. It was sieged by General Browne and completely 'beaten down'.

Many towns were turned into strongpoints which could be held against the enemy, disrupt his advance and protect lines of communication. To combat the threat of artillery, earth ramparts were constructed well outside the surviving medieval defences, often incorporating the latest military thinking. At Reading, in October 1643, the Venetian ambassador recorded that 5,000 local men had been pressed into service on the defences and the work continued around the clock. It was completed within a month, but no plans survive. Three neighbouring villages were demolished to deprive the attackers of cover. Despite these preparations, the town changed hands three times.

The war years 1642–6 saw on average a doubling in civilian mortality rates in Berkshire: a similar pattern would probably be found throughout the Upper and Middle Thames valley as well as other parts of the country which saw prolonged action. Although the towns, such as Abingdon, Reading and Wallingford, bore the brunt, rural communities were also affected. Military activity, the disruption of normal economic life, high taxation and the requisitioning of food caused widespread privation. Both armies suffered from epidemics and troops carried disease – possibly typhus, though some places saw outbreaks of plague – from town to town where the weakened populace had limited capacity for resistance.

London was encircled by an earthen bank and ditch 11 miles long, punctuated by batteries and forts – a description of the circuit published by William Lithgow in 1643 listed twenty-eight defensive works. Although its precise course is largely lost, it reached from beyond Westminster in the west to Wapping in the east. It leapt the river at Vauxhall, running south of Southwark to the river at Rotherhithe. Booms or chains may have closed the river to shipping. At the heart of this circuit the City wall still stood and there is some evidence that the ditch was re-cut to provide defence in depth. These defences were never tested against the Royalists, and once hostilities were over the earthworks were dismantled and forgotten. Oxford, by contrast, was defended by a carefully engineered outer rampart only 3 miles long, and had to withstand three sieges.

Following the Royalist victory at Edgehill in October 1642, Prince Rupert, the charismatic Royalist cavalry commander, swept down the Thames Valley towards the ultimate prize of London. He captured Abingdon, Aylesbury and Maidenhead, but was checked at Windsor. When the Royalists pushed on, they found Kingston bridge and the town of Brentford had been fortified against them, blocking passage along both banks of the Thames. On 12 November the Royalists managed to drive the defenders from Brentford and won the day. They then sacked the town, sparking fear in London. In consequence, a large body of citizens joined the 'trained bands' or militia which turned out the next day to defend the capital. A Parliamentary force of 24,000, many of them untrained, drew up at Turnham Green to face the advancing army. It was late in the year and the king did not want to alienate Londoners, so after a little posturing he withdrew to Oxford without a fight.

Newbury was the scene of more than one clash. The Parliamentary army under the Earl of Essex was retreating towards the protection of Reading and eventually London after they had successfully lifted the siege of Gloucester. The Royalists under the direct command of the king caught up with them at Newbury on 20 September 1643. After an inconclusive day of fighting, with 1,300 Royalist and 1,200 Parliamentary casualties, Essex was able to continue his retreat. Another inconclusive engagement was fought near Newbury on 27 October 1644. A small Royalist garrison had been left at Donnington Castle, Newbury, following the earlier battle. This elegant fourteenth-century castle, commanding a key point on the London–Bath and Southampton–Midlands roads, was little more than a fortified house, not designed to withstand artillery or serious assault. To strengthen its defences, a star-shaped outer work was quickly thrown up in imitation of the latest military thinking and the neighbouring village was demolished. In July 1644 what proved to be a twenty-month siege began, twice relieved by Charles's army. In 1646, with the castle all but reduced to ruin, the defenders sought terms, and the unfortunate Mr John Packer was left to reclaim his home. Today only the gatehouse still stands with the foundations of the curtain wall showing through the grass.

The Thames remained a formidable military obstacle. Bridges were strategic places, often the scenes of skirmishes as the rival forces struggled for control. Most of the bridges on the Middle and Lower Thames were of timber which allowed a particular defensive tactic to be employed: drawbridges were made in the roadway which could be raised to close the crossing. The bridge at Marlow was fortified and drawbridges were cut, though this drastic action seriously weakened the structure. Drawbridges were also made in the bridges at Caversham, Windsor and Kingston. Bridges could be put out of commission by more drastic means. In September 1644, the Earl of Manchester found the timber bridge at Maidenhead was broken to prevent his passage. In 1688 the fleeing James II once again ordered the townsfolk to break the bridge, this time to prevent William of Orange from advancing towards London; but theirs was apparently only a token act of obedience as he was still able to cross – perhaps they had an eye to the cost of repair on the ratepayers. The wooden bridge at Henley was also badly damaged during the Civil War and the medieval bridge chapel was destroyed, while the timber bridge at Staines had to be rebuilt. The opportunity was taken in 1647 to rebuild the bridge at Kempsford (near Cricklade) in stone.

The Gloucestershire town of Lechlade and its medieval masonry bridge changed hands several times. Radcot Bridge, near Faringdon, another ancient stone structure, was also a scene of action. Abingdon, Faringdon and Wallingford formed part of a ring of defensive outposts around the Royalist headquarters in Oxford. In April 1645 Cromwell was present in person, commanding the siege of Faringdon House, when news was received that a force of Royalist cavalry led by Lord Goring was approaching, so a small force was sent to secure Radcot Bridge against them. They advanced too far, were overpowered, and Goring took the bridge. Cromwell then marched round via Newbridge, several miles downriver, hoping to surprise Goring, but the skirmish was inconclusive. The following spring Faringdon was again besieged, and a Parliamentary force captured the outpost at Radcot House and took control of the bridge to ensure their lines of communication. This phase of the Civil War came to an end in June 1646 with the king's surrender set out in the Articles of Oxford.

Even where there were no bridges, it was vital to secure river crossings. When London was threatened in November 1642, the Earl of Essex linked both banks with a pontoon bridge between Fulham and Putney defended by earthworks at either end in order to prevent the Royalists reaching the capital. Incidentally, this must effectively have closed the river to shipping. Late in the war, in July 1648, Parliament issued a proclamation that the horse ferries at Lambeth, Chelsea, Putney, Brentford, Richmond, Hampton Court, Hampton and as far upriver as Shepperton must be fixed on the Middlesex (northern) bank during the hours of darkness and guarded.

Early in 1648 civil war broke out once again, with Royalist uprisings in Kent and Essex. The Kentish men held various towns for the king, including Rochester, Gravesend and Maidstone, and several castles including Upnor on the Medway were seized. When Maidstone was won back on 1 June through bloody street fighting by a force under Sir Thomas Fairfax, the uprising in Kent petered out. In Essex, meanwhile, the Royalist force was besieged in Colchester from 12 June to 28 August before finally surrendering, marking the end of the second phase of the Civil War. King Charles himself was executed in Whitehall on 30 January 1649.

Fire of London

Another event that had a devastating impact on the country, and particularly on the Thames, was the Fire of London of 1666. War with the Dutch was already sapping the economy, and plague the previous year had claimed perhaps 25 per cent of the population of the City. Then, overnight, the commercial heart of the nation was destroyed – wealth, businesses, the ability to trade, even the basic necessities of life for upwards of 65,000 people made homeless and destitute. Some refugees no doubt found shelter with family or friends, but tens of thousands put up makeshift shelters in the open fields around the city. Wenceslaus Hollar's plan produced later that year shows that 465¾ acres within the ancient walls, including the whole of the river frontage, were ruined. With the loss of London, communities upriver lost a regular market for foodstuffs, fuel and manufactured goods; there were many losers.

With the potential of a blank canvas, the government debated the options. In the event, few radical ideas were implemented: some streets were widened or straightened, building controls restricted the height of buildings and imposed the use of fireproof materials, prices and pay scales in the building trade were regulated to prevent profiteering, and supplies of materials were secured. Rebuilding was underway by the following spring, but it took time. Merchants and tradesmen also had to rebuild their business contacts and their finances.

Public buildings had to be rebuilt, starting with St Paul's Cathedral. Thirty-nine new churches were proposed, though some ancient churches were never rebuilt. Civic and commercial buildings such as the Royal Exchange and the Custom House were designed to be imposing architectural set-pieces. The quays were another priority, though many were the responsibility of their owners. The Corporation took the opportunity to improve the lower section of the River Fleet, lined with broad quays and warehouses. A grand scheme to create a quay running the full length of the Thames frontage from the Temple to the Tower foundered due to the cost of acquiring the land, though piecemeal improvements were undertaken. By 1675 most of the civic and domestic buildings and some of the churches were complete, with St Paul's finally finished in 1710. Though drastic and traumatic in its cause, the result was an architecturally impressive new city that was better suited to the growing ambitions of a world power.

The Dutch Raid

Post-Civil War Britain was an ambitious nation, and international conflict was inevitable. The Dutch raid on the Naval Dockyards at Chatham in 1667, coming as it did a year after the Fire of London, struck at the heart of British maritime pride, undermining her international reputation. In the seventeenth and eighteenth centuries Britain engaged in a number of wars with the Dutch United Provinces, ultimately over supremacy in maritime trade, and by 1667 they had been openly at war for two years. Even so, the British military were totally unprepared for such an audacious move.

Samuel Pepys, the diarist, was a senior civil servant in the Navy Office, roughly the equivalent of a modern Permanent Secretary. On 8 June 1667 Pepys arrived at his office in Whitehall to hear that a fleet of eighty Dutch ships was off Harwich.[2] The militia had already been called out, and all the available western barges (river barges designed to work upriver from London) had been commandeered to make a pontoon for the cavalry across the estuary. Two days later the news was that the Dutch had sailed into the estuary as far as the Nore. That triggered a busy day for Pepys, ordering fireships (to set alight and sail into the enemy fleet), and visiting the shipyards at Deptford and Woolwich. He could hear guns in the distance, towards Sheerness. As a defensive tactic, a line of English frigates was drawn up across the river between the Tilbury and Milton blockhouses. Local commanders were aware that the sailors needed to man the imposing ships moored at Chatham and the troops needed to defend the site were woefully under strength, and there was little artillery or powder. In desperation, valuable ships were sunk in the Medway in a vain attempt to prevent the Dutch from reaching the dockyard.

Over the next few days the news got worse: the Dutch had taken Sheerness, they had cut the chain with its 6¼-inch links that supposedly prevented vessels entering Chatham Naval Dockyard, and burned the fleet in harbour. It is clear Pepys and his Navy colleagues did not know what to do. He ordered more fireships – his diary even speaks of hiring them! Despite the action taking place just 35 miles from London, lack of news paralysed the Naval central command. In the absence of proper information, rumour was rife: was this the prelude to an invasion? Many workers at Chatham Dockyard deserted. The London militia was called out, sent home and called out again. Pepys was worried by the mood on the streets, where the gossip was that England had been betrayed. Inside Whitehall, people blamed one another for years of under-investment. Pepys was sufficiently shaken that he sent his wife to the country with some of their valuables and made several secret stashes of the rest. His entry for 14 June sounds puzzled: 'No news today of any motion of the enemy.' Having spread fear and destroyed or captured ships, the Dutch simply sailed away. It later transpired that they did not attempt to sail further up the Thames because they believed the various riverside batteries were fully operational: they were not! In the aftermath, the commissioner in charge of Chatham Dockyard was arrested and placed in the Tower, and Pepys was afraid he would himself be caught up in the hunt for scapegoats.

On 23 July Pepys received a letter from the base at Gravesend, warning that thirty Dutch men-of-war had again entered the mouth of the Thames on the last tide. When Pepys rushed to inform Sir William Penn, Commissioner of the Navy, he refused to believe the news. Later that day they engaged the British fleet, though Pepys preferred to get his eyewitness report of the fighting from the landlord of the Shipp Inn rather than from official sources.

After the raid, funds suddenly became available to strengthen the defences along the estuary, and the military engineer Sir Bernard de Gomme was commissioned to upgrade the fortifications. Already by 30 June Pepys was inspecting the works. New forts were built on the Medway and at Gillingham. The old Elizabethan fort at West Tilbury was upgraded with a rampart in a modern design. At Woolwich, land was purchased to enlarge the dockyard and military arsenal, and a sixty-gun battery was erected. However, the sense of urgency quickly lapsed and work at the dockyards at Sheerness and Chatham, and on the South Coast at Portsmouth, progressed only slowly. The raid had pointed up the need for batteries around the estuary where the Dutch had been unchallenged, but nothing was done.

Economic Stagnation

The condition of the river had deteriorated since the medieval period, and continued to deteriorate against a background of war and national disaster. By the start of the sixteenth century, serious commercial traffic upstream of Henley had dwindled to nothing and the prosperity of towns such as Oxford had suffered. The merchant Thomas West of Wallingford was unusual in the 1560s in that he still sailed as far as Burcot before transferring his Oxford-bound goods to a wagon. The situation became so bad that an Act of 1604 appointed eighteen commissioners (all local landowners) to reopen the river from Burcot (near Wallingford) to Oxford, funding their schemes from an increase in local tax. The Act sweetened this pill with talk of commercial benefits, mentioning Headington stone moving downriver from Oxford and coal passing in the opposite direction. Some progress was made, but in 1623 a new Act set up a slimmed-down commission of eight members. A wharf was built at Folly Bridge in Oxford, and the newly introduced technology of the pound locks (familiar today on canals) was employed to carry shipping around obstructions at Culham, Iffley and Sandford. Even then, Culham lock collapsed in 1650!

John Taylor (1578–1653), known as the 'Water Poet', was a self-educated wherryman and member of the Watermen's Company. During his life he made several journeys around the country, publishing his observations and thoughts in poetic form. *Thame Isis*, published in 1632, recounts a trip down the Thames from its rival source at Coberley on the River Churn. On the way he lists the obstructions to shipping and other abuses which he sees, and they are not confined to the upper river. For example, he notes a fish weir at

Nuneham Courtenay, that the lock at Whitchurch needs repair, that the river is choked with weed below Caversham, while the threshold to the lock at Sonning is too high, causing barges to ground. He reports that five passengers were recently drowned near Boveney due to a dangerous 'stop'. It is the age-old complaint: the national interest versus private property. Clearly no-one was investing, no-one was planning, no-one had authority; and the commonweal suffered. He pulls no punches. It may not be great poetry, but surprisingly it did sell – more a literary curiosity than a gem. And it paints a graphic picture of the state of navigation at the time:

> Shall Thames be barr'd its course with stops and locks,
> With mils, and hils, with gravell beds, and rocks:
> With weares, and weeds, and forced ilands made,
> To spoile a publike for a private trade?[3]

Daniel Defoe, author of *Robinson Crusoe* among other works, published *A Tour Through the Whole Island of Britain*, based mostly on his travels in the 1680s. He was interested to note the quantities of food and other produce regularly sent down the Thames to London. Cheese from Gloucestershire and Somerset travelled overland to the Thames, bacon from Wiltshire, and malting barley was bought in Abingdon and Faringdon. Barges from wharfs on the Kennet at Reading carried 1,000–1,200 quarters of malt at a time (i.e. 120 tons), while Marlow was important for malt and meal, as well as beech wood, and brassware from the Temple Mills. Henley and Maidenhead also traded malt, meal and timber. Merchants were managing to trade, but conditions were difficult.

For artists and intellectuals in this unsettled period, an idealised Thames symbolised all that was desirable in an idealised nation. For Edmund Spenser (1552–99), in his poem *Prothalamion*, it was 'silver streaming', with the refrain, 'Sweete Thames! runne softly, till I end my Song.' Robert Herrick (1591–1674) called it 'silver-footed' with crystal waters, while for Francis Quarles (1592–1644) it was 'silver-breasted'.[4] At a time of religious upheaval, civil war and foreign conflict, England's river could stand as a metaphor for peace and purity, just as a formal garden served to deny social and political disorder for a wealthy landowner.

8

The Working River

Industry and Empire, Seventeenth Century to the Present

Unprecedented Growth

For 250 years, since at least the 1750s, the world has been changing at an ever-faster rate. Britain was a leader in this process, and often stood at its heart. The agricultural and industrial revolutions offered huge potential for wealth creation, replacing familiar and slowly developing ways of life with whole new social orders. Power shifted, often uncomfortably, to new classes of entrepreneurs and financiers. Empires were forged, creating new markets and opportunities, followed by the postcolonial legacy. Two world wars and the Cold War remodelled the political, economic and social landscape. Even the Thames has not remained unchanged. Used and abused, it has been taken for granted and adapted to human need.

The vigorous nineteenth and twentieth centuries saw the population of Britain multiplied six times. It also saw a move from country to town, and the development of the suburbs. This growth is despite the numbers who emigrated to the colonies and the impact of two world wars. This had a huge effect on the Thames valley.

Table 2: Population figures from the census (rounded)

Census year	Britain	London	LB Harrow	Reading	Oxford
2001	49.1 m	7.1 m	207,300	143,100	134,200
1991	48.0 m	6.6 m	203,700	136,000	130,500
1981	46.6 m	6.7 m	196,100	130.900	107,600

1971	45.8 m	7.4 m	203,300	139,500	125,100
1961	44.0 m	7.9 m	210,400	125,200	115,00
1951	41.0 m	8.2 m	217,800	112,300	105,900
1941	No census	No census	No census	No census	No census
1931	37.3 m	8.1 m	98,700	95,300	83,100
1921	35.2 m	7.3 m	64,400	89,700	72,200
1911	33.6 m	7.1 m	42,000	84,300	62,900
1901	30.5 m	6.5 m	22,700	72,900	57,400
1891	27.2 m	5.5 m	12,200	63,000	52,400
1881	24.4 m	4.7 m	10,300	47,300	46,400
1871	21.3 m	3.8 m	8,800	39,500	41,100
1861	18.7	3.1 m	7,400	31,600	35,800
1851	16.7 m	2.6 m	5,900	23,800	30,600
1841	14.8 m	2.2 m	5,800	21,100	27,800
1831	13.0 m	1.8 m	5,300	14,500	24,200
1821	11.1 m	1.5 m	4,300	14,500	18,100
1811	9.5 m	1.3 m	3,900	12,200	14,500
1801	8.3 m	1 m	3,200	10,700	12,700
1750	5.7m estimate[1]	650k estimate	Not estimated	Not estimated	Not estimated
1700	5.0 m estimate[1]	575–600 k estimate			
1650	5.2 m estimate[1]	350–400 k estimate			
1600	4.1 m estimate[1]	200 k estimate			
1540	2.7 m estimate[1]	50 k estimate			
1340*	Not estimated	40–50 k estimate			
1066	Not estimated	25 k estimate			
Boudicca	Not estimated	30 k estimate			

* On the eve of the Black Death.

On the threshold of the nineteenth century, when the first national census was taken, the population of London had just broken the 1 million barrier. The built-up area was tightly circumscribed, consisting of the City, Westminster, a very limited suburban growth to the north and west, and some development in Southwark and along the South Bank. A very real limit on distance was imposed by the fact that most people still walked to work. As a result, population density in the central districts was high, even for the emerging middle classes. This was a century of real change in British society, and by the close the population of the metropolis had increased over five times to 6.5 million. The urban area had also increased many times over, and the concept of the residential suburb had been invented. Many factors contributed to this growth: the international pre-eminence of Britain and London as its capital, maritime trade, industrial and financial development, and last but not least the effect of the railways as they loosened the ties of distance. Already by 1849 *The Builder* could observe that 'those parties who can afford it are beginning to move off a little way into the country along the different lines of railway'. Cheap and expanding public transport allowed the urban fringe economically to move ever further outwards, though long-distance commuting was not yet viable.

Growth slowed in the twentieth century, due in part to such brakes as the Great War and the Depression. The 1931 census showed a cumulative rise in the first three decades of only about 1.4 million, though numbers continued to rise until the start of the Second World War. Wartime destruction and post-war austerity saw population and economic life plateau, and by the time the economy started to work once more in the 1960s the situation was very different. It was now possible to commute to work from pleasant towns in a wide arc across the estuary, home counties and Thames valley, while the policy of developing new towns such as Harlow and Stevenage saw whole communities relocate away from the capital. Soon the docks began to close, and many industries found it was no longer either necessary or economic to manufacture in the South East. The cumulative result of these changes has been to cause the number of people living in London to drop, although many more work than sleep in the capital. The 2001 census found the number living within the Greater London area had fallen to 7.1 million, only 600,000 more than in 1901. At the same time, the urban area has spread well beyond its earlier limits; consequently the population density is much lower.

The area now covered by the London Borough of Harrow illustrates the impact of improved public transport in opening up areas where London workers could live. Throughout the nineteenth century this district, so close to the City, was largely rural, focusing on agricultural produce for the London market. With the extension of the underground lines to join up these isolated settlements, 'Metroland' was spawned. The suburbs followed the lines, and from 1891 the whole area began to be developed, reaching a peak in the 1920s and 1930s and again with post-war rehousing.

Oxford and Reading were similarly sized Thames-side towns

at the dawn of the industrial age. The pattern of growth in nineteenth-century Reading compares closely with London, with the population multiplying sixfold. The twentieth century, however, tells a different story. After the Second World War Reading continued to grow, latterly as a result of the 'Silicon Valley' phenomenon as new electronic technologies found a home. The town also benefited from both businesses and commuters moving west from London along the line of the old Great Western Railway in search of space. By contrast Oxford, with a smaller manufacturing base and a greater emphasis on the university as an employer, and at a greater distance from London, saw only a fourfold growth during the nineteenth century.

Industrial River

The Industrial Revolution brought major change to many parts of the country, and the Thames valley was far from exempt although it was generally spared the heavy industry that is found in Midlands and Northern towns. The Upper Thames remained a rural backwater for much of its length, although Morris based its car manufacturing at Cowley just outside Oxford and across the river at Abingdon.

The rural Upper Thames was the scene of an interesting experiment to apply industrial methods to agriculture. In 1859 Robert Tertius Campbell, who had recently returned from Australia with a substantial fortune, bought the run-down Buscot Park Estate near Faringdon. This 3,500-acre estate lay beside the Thames and boasted a cheese wharf for shipping to London. Campbell did not simply want to be accepted as a country gentleman: he was driven by an idea. His plan was to make sugar and distil alcohol from sugar beet. He drained the land and created an irrigation system powered by waterwheels. Next a distillery was added, with a narrow gauge railway to haul the beet. A mill for oil cake, a fertiliser factory, a gasworks and a vitriol works followed. A telegraph system speeded communications around the estate. Dairy cattle converted the by-products into cheese for export to London, carrying on a local tradition. Other stock were fattened 'scientifically'. He erected innovative cast-concrete barns and used steam ploughing engines on his land. Everything was modern. At first he seems to have turned a profit, but sadly after a decade he ran into financial difficulties and was forced to close the distillery, selling off what he could. He had stretched himself too far financially without due regard to commercial returns. When Campbell died in 1887 the estate was sold, with most of the proceeds going to settle his debts.

By contrast, the towns of the Middle Thames saw considerable development. In the medieval and Early Modern periods, woollen textiles had been the mainstay of Reading's economy. The Oracle was set up in the seventeenth century to provide workshops for a variety of textile crafts. The legendary Jack o' Newbury was part of this trade, a composite figure based on a dynasty of wealthy Tudor clothiers all called John Winchcombe who lived in nearby Newbury. By the nineteenth century Reading's industrial base was diverse, with the usual range of food-related industries such as brewing, building industries such as brickmaking, boatbuilding due to the town's location on the Kennet and Thames, printing, and small-scale engineering works. The firms with which the town was to become synonymous were nineteenth-century creations: Suttons Seeds and Huntley & Palmers biscuits.

It was water power that launched the Industrial Revolution; soon the technology was adapted to many different industries and some mills became large industrial complexes. The many tributaries of the Thames to the west of London and the Lea to the east were harnessed for power. Brentford was an important milling town. Gunpowder mills at Bedfont and Hounslow, paper and corn mills at Harefield converted into copper mills in 1803, corn and oil mills at Tottenham, a mustard mill at Staines, corn mills at Isleworth, and paper mills at Bromley-by-Bow; these are indicative of the versatility of the technology, and it was not unusual for mills to switch their business. By the closing decades of the nineteenth century, many mills had supplemented their traditional waterwheels with steam to ensure a regular source of power.

The potential of tributaries on the South Bank was also exploited. Once again, many mills were small concerns, often grinding corn for local consumption. Large industrial complexes also developed, such as the gunpowder mills on the River Darent at Dartford, or the paper mills on the River Cray at St Paul's Cray and St Mary Cray.

Not everyone bought into the Industrial Revolution. William Morris established his Arts and Crafts textile factory in the leafy Surrey suburb of Merton. The old workshop he found was Merton Abbey, a former silk-weaving factory set up by Huguenot refugees beside the River Wandle. Here he dyed and printed textiles, wove tapestries and carpets, and made glass. His firm, Morris & Co., set standards in design, famously supplying the shop Liberty of London. Morris himself was a socialist with a romantic belief in craftsmanship and the medieval guilds. He also loved the Thames, latterly dividing his time between his two riverside homes, his townhouse in Hammersmith named 'Kelmscott' and Kelmscott Manor near Lechlade.

From the early nineteenth century the Lower Thames developed as an industrial region to rival any in Britain. Though it lacked the advantages of nearby raw materials and fuel which its rivals possessed, it had the very real advantage that through the docks it had ready access to world markets. In addition, it had a plentiful labour force and offered a large market in its own right.

At the same time that the Thames was developing as a world port, it was also emerging quite naturally as a centre for shipbuilding and repair. In the period up to the Industrial Revolution, the Naval dockyards were the largest industrial enterprise in the land, and the Medway and Lower Thames was a key focus of this activity. Commercial shipbuilding was on an altogether different scale, with small yards employing traditional techniques. Although the shipbuilding trade was dispersed around the coast, London had for centuries been the leading shipbuilding area in the country. At the start of the nineteenth century there were fourteen commercial firms of importance on the Thames, five at Rotherhithe, three at Limehouse, others at Deptford, Northfleet, Wapping, Blackwall and Shadwell, in addition to the Naval dockyards at Chatham, Sheerness, Woolwich and Deptford. Tonnage statistics show that the Thames made 13 per cent of all British output in 1791 and 11 per cent in 1820.

The advent of iron ships changed the picture. Many of the Thames yards were small and often unable to invest in the new technology and skills required, so chose not to enter the market. However, between 1832 and 1846 a number of entrepreneurs did build iron ships on the Thames. Some moved to the Thames having previously had businesses elsewhere, such as the pioneers David Napier, who had built ships on the Clyde, and William Fairbairn, who had worked in Manchester. They were both attracted to undeveloped sites near Millwall, in part because the by-laws regarding 'noxious' industries were less stringent in Essex than in London and Middlesex. Other shipbuilders followed, with yards at Blackwall and Limehouse and across the river at Deptford and Greenwich.

I. K. Brunel chose John Scott Russell's shipyard at Millwall for his gigantic ship, the *Great Eastern*. At 18,914 tons, it was four times the weight of any previous boat. Even its ordinary components were much larger than was normal, causing technical and logistical problems for the yard – for example, the propeller shaft weighed 60 tons. Russell wanted to build the *Great Eastern* in a specially dug dry dock, but Brunel favoured a slipway. Due to its sheer size, this meant the ship had to be launched side-on to the river; and when the great day came on 3 November 1857, it failed, as well as causing the very public death of an employee. The *Great Eastern* was not finally launched until 31 January 1858, and the whole enterprise bankrupted Russell.

Shipbuilding was a precarious business and prone to failure. With strong competition from the Clyde and Belfast in particular, the Thames began a decline in the 1860s, two decades later constructing only 2.5 per cent of UK tonnage. By the First World War the industry had disappeared; only barges and small vessels were being built on the Thames, with several yards switching to repairs. The naval yards, well positioned in the estuary and patronised by a wealthy client, continued into the late twentieth century.

Within the London conurbation, food processing, including brewing, remained a major concern throughout the nineteenth and early twentieth centuries. A huge variety of other manufacturing industries have grown up throughout the region, though many remain comparatively small-scale. Pottery manufacture included the Fulham Pottery, established by John Dwight around 1672, which continued under different management until it relocated to Battersea in 1986. Heavy industry in Southwark included Grey & Marten's lead works, which imported its raw material directly to its own wharf. Electricity generation to meet the capital's huge appetite for power created several landmark buildings. The vast newspaper industry traditionally occupied Fleet Street until the 1980s when it became one of the first industries to relocate to vacant sites in the Docklands, in this case as part of a major restructuring. London has a large service sector, while the City in particular is home to an internationally important financial services sector.

Industry was attracted to the lonely shores of the estuary where land was relatively cheap but still near the capital. The river offered an ideal method of transporting bulky raw materials and finished goods and the docks were conveniently close. A plentiful supply of water was available, while industrial waste could be disposed of easily. In 1925 Ford, the American car giant, opened a European factory beside the river at Dagenham, with its own riverside wharf. Tate & Lyle likewise established a huge sugar refinery at Plaistow, again with its own wharves, while Proctor & Gamble had a large factory at West Thurrock. The estuary was a cradle of the early aircraft industry, with Short Brothers on the Isle of Sheppey. Oil refineries and storage facilities line the lower reaches, and the by-products are used by a range of industries.

Fishing was an important industry on the Thames for millennia. It was still rich in fish at the close of the eighteenth century, but this changed quickly early the following century. Medieval Woolwich was typical of many of the settlements east of London, being primarily a fishing village, while upriver of London settlements such as Chiswick and Strand-on-the-Green were also fishing villages. Fish was landed at Billingsgate for over 1,000 years. The river was well stocked with salmon. Whitebait, the fry of the herring, were common as far upriver as London. Along with other common species, porpoise and even whale were occasional visitors. Freshwater species were also plentiful, including perch, roach, rudd, bream and pike. Excavation found that fish had played an important part in the diet at the medieval Hospital of St Mary Spital; a range of marine and freshwater species were eaten, with herring and plaice being the most common. Some of the estuary towns were known for their specialities, such as Gravesend for shrimps, Whitstable for oysters or Leigh-on-Sea for cockles.

Upriver also, fishing had long been an important economic activity. Fish traps from the Saxon period have been excavated, while fish weirs were one of the age-old hazards to navigation, mentioned as early as Magna Carta and still causing a headache for the authorities in the eighteenth century. Eels were a major seasonal resource. During the autumn 'eel run', millions of eels swan down the river to the sea where they spawned in the estuary. Each spring, elvers in their tens of millions made the return journey, and the shallow margins of the river could be black with their bodies. They were caught using traps known as 'eel bucks', large baskets on wooden frames which could be lowered and raised in and out of the river. Even at the end of the nineteenth century, hundredweights could still be taken in a night; mature eels in the autumn were all of good size – usually over 1 lb – while in the springtime elvers were just inches long. Eel pie and jellied eels were traditional foods of the East London poor.

Port of Empire

London's maritime trade boomed. By the end of the seventeenth century, its quays were handling 80 per cent of the nation's exports and 67 per cent of its imports. A century later, London's position as the nation's foremost international port was being strangled by vested interests. London still had only 1,400 feet of wharves and quays, while the much smaller port of Bristol had 4,000 feet. These were the 'legal quays', the twenty quays on the north bank designated by Elizabeth I through which all cargo was to be discharged for customs clearance. The result was congestion in the Thames and delays in unloading ships. Larger vessels discharged their cargoes onto barges and lighters in mid-stream, but those barges still had to queue for the legal quays. In response to petitions from merchants and ship owners, several wharves on the Southwark bank were designated 'sufferance wharves', temporarily licensed for customs clearance. This concession improved the situation slightly, but the basic problems remained.

A transformation in the way in which shipping was handled began with the opening of the West India Docks in 1802. Two vast basins were cut across the loop of low-lying wasteland to the east of the City known as the Isle of Dogs to create 54 acres of water surrounded by purpose-built warehousing. A lock at each entrance controlled access to the river in order to maintain a constant water level in the dock. The venture was a huge success, allowing vessels to be discharged in a space of days rather than weeks. The volumes of trade were high: in 1848, the Docks loaded or unloaded over 3,000 ships.

West India Docks was quickly followed by London Docks. This was at Wapping, much closer to the City. A valuable twenty-one-year monopoly on vessels carrying rice, tobacco, wine and brandy, other than those from the West or East Indies, gave it a huge commercial kick-start. The plan allowed for 27 acres of water entered by a river lock, together with state-of-the-art bonded warehouses. In May 1849 the warehouses held 170,000 tons of goods, and had space for 60,000 pipes of wine. Security was taken seriously, and the whole site was surrounded by a high wall and given its own police force. In 1828 St Katherine's Dock was squeezed onto a 23-acre site between London Docks and the Tower of London. 1,250 houses, a brewery, the ancient hospital and the twelfth-century church of St Katherine were all demolished to make way. It was, however, a small dock at a time when shipping was rapidly increasing in size.

The long-established East India Company was a wealthy and powerful organisation, and its vessels were the largest using the port of London at that time. Tea, silk, spices and Chinese porcelain were among its most valuable imports. In 1803 it obtained an Act of Parliament to build new docks at Blackwall. Prior to this their ships had unloaded in mid-stream, and their goods were stored in warehouses in Cutler Street. As part of the proposal for the new dock, it was revealed that an average of £2,100 worth of tea alone was stolen each year under the existing system: a secure enclosed dock would eliminate this drain on profits.

A complex known as the Surrey Commercial Docks developed in the first decades of the nineteenth century in a bend on the South Bank alongside Limehouse Reach. This vast system eventually covered 300 acres and was operated by four separate companies, only finally merging in 1864 in the face of increasing competition and the need for economies of scale. Mergers were by this date the only way of maintaining viability, until in 1909 the newly formed Port of London Authority assumed responsibility for the tidal river and all its docks.

Other enclosed docks were developed in response to the growing size of ocean-going ships. The Royal Victoria and Royal Albert Docks were opened in 1855 and 1880 respectively. They lay further east, on the Plaistow Marshes. The Royal Albert alone was three-quarters of a mile long with 3 miles of quayside. Finally, in 1912, work began on the King George V Dock, though this was delayed by the war and not completed until 1921. Meanwhile, the East & West India Docks Company was feeling the competition of these new docks, so decided to build a deep-water dock of its own at Tilbury, 26 miles downriver of London. Opened in 1886, it was linked to the capital by rail.

The new system of enclosed docks, with its rapid turn-around of shipping, was highly profitable. Enhanced security had almost eliminated theft. Official returns for the Port of London in 1842 show that customs duties amounted to almost £12 million. Yet, towards the close of the nineteenth century, competition and lack of investment were driving the port into decline. At the same time, other ports such as Liverpool, Manchester, Glasgow and Newcastle were competing for a slice of the business. However, by 1913, revitalised by the Port of London Authority, London handled about a third of all trade through British ports, totalling 20 million tons of cargo annually with a value of over £400 million. Growth continued after the war, handling 35 million tons of cargo by 1930 and employing 100,000 people.

The Pool of London, the section of the Thames below London Bridge, continued to function as an active dock well into the twentieth century. A directory to *London Wharves and Docks* published in 1954 still listed over 500 commercial wharves with their specialisms. Some ship owners exploited the 'free water' clause, which allowed barges and lighters free access to the docks to deliver or receive goods, to convey cargoes to cheaper warehousing at the improved riverside wharves.

The novelist Joseph Conrad graphically described the sensations felt by a hand as a ship berthed in a London dock after a long sea voyage:[2]

Black barges drifted stealthily on the murky stream. A mad jumble of begrimed walls loomed up vaguely in the smoke, bewildering and mournful, like a vision of disaster. The tugs backed and filled the stream, to hold the ship steady at the dock-gates; from her bows two lines went through the air whistling, and struck the land viciously, like a pair of snakes. A bridge broke in two before her, as if by enchantment; big hydraulic capstans began to turn all by themselves, as though animated by a mysterious and unholy spell. She moved through a narrow lane of water between two low walls of granite, and men with check-ropes in their hands kept pace with her, walking on the broad flag-stones. ... 'Let go your quarter-checks! Let go!' sang out a ruddy-faced old man on the quay. The ropes splashed heavily falling in the water, and the *Narcissus* entered the dock.

The stony shores ran away right and left in straight lines, enclosing a sombre and rectangular pool. Brick walls rose high above the water – soulless walls, staring through hundreds of windows as troubled and dull as the eyes of over-fed brutes. At their base monstrous iron cranes crouched, with chains hanging from their long necks, balancing cruel-looking hooks over the decks of lifeless ships. A noise of wheels rolling over stones, the thump of heavy things falling, the racket of feverish winches, the grinding of strained chains, floated on the air. Between high buildings the dust of all the continents soared in short flights; and a penetrating smell of perfumes and dirt, of spices and hides, of things costly and of things filthy, pervaded the space, made for it an atmosphere precious and disgusting. The *Narcissus* came gently into her berth; the shadows of soulless walls fell upon her, the dust of all the continents leaped upon her deck, and a swarm of strange men, clambering up her sides, took possession of her in the name of solid earth. She had ceased to live.

London was a city of great contrasts. Henry Mayhew conducted a survey into the London poor, publishing his findings as a series of open letters in the *Morning Chronicle*.[3] In October 1849 he wrote about the plight of dock workers. This was a group which had a reputation for vice and profligacy, but he was shocked by the conditions in which they worked, arguing that the unreliable nature of their work was not conducive to developing regular habits of life.

Mayhew estimated that 20,000 men lived from their work at the docks. They were regarded as unskilled labour, little more than 'human steam-engines', and were paid accordingly at or even below subsistence level. The real evil, however, was that the work was casual, on a daily, or even an hourly, basis. Its availability depended on how busy the dock was on that day. London Docks, for example, might take on between 1,000 and 3,000 hands, with a permanent staff of only 400–500 labourers. Each morning the casual labourers would crowd around the gate waiting for the foreman's 'call-on'. Those who were not chosen might hang around in case extra hands were needed later in the day or else drift away to look for a drink or food. He concluded, 'It is a sight to sadden the most callous, to see thousands of men struggling for only one day's hire.'

Mayhew analysed the trend. He was told that an easterly wind prevented ships from sailing upriver, so at such times business was slack. Figures supported this observation: on 26 May 1849 a high of 3,012 hands had been employed, while on 30 May this had dropped to 1,189 – due to the wind. In other words, 1,823 men at London Docks alone depended for their living on wind direction! This could be multiplied across the whole dockland and measured in human misery. When daily rates of pay were added to the calculation, the desperation of the dockers became clear. Casual labourers earned two shillings and sixpence a day in the summer, reduced to two shillings and fourpence in winter due to shorter daylight hours. For extra hands taken on during the day, the rate was fourpence per hour. The accounts revealed that on average a labourer earned only five shillings a week. This was against sixteen shillings and sixpence a week for the lucky few who formed the permanent complement. Craftsmen such as coopers and smiths earned commensurately more.

Work in the docks was hard and physical. In the absence of steam-powered equipment, cranes and winches were driven by a treadwheel or lever. Other men pushed laden carts an average of

30 miles a day. It was dangerous work: accidents such as falling or being hit by a crate were common. Yet despite the temptations of handling rich goods all day, heavy security including a search at the gate had almost eradicated theft. These 'human steam engines' were running on empty.

Their poor rates of pay and conditions put dock workers in the forefront of the growing trade union movement from the 1870s onwards. The first major dock strike closed the docks for a month in 1889. Their main demand was a 20–25 per cent increase in the hourly rate of pay to sixpence. In a labour intensive industry this was always going to be resisted, but after an arbitration committee was set up, including the Bishop of London and the Roman Catholic Cardinal Manning, the employers agreed to the demand.

At the end of the First World War dock workers were still poorly paid and their union was demanding a minimum wage. Ernest Bevan (later Minister of Labour) championed their cause. In evidence to the inquiry, he bought food to the exact amount allowed for a family dinner, prepared it, and served it before the court, asking whether this was sufficient 'to sustain the strength of a docker hauling 71 tons of wheat a day on his back'. The inquiry was persuaded, awarding the minimum wage of sixteen shillings a day that the unions were demanding. However, in the Depression that followed, the day rate dropped back to ten shillings.

The immediate post-war period was one of expansion and optimism for London's docks, but by the 1960s it was clear that the western docks had no future. The end, when it came, was rapid, with a rash of closures by the end of the decade. West India and Millwall Docks closed in the 1980, as did the three 'royal' docks. By this date the warehouses that lined the City and Southwark shores were supplied by road rather than water, and their wharves were obsolete. The once-busy port fell silent, a victim to the growth in the size of shipping, the new practice of containerisation, RORO ferries and the ease of road and rail transport. Other ports around the coast were better placed to catch this new business. Recently a specialised container terminal, the DP World London Gateway Port, has been developed on the north bank of the estuary near Stanford-le-Hope. This involved dredging a new deep-water channel 100 km long from the port well out into the open sea.

In response to hundreds of acres of derelict dockland within just a few miles of the capital, the London Docklands Development Corporation (LDDC) was established in 1981. The LDDC was tasked with the regeneration of the Docklands, including the Isle of Dogs: as the Act put it,[4]

> to secure ... regeneration ... by bringing land and buildings into effective use, encouraging the development of existing and new industry and commerce, creating an attractive environment, and ensuring that housing and social facilities are available to encourage people to live and work in the area.

The London City Airport was opened in 1987 on the site of the Royal Docks. Commercial development took place around the West India and Millwall Docks, including the iconic Canary Wharf complex. Housing was also built, including both social housing and exclusive riverside properties. The public transport system was improved with the Jubilee Line extension and the Docklands Light Railway, as well as by a new river bus service. Gradually this formerly depressed stretch of the Thames began to reinvent itself as a commercial hub and a place for water sports such as windsurfing.

The Canal Age

The condition of the river for navigation had continued to decline during the seventeenth century, defying all attempts at a solution. Poor navigation was not in the public interest, so yet another Act of Parliament was passed to crack this nut. The Thames Navigation Commission was established in 1751 with a brief to manage the river from London Bridge to Cricklade, and explicitly to deal with the obstructions of weirs, fisheries and watermills. This was the latest of many statutory attempts to resolve the battle, already old in Magna Carta, between local landowners and long-distance navigation. Once again the Commission lacked the powers to prevent 'abuses' by the owners of weirs, locks and the towpath. Further Acts followed in 1771 and 1774 to strengthen the Commission's hand, with some success, and by 1804 twenty-six pound locks had been built. A navigation channel and pound lock were created to bypass the difficult bend and mill at Sutton Courtenay, and the new Sutton bridge was extended to span the cut. It was a start.

In his *General View of the Agriculture of Berkshire* of 1804, William Mavor listed that county's chief exports to London. Large quantities of malt together with 20,000 sacks of flour were annually sent from Reading alone. Elsewhere, corn, wool, timber and woodland products made up much of the downstream cargo, together with considerable quantities of cheese from around Lechlade. On their return upriver, coal from Newcastle was the largest single item of freight. Mavor noted that coal from Staffordshire and Wales was barred by statute from being traded further downstream than Reading, presumably to protect the Newcastle trade. The benefits of trade were two-way. The Thames was a cultural gateway for the people of the Middle and Upper Thames as 'the productions of the East and West Indies, the Baltic, the Mediterranean, and the South Sea, through the port of London' were carried upstream.

Mavor noted that the standard barge, called the Newbury, measured 109 feet by 17 feet with a draft of 3 feet 10 inches, and a capacity of 128 tons. Travelling against the stream required between eight and fourteen horses and a complement of six men and a boy. The bargemen used stout poles to keep the vessel in the channel. Downstream barges were carried by the current, and with just a single horse could average 3½ mph.

A new development in the second half of the eighteenth century eventually cut the Gordian knot, releasing the Thames from its role as the nation's chief commercial highway. Britain was rapidly gearing up under the influence of the Industrial Revolution, and a new breed of entrepreneur was emerging. Bulk transport was one of the keys to commercial success, so became the focus for an effort that was to bring national and international markets within reach of almost every town in the country. The answer was manmade waterways.

The first canal was commissioned by the Duke of Bridgewater in order to carry coal from his mines at Worsley into Manchester, a distance of only 10½ miles. An engineer named James Brindley was given the task, and the Bridgewater Canal was opened in 1761. Brindley overcame many difficulties, including a significant drop in altitude and the need for an aqueduct to cross the River Irwell. As a measure of the success of the canal, the price of coal in Manchester was halved, entirely as a result of reduced transport costs.

The potential benefits of canals led to canal mania. One of the most important of these early canals, linking the Midlands to London and its docks, was the Oxford Canal. Authorised by Parliament in 1769 (only ten years after the Bridgewater Canal scheme was approved) and built by the great engineer James Brindley, it snaked for 91 miles from its junction with the Coventry Canal, reaching the Thames at Oxford in 1790. There freight was transshipped from canal to river barges and the river led down to London and its docks. This began to put pressure on the need to improve the Thames navigation.

In 1783 an Act was passed for an even more adventurous scheme. A canal was proposed to link the headwaters of the Thames with the River Severn, which involved crossing the Cotswolds and would cost £200,000. The canal left the Thames at Lechlade and climbed via twenty-two locks. On the other side of the Cotswolds, forty locks climbed from the Stroudwater Navigation at Wallbridge. East and west were linked via an astounding feat of engineering, the 3,817-yard Sapperton Tunnel. This tunnel took five and a half years to build, and the first vessel passed through on 19 November 1789. It was almost a canal too far, as water shortages high on the limestone hills and repairs often meant closure. Water had to be pumped from the aquifer at Thames Head, the highest point on the canal, to prevent it draining. At first a wind pump was used, though this was quickly replaced by a steam pumping engine. In 1854 a new Cornish engine was installed which could pump 3 million gallons of water a day! To combat some of the technical problems, an 8½-mile spur was built to join this canal with the Wilts & Berks Canal at Latton Basin, bypassing the river above Abingdon.

An earlier, though still ambitious, project was the Kennet & Avon Canal. At either end, it was a relatively simple task to improve the existing rivers. The first section, from Reading to Newbury, known as the Kennet Navigation, was constructed in 1718–23. The Bristol Avon Navigation followed in 1725–7. More challengingly, the central section from Newbury to Bath involved cutting a canal through hilly topography. With seventy-nine locks over its 57-mile length, it was opened in 1810, the final piece in a chain linking two of England's greatest seaports, London and Bristol.

At the start of the nineteenth century the Grand Junction Canal (later part of the Grand Union) from the Midlands reached the Thames at Brentford, drawing away much of the traffic from the Oxford Canal. It was an immediate success, with an annual gross revenue in 1818 of £170,000. The Grand Junction turned the country village of Paddington into a thriving transport hub. Previously, the area had been noted for market gardening and nurserying, and possessed 'some of the noblest elm trees in Middlesex'. The canal created a large basin surrounded by extensive warehousing, and already by 1819 the settlement was developing a reputation as a market for a range of goods brought down from the Midlands and the North West. The Regent's Canal, opened 1820, extended the route around London to the Thames at Limehouse Basin, allowing easier transshipment to seagoing vessels, and linking with the Lea and Stort Navigations. Previously, flour, malt, bricks and coal among other goods had been transhipped at Brentford from barges to Thames lighters for the final part of their journey.

Many businessmen wanted a share in the benefits of ready access to the Thames and onward through the nationwide network. The Thames & Medway Canal opened in 1824, incorporating a tunnel which, at 3,931 yards, was even longer than the Sapperton Tunnel. The Croydon and Grand Surrey Canals opened up the area south of the Thames opposite London. The River Wey had been improved for navigation in the seventeenth century, but the Basingstoke Canal branched off it in 1794. Clear passage down the Thames was a common requirement for all these ventures, providing the impetus to find solutions. After enumerating the work of the Thames Navigation Commission, William Mavor could still only conclude, 'Yet, after all, it must be confessed, that less has been done towards improving this valuable navigation, than its allowed importance demands.'

The Road Lobby

'It will open up the Southern parts of the Kingdom,' declared the promoters of the Burford–Lechlade–Swindon Turnpike Trust. Despite the new canal network, roads remained a vital component in the national transport system, often increasingly connecting with canal wharves. The Thames & Severn Canal had made Lechlade a boomtown, but the main roads required improvement. On 15 October 1791 a group of gentlemen met in the King & Queen Inn, Highworth, and resolved to form the Burford–Lechlade–Swindon Turnpike Trust. The Earl of Radnor put down £300, and Mr Ambrose Goddard and Mr Edward Loveden MP each invested £100. Subscriptions were advertised, and the following year Parliament approved a petition signed by over 100 locals. The new turnpike was to include a bridge to replace the Bell Lane ferry, which was a bottleneck. The Thames Commissioners stipulated the bridge must not impede navigation, so it was given a 40-foot semi-circular arch to allow masted barges to pass, as well as a towpath, and floodwater openings were created to either side. The bridge, like the turnpike and the canal, was a commercial venture and tolls were charged: sixpence per cart, twopence per horse and a halfpenny per pedestrian – it was known as Halfpenny Bridge. A toll collector's cottage stands on the bridge. Income was soon hit by the railways, but the business continued until 1875 when the bridge passed to the local authority and was released from toll.

Private turnpike schemes, though authorised by Acts of Parliament, were the local response to the poor quality of main roads. They seldom achieved much, concerned as they inevitably were with investments and profits. The Brentford Turnpike Trust had been established in 1717 to improve the Bath road from Counter's Bridge, Kensington, to Baber's Bridge, Hounslow, but Brentford High Street and the bridge over the River Brent remained a notorious bottleneck. Even so, eighty-three coaches a day passed along the High Street by the start of the nineteenth century. In the early 1840s the first railways bypassed the town and the number of coaches fell by 90 per cent as market forces embraced the superior new mode of transport.

River crossings were the weak points in the road network. A

bridge was erected at Kingston in about 1170. Remarkably, this remained the first bridge upstream of London until the eighteenth century. During these centuries the nation changed out of all recognition, and London became a world city. The virtual absence of road bridges along this important section of the river was stifling both the city and the country, but powerful vested interests sought to maintain the status quo. The City of London collected tolls from London Bridge, the Company of Watermen were jealous of their business, and many local landowners took the revenues from the various ferries which operated along the length of the river – for example, the Archbishop of Canterbury drew a significant income from the Lambeth horse ferry. However, pressure for change was mounting; eventually the dam had to burst.

The first new bridge on this part of the river in almost 600 years linked Putney and Fulham. Royal assent was granted in 1726 and a Company of Proprietors of Fulham Bridge was established with powers to raise £30,000 in shares. However, the rights to the horse ferry were owned jointly by the Bishop of London (as Lord of the Manor of Fulham) and the Duchess of Marlborough (Lord of the Manor of Wimbledon), so compensation for loss of earnings first had to be negotiated. The company chose the plans by Sir Jacob Ackworth for a timber bridge, letting the contract to Thomas Phillips for £9,455. Phillips began in March 1729 and work was completed within the year. In common with most bridges at the time, this was a business generating income from tolls: these ranged from a ha'penny for pedestrians to two shillings and sixpence for a coach-and-six. Inevitably, given its location, it was a profitable venture.

As the power of vested interest failed, a rash of bridges over the London Thames followed. The need for a bridge at Westminster had long been obvious, but any plans had been quashed by the City Corporation and the Company of Watermen. An Act was finally passed in 1736, and the watermen and the Archbishop of Canterbury, who owned a horse ferry, were handsomely compensated. A huge cadre of 175 commissioners were appointed, with the intention of raising the necessary £120,000 by public lottery – for this reason dubbed 'the Bridge of Fools' by novelist Henry Fielding. A design by the elderly Nicholas Hawksmoor was rejected. Then, in 1738, a young Swiss engineer named Charles Labelye was appointed. He used the latest technology, building masonry piers within cast iron caissons. When the first pier showed signs of settling and a stone fell from an arch, part of the bridge had to be dismantled. It was finally opened with due ceremony in November 1750, but needed constant costly attention until it was eventually replaced a century later.

This experience did not chasten the enthusiasm for bridges within London. Blackfriars Bridge was the brainchild of the City Corporation, conceived as a magnificent new entrance to the City. It was to be of Portland stone, with its design influenced by Piranesi. Once again, the watermen were compensated. This project was under-funded from the start, and for a while it operated as a footbridge only, with a temporary timber footway. Opened in 1769, it was never a commercial success and was freed from tolls as a public gesture in 1785. Then in 1771–2, a timber bridge between Battersea and Chelsea was built to designs by Henry Holland, again with Thomas Phillips as contractor. With nineteen spans, its arches were narrow and difficult to navigate, making it vulnerable to impact damage. This was resolved by creating two navigation spans of 77 feet and 71 feet respectively, making use of the new technology of iron girders. Tolls produced a modest income, sufficient for maintenance and operation.

Pressure for the convenience of bridges was also felt upriver. A timber bridge was built at Kew in 1758–9, with six piers and a navigation span of 50 feet. Already by 1782 it needed to be replaced, and a stone bridge by James Paine at a cost of £16,000. This sum was raised by means of a tontine: as each subscriber died, his share of the interest was divided between the survivors until only one was left in receipt of the full-interest payment. After several false starts, the elegant bridge of five semi-circular arches at Richmond, faced in Portland stone, was opened in 1777. A second tontine was required to cover the overspend. At Hampton Court, a bridge replaced two ferries. Built of timber and opened in 1753, it was uniquely designed in the fashionable Chinese style. Users complained it was too steep and the tolls were higher than the previous ferry fare. It proved not to be sufficiently robust, and was rebuilt on a gentler gradient in 1788. Just a few years earlier, a bridge was built at Walton, not far upstream. This unusual timber bridge was described as 'mathematical' by its designer, William Etheridge, who had already built a rather smaller 'mathematical' bridge at Queens' College, Cambridge. The purpose of the design was to allow timbers to be replaced individually. This skeleton of a bridge caught Canaletto's eye: he painted it in the 1750s. Sadly, it suffered the fate of many wooden bridges over the Thames, being replaced in masonry thirty years later. Many towns further upstream already had bridges, though this century saw timber bridges at Datchet and Whitchurch. Three late eighteenth-century stone bridges on the Upper Thames, at Swinford, Tadpole Bridge and Ha'penny Bridge, Lechlade, formed part of larger turnpike schemes. Swinford and the Dartford Crossing remain the only toll bridges on the Thames.

Though it was a source of wealth for London, the river was also a barrier: as the nineteenth century progressed, ever more people wanted to cross. Vauxhall Bridge was opened in 1816, to help open up the South Bank for development. Waterloo Bridge was built by John Rennie for the Strand Bridge Company in 1817 and named in honour of the Duke of Wellington's great victory against Napoleon two years earlier. Southwark Bridge, also by Rennie, followed in 1819. Also built as a commercial venture, it had no obvious road links at its southern end, so was never an economic success. The ancient London Bridge had been altered in the 1750s in an attempt to improve traffic flow. The buildings on the bridge were pulled down and the deck widened by 13 feet on each side to give a total width of 46 feet: previously the carriageway had been only 12 to 15 feet wide. It remained London's premier bridge: on one (typical) day in July 1811, 89,640 pedestrians, 5,418 horse-drawn vehicles and 764 horses crossed, all of whom paid tolls. It was finally replaced in 1831, again by Rennie. Hammersmith Bridge (1827), Chelsea Bridge (1858), Lambeth Bridge (1862) and Albert Bridge (1873) were all suspension bridges. Wandsworth Bridge, a lattice girder construction, was built on the cheap in 1873: the *Illustrated London News* reported, 'No attempt has been made to produce architectural effect, the structure being substantial rather than ornamental.' It later suffered from weight-limit problems and its replacement was finally opened in 1940.

The two eighteenth-century timber bridges at Battersea and Putney were both renewed in stone towards the end of the century. The Metropolitan Toll Bridges Act of 1877 finally brought these crucial elements of civic infrastructure under public control, enabling the Metropolitan Board of Works to buy the remaining bridges and free them from tolls. The century was brought to a fitting close in 1894 with Sir Joseph Bazalgette's Tower Bridge, with its innovative opening caissons to allow larger ships into the Pool of London. By the start of the new century, fourteen road bridges crossed the Thames between Hammersmith and the City. In addition there were seven railway bridges between Barnes and the City. Footbridges were built alongside the Hungerford, Cannon Street and Barnes railway bridges; a suspension footbridge, since demolished, serving Hungerford Market, was constructed by Brunel in 1845.

In addition to bridges, the Victorians tunnelled under the river. Despite the considerable engineering challenges, one great advantage was that a tunnel would not interfere with shipping in what was the busiest stretch of water in the world. The early years of the nineteenth century saw two failed tunnels, one intended to link Gravesend and Tilbury, the other between Rotherhithe and Limehouse. In both cases flooding proved insoluble. Then, in 1825, the engineer Marc Isambard Brunel (father of Isambard Kingdom Brunel) developed the Great Shield, a tunnelling machine that moved inside an iron tube. Work was painfully slow, but the tunnel between Rotherhithe and Wapping opened to popular acclaim in 1843. Unfortunately, after so much investment it fell out of use until it later was recycled as a railway tunnel. A second tunnel linked Tower Hill with Tooley Street (Southwark). Opened in 1869, it was already redundant due to the construction of Tower Bridge. In 1902 another foot tunnel, linking the Isle of Dogs with Greenwich, was designed to attract dock workers from across the river. Two road tunnels, the Blackwall Tunnel (1896) and the Rotherhithe Tunnel (1908), obviated the need for long bridges. To complete the record, the Dartford Crossing is the most easterly fixed crossing on the Thames. Two tunnels (opened in 1963 and 1980) and a suspension bridge carry the M25 over the river. Despite a toll being charged, over 50 million vehicles a year use the crossing.

In an age when bridges and tunnels had replaced ferries, Woolwich Free Ferry was established by Act of Parliament and opened on 23 March 1889. Once again, compensation was payable to watermen and other ferry operators. The ferry was operated by the Metropolitan Board of Works as a tool to help develop the area, and unsurprisingly has always been very popular. By the end of 1895 it had carried almost 26 million passengers and over 1.6 million (horse-drawn) vehicles, with a maximum of 54,484 passengers in one day; the ferry now carries over 2.5 million passengers annually.

The Railway Age

A new technology swept the country in the 1830s and 1840s – the steam railway. This was destined to have an even greater impact than the canals had had over the previous 100 years, due to its greater speed, greater flexibility and its ability to carry passengers. However, the promoters of the two modes of transport shared a similar psychology, leading to a scramble for investment and an economic 'bubble'. London soon sat at the heart of the burgeoning railway network.

In the 1830s the capital's population stood at just under 2 million, squeezed into a comparatively small area. The pressure for housing was driving the outward spread of the suburbs. Property prices south of the river were comparatively modest and greenfield sites presented an opportunity to escape from the evils of urban overcrowding. The catch was that most people had little option but to walk to work: in 1836 75,000 pedestrians crossed Blackfriars Bridge daily and 100,000 crossed London Bridge. This imposed a very real constraint – 2 miles was a reasonable walking distance – though it was one that the new technology of the steam railway could address. In 1836 the London & Greenwich Railway was opened. Although it was only 3¾ miles long, running to a terminus on the southern approach to London Bridge, this small suburban venture pointed the way for London's suburban expansion.

From 1839 the London & Croydon Railway ran 10¼ miles to London Bridge, sharing the last section of the line and its terminus with the London & Greenwich. The South Eastern Railway was approved in 1836 and the London & Brighton the following year. All four companies initially planned to share the line and station at London Bridge. Other lines and companies quickly followed, eventually criss-crossing the southern suburbs with commuter services. Where the railways went they opened up new areas for suburban development. By 1846 London Bridge Station was handling 625,000 passengers a year, rising within four years to over 5½ million. The SER opened the North Kent line in July 1849, serving the Thames-side towns. The Medway Canal was superseded, its famous tunnel being drained and a railway laid. Prior to this, the Medway towns alone had supported sixteen stagecoach services a day to London and passenger steamers ran from Gravesend pier, while a fleet of barges and wherries provided a regular freight service taking twenty-four hours.

Parallel developments took place north of the river. The Eastern Counties Railway Company was authorised in 1836 to build a line to Norwich, establishing a terminus at Shoreditch (later called Bishopsgate) on the eastern edge of the City. Meanwhile, the Blackwall Railway had a station at Fenchurch Street. These two companies jointly formed a line to Tilbury and Southend, reaching the latter in 1854, and opening up the Essex shore. Particularly in the more built-up areas north of the river, thousands of homes had to be demolished to make way for new lines while viaducts carried the smoking trains above workers' housing. Startled by the speed and scale of developments, the Royal Commission on London Traffic decreed in 1846 that railways should not penetrate the inner-city area. Soon a ring of termini had sprung up around the City, each the focus for a growing network of mainline and local services which poured workers into the metropolis six days a week. Acts of Parliament were required to build or extend a line, but otherwise the growth of the system was uncoordinated as companies and investors scrambled for opportunities and profits.

The possibility of through traffic was opened up by the Metropolitan Extensions Act of 1860 which allowed the London, Chatham & Dover Railway to cross the river and join the Metropolitan Railway at Farringdon Street. The South Eastern Railway also penetrated the City and Westminster with new termini on the north bank at Charing Cross (1864) and Cannon Street (1866). Further west, bridges at Battersea, Putney, Barnes, Kew, Richmond and Kingston were essential for civic pride, linking towns on the Surrey bank with the more developed suburban network to the north.

By the end of 1832 commercial pressure was mounting for a railway link between Bristol and London, and the Bristol-based committee secured an Act of Parliament three years later. Isambard Kingdom Brunel, a mere twenty-six years old, was appointed as engineer. The Great Western Railway opened as far as Maidenhead in 1838, and fully in the summer of 1841. Its route followed the Thames Valley from its London terminus at Paddington as far as Didcot, where it struck out towards Bath and its final destination of Bristol. A branch line from Didcot ran north to Oxford. The Cheltenham & Great Western Union Company ran its own line from Gloucester to connect with the GWR at the new railway depot of Swindon. This new railway opened up the Thames Valley in a new way, bringing the eastern towns in particular within easy reach of London.

The London Underground Railway was a pioneering innovation and the first underground railway in the world. It was to revolutionise transportation within the core of the capital, with its tentacles helping to create the suburbs. Work on the Metropolitan Railway began in 1860, and the first section ran from Paddington to Farringdon. It was an immediate success, despite the discomfort of smoke and steam in enclosed spaces. Outside the urban core trains could run overground, and the far-sightedness of the companies ensured that their lines extended well beyond the current suburbs, linking outlying towns and villages in a way which would promote growth. The Metropolitan Line took a lead in encouraging commuters to improve their quality of life by moving out to the country just a short train journey from work. This was 'Metroland', a place where suburbanisation progressively destroyed the rural idyll it was advertised around – what Sir John Betjeman, who had a love–hate relationship with these north-western suburbs, memorably called 'our lost Elysium'.[5]

The area now covered by the London Borough of Harrow illustrates the impact of improved public transport in opening up areas where London workers could live (see Table 2). Throughout the nineteenth century this district, so close to the City, was largely rural, focusing on agricultural produce for the London market: Perrivale before the First World War was described as a 'parish of enormous hayfields' – Betjeman again.[6] Its population remained below 10,000 until around 1880. With the extension of the underground lines to join up its isolated settlements, 'Metroland' was spawned. The suburbs followed the lines, and from 1891 the whole area began to develop, reaching a population of 100,000 in the 1930s and breaking 200,000 with post-war rehousing.

Prison Hulks and Smallpox Boats

No discussion of the Thames would be complete without reference to prison hulks, made infamous by Charles Dickens. The bleak expanses of the estuary were felt to be a world apart, so when the American War of Independence forced a halt to the transportation of prisoners to the New World, they were held as a temporary measure in decommissioned Naval ships moored in the lower reaches. After 1784, with Australia as the new penal destination, transportation recommenced, and the hulks were retained to hold convicts awaiting transportation, as well as some who were not due to be transported. Overcrowding and insanitary conditions contributed to a high death rate among inmates. Despite mounting opposition, hulks continued to be used into the second half of the nineteenth century, gradually being replaced by a more extensive prison system. In 1851, 1,800 convicts were still being held in four hulks, two at Woolwich and two at Portsmouth. Convict hospital ships continued in use at Woolwich until the *Defence* was destroyed by fire in June 1857. Transportation was finally ended in 1867.

In addition to criminals, the lower river has been used to segregate sufferers with contagious diseases. Smallpox in particular was feared, and isolation was essential. The London Metropolitan Asylum Board was responsible for fever, smallpox and insanity hospitals for the poor. In order to cope with the sudden influx of patients during the periodic epidemics, the Board bought a remote plot of land by the river at Dartford. The former Naval vessels *Atlas* and *Castalia* were converted for use as floating isolation hospitals with up to 300 beds, and *Endymion* as an administration block. To minimise contact with the healthy population, fever or smallpox patients were usually taken from Rotherhithe or Blackwall by ambulance steamer: in 1913 (not an epidemic year) the service carried 1,368 patients. Stores were also mostly brought from London due to local fears of infection. In 1902 a purpose-built hospital was constructed on-shore and the ships were scrapped. They had had a good record, the mortality rate during epidemics running at 13 per cent compared with a national average of 25 per cent.

9

The Defended River

A Weak Link in the Nation's Armour

British Sea Power

It was Henry VIII who first clearly saw the importance of sea power, augmented by innovations in gunnery, to his island nation. In the period up to the Industrial Revolution, the Naval dockyards developed into the largest industrial enterprise in the land, and the Lower Thames was a key focus of this activity. Repair, refitting and victualling yards all grew up around the Medway and the tidal river, notably at Chatham, Woolwich, Deptford, Sheerness, Erith (victualling yard) and Purfleet (powder store).

The Medway was recognised as a safe haven, and many Naval vessels were wintered there. It was also a convenient place for routine maintenance, and storehouses were rented. By the 1570s Chatham was emerging as a Naval ship yard, and it was thought necessary to defend the mouth of the Medway with artillery. Next century Chatham became the country's pre-eminent Naval dockyard. Deptford and Woolwich both remained highly valued, while Portsmouth on the Channel coast retained a strategic importance, but Chatham offered a safe anchorage near the open sea yet convenient for London. In the first years of the seventeenth century the dockyard suffered from lack of investment and corruption: a commission of inquiry into the Master shipwright, Phineas Pett, identified considerable abuses. A completely new dockyard was built along modern lines on an 80-acre site between 1619 and 1626. By the 1660s around 800 men were employed, though the work was largely seasonal. During the Dutch wars

Chatham was highly active, with twenty-two men-of-war launched in 1654 alone; although the humiliating Dutch raid of 1667 marked a low point in the yard's fortunes.

Over the next two centuries, with frequent conflicts around the globe and a rapidly growing Empire, the Navy had a major role to play. Chatham and the other Thames yards were constantly busy with repairs, refits and the building of new ships: HMS *Victory* was built there. At the conclusion of the Napoleonic War, the dockyards were employing 3,000 men, but in peacetime this figure was rapidly reduced by a third. This caused considerable hardship in the town. Iron ships were the new future, though it was not until the 1860s that the dockyards experienced another great expansion to handle this technology. By 1903, 10,000 were employed. Chatham adapted to each innovation, and from 1908, fifty-seven submarines were built. After the First World War the Navy was run down and Chatham also suffered, exacerbated in the 1920s by the Depression. It geared up again in 1939.

The Crown purchased a shipyard at Woolwich in 1512, later known as Gun Wharf, to build the man-of-war the *Great Harry*. Later that century a ropeyard was established nearby. A survey of 1633 lists timber yards, the dry dock and galley dock, houses for the master builder and 'clerk of the cheque', storehouses, the plank yard, smith's forge, sawhouses, cranes and a wharf, all surrounded by a 9-foot-high fence; the wharf is said to be 'much ruined' and in urgent need of repair. Two docks were capable of servicing two vessels simultaneously. The fortunes of this yard fluctuated with British foreign policy. In the 1650s war with Holland prompted its enlargement and refurbishing, and by 1665 a quarter of the town's population of 1,200 worked in the shipyard. Following the Dutch raid of 1667, the dockyard was further enlarged onto a reclaimed riverside marsh; though between wars the number of men employed tended to slump. With a strong emphasis on self-help, unemployed shipwrights built a windmill in 1758 to grind wheat for an early co-operative. The early eighteenth century saw four new slips constructed on reclaimed land, together with other improvements. Both the American War of Independence and the Napoleonic War saw further expansion, and the development of steam required further refitting. However, the dockyard lacked capacity for ever-larger ships, and was finally closed in 1869 by Gladstone's government as part of defence cuts, though the neighbouring arsenal continued to thrive for another 100 years.

Foremost among the many military armament establishments along the Lower Thames was Woolwich Arsenal. The Royal Artillery barracks were established in the town in 1773 and the Royal Military Academy a few years later. Following the setting up of a Naval dockyard, ordnance was first stored and then manufactured. The enterprise grew, its fortunes fluctuating with the international situation, and finally peaking in the First World War when it covered 1,285 acres and employed 75,000 people including 28,000 derogatorily termed 'munitionettes' (i.e. female munition workers). A terminal decline after the war ended with closure in 1967. This was a body blow to local employment, and schemes for regeneration are being developed.

As Britain grew in stature as a world and imperial power, the Naval dockyards and other facilities along the estuary continued to develop. An extensive powder depot was established at Purfleet in the mid-eighteenth century. As always, however, the fortunes of the shore-based defences fluctuated with the perceived level of military threat. New batteries were built, then left to decay. In response to an invasion scare in 1804 during the Napoleonic War, a flotilla of warships was temporarily stationed in the Lower Hope in support of the batteries. In broader strategic terms the high command presumably thought the Navy could defend both itself and London, despite the lessons of 1667.

Technological innovation repeatedly forced military thinking to be reviewed. When the Royal Commission on the Defence of the United Kingdom reported in 1860, it made a raft of recommendations to modernise the system of defence around the dockyards of the estuary. The old forts at Tilbury, New Tavern, Coalhouse and Shornemead were upgraded and a new fort erected at Cliffe, though marshy ground caused structural problems leading to delays. A battery, known as Slough Fort, was built near the mouth of the Medway, with others around Grain and Sheerness. New designs of heavy gun were deployed, together with shore-based torpedo stations and mines in the river. Rather than upgrading the tactically out-dated Chatham Lines, five detached forts were constructed to cover the landward approaches. Towards the end of the century a string of forts and mobilisation centres were built along the scarp of the North Downs to protect the capital from invasion along the Channel coast.

Two World Wars

During the First World War the air threat against British towns and cities was limited due to the distances involved and, first using Zeppelins and later aircraft, was mostly directed towards London. The major perceived threat was still naval, with torpedo boats and mines being a danger. It was fifty years since the Royal Commission had reported, but the estuary remained a weak point and the Naval dockyards at Sheerness and Chatham remained military targets. To counter this, ships were stationed in the estuary to intercept potential enemy raiders, while anti-aircraft guns and fighter planes guarded against Zeppelin raids. The land approaches to the Naval bases were defended in case of a landing, and a pontoon of boats was held in readiness to close the river between Gravesend and Tilbury and to facilitate troop movements. It later transpired that the German High Command had planned to make a landing in the estuary as part of a projected general invasion of England, though it is also clear that they regarded its defences as formidable.

After the war most of these precautions were discontinued, and the defence of the Naval bases switched to long-range batteries on the Isles of Grain and Sheppey, which were designed to be effective against shipping.

The Second World War presented a very different picture, as the conflict was carried to the British homeland. From June 1940 Britain stood alone. The Allied Army had suffered a crushing defeat in Europe, though a large number of British and French troops had been successfully evacuated from Dunkirk. A German invasion to drive home the advantage they had won on the Continent was expected imminently. The Prime Minister, Winston Churchill, gave his famous 'We will fight them on the beaches' speech to rally the nation.

Among the many preparations for the anticipated invasion was a 300-mile-long anti-tank defence known as the GHQ Line. This was the brainchild of General Sir Edmund Ironside, Commander-in-Chief of Home Forces. This defensive line was to protect London and the Midlands from an enemy advance from landings on the east or south coasts. Starting on the River Welland north of Peterborough, the Line reached the Thames estuary near Benfleet. Across the river, it continued through Kent before running south of the North Downs, hitting the Thames again at Reading. Here the Line forked, with one branch following the River Kennet to reach the Severn Estuary at Burnham-on-Sea. The second branch followed the Upper Thames as far as Cricklade before turning south to rejoin the Kennet Line. The important port of Bristol was protected by an extension. Where possible, the Line made use of existing natural and manmade features, such as rivers, high ground and railway embankments. A total of 112 miles of anti-tank ditch, 20 feet wide and 8 feet deep, was dug to block any gaps. The Line was defended by 1,448 concrete and steel pillboxes, most of which were designed for infantry use, while a number housed 2-pounder or 6-pounder guns. The Line was built by both the military and civilian contractors, and, as a measure of national urgency, it was almost completed within two months. Once again, the Thames had a pivotal role in the defence of the country.

As the feared invasion did not materialise, military leaders took stock of their options. By the autumn of 1940 the GHQ Line was downgraded and defensive effort focused on the coast. However, it remained operational as a last line of defence, and Home Guard units continued to help man the key crossing points. Elsewhere across the country, more than 18,000 pillboxes were built at nodal points on the transport network, coastal defences, local stop lines and essential installations. How long any of this could have withstood a full-blown blitzkrieg is debatable, but Britain stood defiant.

The Thames estuary continued to be a vulnerable point for invasion, while the river itself was a potential navigation aid for enemy aircraft bound for London. Aware of this, a further long-range battery had been built on Canvey Island at the time of the Munich Crisis in 1938. Once war was declared, a system of anti-aircraft defences, including batteries, observation posts and a central control room, was established along the river to protect the capital. Radar was another essential tool. Then, in 1942, the remarkable off-shore installations called Maunsell Forts (after their designer Guy Maunsell) were constructed. Each fort consisted of seven interconnected steel blockhouses raised above the waves and heavily armed. Three anti-aircraft forts guarded the mouth of the estuary, one at the Nore and two further out at Red Sands and Shivering Sands. They recorded a number of successes, though their very presence may have discouraged German aircraft from flying the Thames route. (Following their decommissioning after the war, several operated as pirate radio stations.)

Other measures included defending the beach and seafront against landings, with barbed wire, anti-tank blocks, minefields and pillboxes. For example, 1,805 anti-tank blocks were placed along the seafront at Southend: seaside holidays were over for the duration. A long boom protected Shoeburyness, while another 1¾ miles long could be thrown across the river between St Mary's Bay on the Isle of Grain and Canvey Island. An anti-submarine net was stretched strategically between Shoeburyness and the Isle of Sheppey, where deep water channels converged, with three gates to allow shipping to pass.

Although the Allied commanders were not to know it, Operation *Sea Lion*, the German invasion plan, focused on the Channel coasts of Kent and Sussex; the Thames estuary was not part of the initial plan. Even so, it was essential to be prepared for every possibility as the enemy would spot a weak link. After the war, the defences were quickly run down as the nation faced the challenges of reconstruction. The next threat to national security, the Cold War, would require a very different set of tools.

The systematic bombing of industrial and civilian targets that began in 1940 marked the beginning of a new strategy. The Blitz, from September 1940 to May 1941, was a major bombing offensive against London. It opened on 7 September with a heavy raid which targeted the docklands in an attempt to put them out of action. After a lull, the tempo of bombing picked up again in 1943 with the use of flying bombs from 1944. By the end of the war, almost 30,000 Londoners had been killed and over 50,000 injured. The final tally included 40,000 homes destroyed and over a million damaged. London County Council compiled maps of bomb damage which reveal the devastation of some areas and the gap-toothed nature of damage in others. These show that the City, Southwark and the docks on both banks were particularly targeted.

Outside the metropolis, the riverside towns experienced only isolated raids – though there were still casualties and damage to property and infrastructure. The dockyards in the estuary were attacked, but with surprisingly limited results: at Chatham, fifteen workers killed and 107 wounded out of 13,000. Upriver, even Reading was considered a safe place and some government departments transferred there from London. Its only air raid came on 10 February 1943 when a single plane dropped several bombs and caused significant casualties. Oxford was deliberately spared because Hitler planned to make it his capital.

The Peace Dividend

Lessons were slow to be learned. Following each scare funds rapidly dwindled and the various installations declined, causing hardship in the towns and the loss of skilled labour, only to be hurriedly upgraded again. The closure of Woolwich Arsenal in 1967 and Chatham Dockyard in 1984 brought an end to 450 years of military industry on the Lower Thames. Having lost their traditional purpose, both communities have found regeneration a challenge, though new commercial docks at Chatham handle in excess of 1 million tonnes of cargo a year.

10

The Recreational River

Frost Fairs, Pleasure Gardens and Poetry

A National Stage

The Thames has long been a working river; it has also been a place for relaxation and enjoyment. At times its pleasures have been restricted to the wealthy, while at others they have been open to all. The popular perception of the river was changing too. Once simply a place of work or a rustic backwater, it was increasingly valued for its natural beauty and tranquillity or just plain fun.

The river through London provided an ideal setting for civic and national pageantry, with scope for crowds of spectators to line both banks. King John made the Mayor of London into one of the first elected offices, and required the newly elected mayor to swear an oath of loyalty to the Crown at Westminster each year. Thus began the annual spectacle of the Lord Mayor's Show. What began as an official journey upriver to Westminster, had become by the sixteenth century one of the unmissable London events. The pageantry became increasingly splendid with the procession extending for over a mile as each of the livery companies accompanied him with their own ornate barges. The Venetian Canaletto, among others, painted the Lord Mayor's barge as it passed Westminster Bridge. This tradition came to an end in 1857 when the City ceded responsibility for the Thames below Teddington to the Thames Conservancy, and the celebration transferred onto dry land where it was no less exuberant.

Royalty chose the river for national events. The traditions surrounding the coronation of a new monarch included a waterborne procession from the Palace of Westminster to the Tower of London, followed by a return by road to Westminster Abbey. Charles II reintroduced this tradition at the Restoration, but was the last monarch to make the journey as the Tower ceased to function as a symbolic focus for royal power. The Thames was also a fitting means of bearing the coffin of the national hero, Admiral Horatio Nelson, to St Paul's for his state funeral. He was granted the honour of being carried in the royal barge on his final journey from the Royal Naval Hospital at Greenwich. A flotilla of small boats rowed alongside the victor of Trafalgar's official cortege to pay their last respects.

The wealthy and powerful used the river for recreation, often owning their own splendid barges. George Frederick Handel's *Water Music* was commissioned by no less a person than George I. It was premiered on the river as a private entertainment for the king and his court on the evening of 17 July 1717 as their barges slowly sailed upstream to Lambeth or Chelsea. George so much enjoyed the piece that he had it played three times during the trip. Handel continued to enjoy royal patronage. George II commissioned *Music for the Royal Fireworks* from him, to be played in Green Park, London, on 27 April 1749 in celebration of the ending of the War of the Austrian Succession which had embroiled most European powers. A few days later the music was repeated at a firework display on the river beside the Duke of Richmond's house at Whitehall. A popular etching of the occasion was published.

This tradition of civic pageantry was continued in 2012 with Her Majesty the Queen's Diamond Jubilee Thames Pageant. On 3 June a flotilla of up to 1,000 boats of all sizes was assembled to celebrate the sixtieth anniversary of Her Majesty's ascension to the throne. Led by the royal barge, the *Spirit of Chartwell*, the colourful flotilla of invited craft sailed through central London from Albert Bridge to Tower Bridge. Watched from the banks and bridges by an estimated 1 million people, despite the rain, the event was accompanied by music and by specially cast bells, concluding with a firework display.

A Privileged Landscape

Royalty had always had access to prime locations on the river both above and below London. Perhaps the most famous was Hampton

Court Palace. Located on the north bank of the Thames, it was within easy reach of the capital. In 1514 Archbishop Thomas Wolsey, soon to be made cardinal, leased the old manor house of Hampton Court and began creating a grand mansion which was to become pre-eminent in England. On Wolsey's fall from power, Henry VIII accepted the house as a 'gift' and continued its development.

Following the Dissolution of the Monasteries by Henry VIII, large estates on the banks of the Thames came onto the market, allowing the Thames to become the playground of the super-rich. For the wealthy, houses along the bank upriver of London combined the convenience of easy water transport to the City with a healthy and spacious lifestyle. Having royal neighbours was a further attraction. These aristocrats were in the main not simply fashion conscious but fashion leaders. With money to burn, they experimented with the latest ideas in architecture and garden design.

The royal family had several country retreats along this section of the Thames. George III and his queen, Charlotte, enjoyed an idyllic and secluded country existence at their summer home, Richmond Lodge. The king's mother, Augusta, lived conveniently nearby at the White House, Kew. After her death the royal couple moved into the White House and Richmond Lodge was demolished. The accommodation was cramped and uncomfortable, however, and the royal family was growing quickly; it was even necessary to board-out some of the royal children. The king conceived the idea of a new palace, which James Wyatt was commissioned to design. It was to be in the Gothic style, more in keeping with the royal estate, and would stand on the site of the White House. So in 1802 the White House was pulled down and the royal family moved temporarily into the Dutch House (Kew Palace), next door. This was a palace in miniature, and had begun life with more humble pretensions. This Dutch-influenced red brick house was built in 1631 for a London merchant, Samuel Fortrey, and was leased and then purchased by the Crown as a home for Frederick, Prince of Wales, the eldest son of George II (and father of George III). After Frederick's death in 1751, the future George III was brought up at Kew while his mother continued to develop the gardens, engendering in him a great love for the spot. Sir Joseph Banks, a leading naturalist, became the unofficial director of the royal botanic garden after Augusta's death, sending plant hunters to remote parts of the world to collect specimens. In 1841 the gardens were given to the state and increased in size. George's castellated palace was never completed, and after standing empty for some years it was blown up in 1827–8. Consequently, Kew Palace was reprieved, though it was never again a royal home.

Among the leading nobility, the Percy family, Earls of Northumberland, acquired a former Bridgettine convent at Syon, Isleworth, in 1604, which after the Dissolution had briefly been owned by the Duke of Somerset. The Percys turned it into a truly grand house, engaging Robert Adam in the 1760s to create some stunning interiors. Although their main seat was Alnwick Castle in Northumberland, and Northumberland House was maintained as their London townhouse until it was demolished in 1874 to make way for a much-needed thoroughfare between Charing Cross and the newly built Victoria Embankment, Syon House was a convenient out-of-town residence. The nun's cloister forms the courtyard of the present house and other portions are embedded within the fabric, while the gilded lion on the roof was transferred from Northumberland House. Capability Brown was commissioned to work on the grounds, while a neighbour, the Earl of Holdernesse, employed him at Syon Hill.

A rather different story is associated with a former Cistercian abbey on the Thames at Medmenham. By the time of its dissolution it had declined sadly, boasting only a single monk and his abbot; but its post-monastic incarnation was to be thoroughly sacrilegious. Like so many others, the buildings were converted into a country house, later leased by Sir Francis Dashwood. Dashwood founded the secret society later known as the Hell Fire Club at his family home, West Wycombe Park. In 1751 Medmenham Abbey became the new meeting place for the Club. This was the most notorious of several similar societies. Under the mocking guise of a 'brotherhood', Dashwood's high-society friends indulged in a programme of orgies which shocked even the lax Georgian era. Rumours circulated of black masses and devil worship, and initiates included prominent politicians as well as rich young bucks: Dashwood was himself an establishment figure, briefly Chancellor of the Exchequer.

As the seventeenth century gave way to the eighteenth, the Stuarts to the Hanoverians, English taste in gardening also gradually changed. The formal, heavily ordered style which had been so influenced by Versailles was replaced with a more 'natural' landscape drawing loosely on Classical roots. This was an age when the Classics formed the core curriculum for the educated upper classes, and many gentlemen made a Grand Tour as a sort of finishing school; so what was more natural than to re-create Arcady in the settings for their country houses, both large and small. It was a peculiarly English envisioning of nature domesticated, often complete with herds of deer or rare cattle. Where possible, the house itself was placed on a rise to enjoy the view over a seemingly natural mix of gardens and parkland, punctuated by eye-catching Classical ruins and other features. Vistas were carefully designed like stage sets and water was managed to dramatic effect. A particular asset was a privileged view of the Thames.

This philosophy was taken to an extreme by Philip Southcote, related by marriage to the aristocracy and a member of the fashionable set. Around 1735 he acquired an estate in the Thames valley near Weybridge. Here, at Woburn Farm, he experimented combining the new style of gardening with non-intensive farming. This was termed the *ferme ornée* or ornamental farm, with a 35-acre garden and 110 acres of ornamented farmland, mostly pasture, bound together by a series of walks punctuated by ruins and rustic features. Though his garden is now lost, its influence was considerable.

Chief among the designers of the landscape garden in the early eighteenth century were William Kent, Stephen Switzer and Charles Bridgeman. It was also an age of gentlemen amateurs as arbiters of taste, and the new profession of 'gardening writer' emerged with practitioners such as the memorably named Batty Langley, whose *New Principles of Gardening* went into many editions. As the century progressed, Lancelot 'Capability' Brown became a giant. His mantle was picked up by Humphrey Repton, another great landscaper of parks. Together with their followers, they transformed the English countryside. By the close of the century a German traveller, J. W. von Archenholz, noted in *A Picture of England* (1790) that the whole country seemed to be filled with parks enjoying picturesque views and pretty villages designed to be seen from a distance – close to, of course, rural poverty was obvious.

When Henrietta Howard, Countess of Suffolk (and mistress of George II while he was still Prince of Wales), created a house for her retirement from court, it was natural she should choose a location in the Thames valley within reach of London and surrounded by other grand houses. Marble Hill House, Twickenham, became the classic statement of the English Palladian Villa, probably designed by the 'architect earl', Henry Herbert, 9th Earl of Pembroke. Building began in 1724 and progressed swiftly, though the countess was not free to take up residence until 1734. Its extensive gardens were laid out by Charles Bridgeman, later Royal Gardener. From the south front of the house, the view stretched across an oval circus and extensive lawns to the river. The countess later married and Marble Hill became a family home. Regular visitors included the poet Alexander Pope, who advised on the gardens, and the politician, novelist and leader of fashion Horace Walpole, both near neighbours.

In 1747 Horace Walpole (later 4th Earl of Orford), took out a lease on another house in Twickenham, Strawberry Hill. Over the next twenty years he converted the jumble of ordinary buildings into a playful but highly influential Gothic, part castle, part dream. The Gothic elements have been described as a 'skin', composed of ornaments and features. Interior decoration was part of the overall scheme, and Walpole assembled a remarkable collection of furniture and artistic objects. Garden design was another area of experiment. A spacious lawn ran down to the river, surrounded by picturesque elements including a serpentine wood and many garden buildings such as the Chapel in the Wood.

Lord Burlington, the 3rd Earl, inherited a Jacobean house at Chiswick and went on to create a hugely influential neo-Palladian villa on the site. As a young man he had made the Grand Tour, returning with over 850 trunks of art and antiquities. The wealthy aristocrat already had a townhouse in Westminster – Burlington House, Piccadilly – when he personally designed a new house to stand alongside his old house at Chiswick which was down-graded to serve the domestic functions. Built between 1726 and 1729, the new Chiswick House was to be a temple to the Arts, providing an exquisite setting for Burlington's art collection and a venue for gatherings of his cultural circle. It was symmetrical in form, and its central saloon was surmounted by a cupola. After Burlington's death, the property passed to the Dukes of Devonshire. They found it inconvenient as a family home, so in 1788 the Jacobean house was demolished and a pair of wings containing the domestic offices were added to the new house. Those wings were themselves demolished in the 1950s to return the house to its original form. As with all of these riverside villas, the gardens were integral to the atmosphere. The extensive grounds explored new ideas of naturalistic and picturesque design, softening the divisions between different areas and opening up vistas. Many garden buildings and monuments provided focuses within this landscape. A public highway ran awkwardly between the house and the Thames, allowing only distant prospects of the river and water meadows. Perhaps partly in compensation for this, a stream called the Bollo Brook which flowed through the grounds was widened to form a private 'river'.

Another Thames-side mansion commanding glorious views that are the equal of any at Richmond, albeit further upstream, is Cliveden, near Cookham. Here, at Cliveden Reach, the river winds dreamily below romantic hanging woods. George Villiers, 2nd Duke of Buckingham, chose this site to build a great house for his mistress, the Countess of Shrewsbury, in the 1660s. His architect, William Winde, first created a large terrace as a foundation, and it is this which still gives the gardens their flavour. The house was remodelled for the Earl of Orkney in the early eighteenth century, while Charles Bridgeman laid out the grounds. The Octagon Temple, perched right on the edge of the terrace above the river, was integral to this scheme. The house suffered two disastrous fires before being rebuilt for the Duke of Sutherland by Charles Barry, recently architect of the Houses of Parliament. Then, in 1893, the wealthy American William Waldorf Astor bought the estate and laid out the gardens. Under the Astors, Cliveden became a centre of European political and literary life, the equal of its glittering eighteenth-century predecessors such as Chiswick House or Strawberry Hill.

Not everyone espoused the new ideas. Ham House was the product of an earlier generation. This red brick mansion was set in an elaborate formal garden of parterres and avenues on the bank of the Thames. Just 10 miles from London, it had been built in 1610 for Sir Thomas Vavasour, Knight Marshal to James I. It came into the hands of William Murray, 1st Earl of Dysart, who remodelled the interior in the 1630s to create some sumptuous rooms. After that the grounds saw only limited changes in line with fashion, and the National Trust has restored it in part to a seventeenth-century layout. In the eighteenth century successive earls seem to have been antisocial, not engaging with the high society of their neighbours – even George III was turned away when he visited unannounced. That said, the 5th Earl did manage to marry the niece of Horace Walpole who lived across the river at Strawberry Hill; it was a whirlwind if rather one-sided courtship. Despite his antiquarian inclinations, Walpole himself found the house depressingly dreary and old-fashioned.

The nearness of this part of the Thames valley to London, together with its natural beauty, attracted many well-to-do families with business in London who could afford to maintain their less ambitious country homes among their elegant neighbours. Towns such as Richmond were well stocked with large houses. The artist Sir Joshua Reynolds lived in Wick House, Richmond, while the actor and impresario David Garrick had a Thames-side villa at Hampton. The poet Alexander Pope leased a house in the river frontage at Twickenham and set about creating a 'natural' Classical garden. His lawn swept down to the river, but due to the cramped nature of the site his main garden was on the opposite side of a public road, accessed via a tunnel (his 'grotto'). Lacking a house as a natural focus in this way gave him free reign. Into the space he squeezed a shell temple, viewing mounts, a grove, bowling green, obelisk (which provided a visual reference point), vineyard, orangery, glass house and kitchen garden. His philosophy of gardening is concisely summed up in his *Epistle to Lord Burlington* (1731):

> Let not each beauty ev'ry where be spy'd,
> Where half the skill is decently to hide.

> He gains all points, who pleasingly confounds
> Surprizes, varies and conceals the Bounds.

Pope's influence was far greater than his 5 acres at Twickenham might suggest. He corresponded with the garden designer Charles Bridgeman and was an influence on another leading designer, William Kent. He also advised on the Countess of Suffolk's garden at Marble Hill and his ideas can be detected in the Chiswick garden of Lord Burlington (the dedicatee of the *Epistle* quoted above).

Pope had made his fortune with a translation of Homer which was so successful that he was freed from the need to chase after patrons. He was also an early victim of the cult of celebrity. His satire, *An Epistle to Dr Arbuthnot*, begins:

> Shut, shut the door, good *John*! fatigu'd, I said,
> Tie up the knocker, say I'm sick, I'm dead.
> The dog-star rages! nay 'tis past a doubt,
> All *Bedlam*, or *Parnassus*, is let out:
> Fire in each eye, and papers in each hand,
> They rave, recite, and madden round the land.
>
> What walls can guard me, or what shades can hide?
> They pierce my thickets, through my grot they glide;
> By land, by water, they renew the charge;
> They stop the chariot, and they board the barge.

Clearly he was pestered by would-be authors demanding that he read their doggerel. Interestingly, the final line quoted makes a reference to his barge. For those who could afford it, travel to the City by private barge was superior to a coach journey and one reason for choosing a riverside property.

Writers and artists, as well as garden designers, taught the cultured classes how they were supposed to think about the river and its setting. They presented a vision of the river from Kew to Hampton as a rural idyll meandering through a landscape of meadowland, woods, private parks and palaces, punctuated by picturesque riverside communities. Artists flocked to paint Thames landscapes. For example, J. M. W. Turner's 1808 *View of Pope's*

Villa at Twickenham during its Dilapidation illustrates an idyllic if slightly misty riverscape, with sheep resting in the foreground and innocent country folk engaged in conversation.

In this favoured setting, the landscape which came to represent perfection more than any other was the view from Richmond Hill. It attracted artists; Sir Joshua Reynolds (better known as a portraitist), who lived on the hill, and J. M. W. Turner both painted the view. Writers were also captivated. In *Heart of Midlothian* (1818) the novelist Sir Walter Scott describes it as 'an unrivalled landscape'. He goes on,

> The Thames, here turreted with villas and there garlanded with forests, moved on slowly and placidly, like the mighty monarch of the scene, to whom all its other beauties were accessories.

The poet James Thomson sang of 'the matchless Thames'. In his long poem *The Seasons* (1727) he expressed his wonder at the distant view over the river:

> Heavens! what a goodly Prospect spreads around,
> Of hills, and Dales, and Woods, and Lawns, and Spires,
> And glittering Towns, and gilded streams, till all
> The stretching Landskip [landscape] into smoke decays!

Perhaps the greatest hyperbole was left to a Prussian tourist, Charles P. Moritz, writing in his *Travels in England in 1782*:

> The terrace at Richmond does assuredly afford one of the finest prospects in the world. Whatever is charming in nature or pleasing in art, is to be seen here: nothing I had ever seen or ever can see elsewhere, is to be compared to it.

Beauty was a magic that could seemingly be sprinkled by the river's touch. In 1746 the great Venetian artist Giovanni Antonio Canaletto moved to England, and for the next ten years he lived and worked here. His reputation was already thoroughly established by his views of his native Venice, and he had long sold to British collectors via an agent. One of his earliest works in this period was of London from the terrace of Richmond House, the riverside home of the Duke of Richmond, a long-term client. It compares interestingly with his famous Venetian views, with a foreground dominated by the sheet of the Thames fringed by a rather flat and low-lying skyline broken only by the mass of St Paul's and the spires of many Wren churches. He also made several studies of the new Westminster Bridge.

By the close of the eighteenth century, the Romantic movement was beginning to win the hearts and minds of the growing middle classes. Beauty, they say, is in the eye of the beholder; in which case, few have had a more beauty-filled eye than William Wordsworth, that unparalleled spokesman for the claims of untamed nature. Yet even he was moved by the view of London and its Thames in the early morning sunlight before the town awoke. *Upon Westminster Bridge*, composed in September 1802, includes the lines:

> This City now doth, like a garment wear
> The beauty of the morning; silent, bare,
> Ships, towers, domes, theatres, and temples lie
> Open unto the fields, and to the sky;
> All bright and glittering in the smokeless air.

and

> The river glideth at his own sweet will.

Canaletto and Wordsworth show that in the eighteenth century the intelligentsia were prepared to interpret anything by the artistic canons of the natural landscape. This was to change in the following century, as the adjective 'man-made' became first an accolade and then a warning.

Frost Fairs

Improvised and uninhibited, the London frost fairs represent the opposite extreme to royal pageantry. The climate has fluctuated several times since the end of the last ice age. Following a warm period in the tenth to thirteenth centuries, the 'Little Ice

Age' extended from the fifteenth or sixteenth century until the mid-nineteenth century, after which the climate began to warm up once again. The Thames at London froze over at least twenty-three times between 1209 and 1814, but has not done so since. 1789 was an exceptional year, when the weather was so cold that the river froze below London Bridge as far as Rotherhithe and remained frozen for two months, and fairs were held at various places.

However, the freezing of the Thames was not due to temperature alone. Equally important was the effect of the old London Bridge on the flow of the river. The bridge consisted of nineteen arches, and each of the stone piers was encased in a 'starling' or breakwater which protected it from the force of the water and from impact with shipping or waterborne debris. As a result, the bridge formed a partial dam, ponding up the river behind it. On the downstream side, depending on the state of the tide, the river level could be up to 6 feet lower. Water burst powerfully through each arch like a mini waterfall, and it was all too common for boats to be upset trying to 'shoot the rapids' as it was known. This constriction of the flow slowed the river down, creating conditions in which it could freeze during a prolonged period of low temperatures. Depending on the precise conditions, the frozen surface of the river was sometimes relatively smooth, and sometimes a jumble of icebergs and fissures. Once Rennie's new London Bridge, with only five arches, was opened in 1831, the river flowed more regularly and so no longer froze.

The frozen river was a spectacle, enhanced by the colours and antics of a fair, as recorded in a number of paintings and drawings from 1677 onwards. Having this huge and egalitarian novelty on the very doorstep of the capital ensured that enormous crowds wrapped up warm to enjoy the fun, and these fairs usually earned a reputation for becoming bawdy in the evenings. A fair usually consisted of lines of tents and booths laid out in one or two 'streets'. Many of the stalls sold food and drink, and riverside taverns would each have their booth. There always seems to have been an enterprising printer producing souvenirs 'printed on the ice'. Around the streets, other attractions were offered to tempt money from the relaxed visitors. Various games such as skittles were played, while entertainers such as musicians or stilt walkers performed. Bull-baiting is shown in several pictures, while primitive forms of merry-go-round and swing-boat can be seen. The 1684 fair advertised a clockwork carriage, and various sledges and wheeled boats offered rides, some probably pulled by watermen whose usual work was suspended. Hog and ox roasts were popular, partly no doubt for their warmth but also because they were such an incongruous idea. The royal family visited in 1684, and a painting of the fair by Abraham Hondius (in the Museum of London) appears to show a military parade which may be in their honour. An engraving of 1739 identifies some stalls, including a goldsmith, printer, milliner, toy shop, seller of Tunbridge ware, and gaming tables. That year the fair also had a unique attraction. Work had begun on the new Westminster Bridge, only two piers projected above the frozen river. Rope bridges and ladders were improvised, and people presumably paid to climb up onto the piers to admire the view of the fair and the City.

Simple Pleasures

London, with its large population consisting of people of all types, inevitably had a huge appetite for entertainment. Throughout the Middle Ages the Southwark shore opposite the City had a reputation for pleasure and low life – crossing the river seemed to grant a symbolic freedom. The early historian of London John Stow researched brothels back to the twelfth century via licences from the fourteenth and fifteenth centuries. The many taverns along the waterfront were a byword for vice, being frequented by rough mariners. Bear-baiting and bull-baiting were popular pastimes into the seventeenth century. In these competitions, trained dogs were pitted against a bear or bull in a fight to the death, with gambling on the outcome. The diarist Samuel Pepys found these 'sports' crude and distasteful.

London's first purpose-built theatres appeared in the late sixteenth century to the north of the City, in Clerkenwell and Shoreditch, but they quickly chose to locate on the Southwark bank: the Shoreditch playhouse named 'The Theatre' was dismantled and transported bodily to Bankside. They shared the same disreputable audiences and shady reputations as the other South Bank pleasures, while distance from the supervision of the City authorities was a further attraction. These buildings were in the round with the auditorium open to the sky, similar to the replica Globe Theatre. A flag flown over the theatre would signal that a performance was scheduled, and it is probable that the play would be only one element in the evening's entertainment. The great names of Elizabethan and Jacobean theatre – William Shakespeare, Ben Jonson, Kit Marlowe – were all at home in this shady world. As theatre became more respectable after the Commonwealth, it relocated back over the river to the West End where its new clientele lived.

The theatres were followed by a new fashion for pleasure gardens. The first was Cuper's Garden, near what is today the southern end of Waterloo Bridge. Opened in the 1630s by Abraham Cuper, gardener to the Earl of Arundel, it offered walks in a fashionable garden, bowling greens, live music, refreshments, and latterly fireworks. A landing stage on the river was known as Cuper's Bridge. A century later it was attracting fashionable society, numbering the Prince and Princess of Wales among its clientele. However, thieves were also attracted, leading in 1753 to the refusal of a public entertainment licence. It reopened as a private garden for subscribers only, but quickly closed again.

This was followed by the New Spring Gardens (later renamed Vauxhall Gardens, giving the word 'Vauxhall', meaning 'pleasure garden', to the language) which opened just before the Restoration in 1660. Londoners took boats across the river to enjoy its landscaped gardens and walks, its shady arbours ideal for lovers' rendezvous, and its art and music. Handel's *Music for the Royal Fireworks* was premiered here to an audience of 12,000 before its official performance in front of the king. Many of the pleasures on offer had previously been the preserve of the wealthier classes; now the gates were opened wide. At first there was no charge for admission, but refreshments were expensive and portions small. In time, the range of attractions was broadened to include various acts and stunts, such as balloon ascents. When Vauxhall Bridge was opened in 1816, it provided easy access to the gardens. With large crowds enjoying their leisure, crime unsurprisingly became a problem, and as more evening events took place the gardens acquired a reputation for licentiousness. At the same time, rival establishments began to adopt and develop the model. Even so, Vauxhall Gardens survived until 1859.

On the opposite bank, Ranelagh Gardens, Chelsea, opened in 1742. A relatively high admission charge ensured a 'better class' of patron: Horace Walpole observed, 'It has totally beat Vauxhall ... You can't set your foot without treading on a Prince, or Duke of Cumberland.' The gardens bordered the river, and one of the earliest regattas was held there in 1775. They included a covered rotunda 185 feet in diameter, painted by Canaletto, which was large enough to hold concerts in all weathers – a wise precaution. In Fanny Burney's 1778 novel *Evelina*, the heroine writes, 'Well, my dear Sir, we went to Ranelagh. It is a charming place; and the brilliancy of the lights, on my first entrance, made me almost think I was in some inchanted castle or fairy palace, for all looked like magic to me.'

Cremorne Pleasure Gardens, also in Chelsea, was a latecomer. Opening in 1845, the attractions included a bandstand and open-air dance floor, a marionette theatre, restaurants, fireworks and landscaped garden walks. Designed to be seen at night by the twinkling of the illuminations, the buildings were more like stage sets than architecture. It closed in 1877. By that date fashion had moved on and families were taking the steamers to the estuary resorts.

Regular events such as balloon ascents were advertised to draw the crowds. One August afternoon in 1861 Miss Young, billed as 'the female Blondin', crossed the Thames from Battersea to Cremorne Gardens on a tightrope supported on four boats midstream. Her first attempt failed because the counterweights holding the rope taut had been stolen! But once the equipment had been repaired the crossing took only seven minutes. Battersea Bridge provided a grandstand for the cheering masses, while many took boats and watched from the water below. Another special attraction was the Cremorne Tournament, a much-simplified version of the Eglinton Tournament of fourteen years earlier. The latter had been intended as the reincarnation of medieval chivalry, with noble knights jousting on horseback, but the weather had turned it into an expensive fiasco. The Cremorne performers, by contrast, were actors and circus performers by profession, but the costume and setting offered a visual spectacle. At a time when Gothic revival was all the rage, it was well received.

Many other tea gardens and minor pleasure gardens catered for different tastes and pockets. In Fanny Burney's *Evelina*, the characters suggest a number of such places for an evening out: White Conduit House, described as a tea garden and 'minor Vauxhall'; Bagnigge Wells, Cold Bath Fields, another minor Vauxhall for tradesmen; Mother Red Cap's in Camden Town; Sadler's Wells; and Saltero's coffeehouse. Other such venues included St Helena, patronised by the Prince Regent, and China Hall tea gardens, both in Rotherhithe.

Riverside pubs are another facet in the kaleidoscope of leisure, and must be the easiest way to enjoy the river. To sit on a terrace or in a garden outside a traditional inn and quietly sup beer or eat chicken-in-a-basket in the sun while watching the swans and boats slip by is a simple pleasure to which many aspire. Every riverside town boasts several of varying quality, as does almost every village, while others are dotted down by old bridges or ferry crossings in remote and peaceful settings.

The Festival of Britain, held to mark the centenary of the Great Exhibition of 1851, was a bold attempt to rejuvenate Britain after five post-war years. A derelict, bomb-damaged site on the South Bank was turned into an imaginative and futuristic attraction. With refreshments, music, fireworks, entertainments and garden walks, it could in some ways be thought of as the lineal descendant of the pleasure gardens which had occupied this side of the river in the eighteenth and nineteenth centuries. It was a cross between a funfair, a cultural event and a trade fair, intended to show off the best of British design while giving people a day to remember. The Royal Festival Hall remains a lasting legacy, while the vast Dome of Discovery and the iconic Skylon were beacons of modernism. The whole family was entertained in the Battersea Pleasure Gardens. Open for only five months from May to September, it drew an astounding 8½ million visitors, while local and travelling exhibitions took the Festival to every part of the country. There was to be no reprieve, as the buildings and structures were broken up for scrap. In many ways it had been a huge success, introducing the populace to a new, bright style and launching the careers of many British designers.

Another great British tradition can be traced back to January 1815 when the first steam boat, the *Margery*, went into operation, running from Wapping Old Stairs to Milton (near Gravesend), and by 1830 fifty-seven steam packets operated on the Lower Thames. Their attraction was that they did not rely on wind and tide. Consequently they were more reliable than traditional vessels, and also faster. This gave rise to a new phenomenon, the day tripper. It was now possible for a family to spend the day at the seaside in Southend or even Margate and return home that same evening. Excursions of this sort soon came within the reach of the growing middle classes, and by the 1830s, 100,000 Londoners were visiting Margate by sea annually. Charles Dickens describes the scene at the steam-wharf of London Bridge or St Katherine's Dock Company on a Saturday morning in summer. A Margate boat lies alongside the wharf, and the Gravesend boat alongside that, linked by a gangplank. Both steamers are crowded to excess and more passengers are being set down by coaches at the entrance. In the chaos people embark on the wrong boat and quickly have to change. Once underway all the menfolk strike the pose of the seasoned sailor, newspapers and picnic hampers are opened, and the holiday commences.[1]

Southend had begun as a resort in the later eighteenth century, but it was the railways that sparked its phenomenal growth. Cheap, fast and reliable, the trains brought working families from the East End for a few hours of fun. In addition to sea and sand, the resort developed attractions such as the amusement park, the kursaal, a cliff railway, Warwick's Revolving Tower (operated 1897–1902) and the longest pier in the country complete with narrow-gauge railway. By the late 1930s Southend received an estimated 5½ million visitors a year, by far the majority still travelling out from London by rail though with increasing competition from the motorcoach trade.

Many poor families in the East End could not afford the trip to Southend, so in 1934 a beach was created in London. Barge-loads of sand were dumped on the muddy foreshore beside the Tower of London and stairs provided access. Despite the fact that London was a major port and the river was badly polluted, Tower Beach remained popular even after the Second World War, only declining as holidays became more affordable. It served a valuable purpose for two decades – though children were advised to keep their mouths closed when they swam!

As the nineteenth century progressed, growth in leisure time and disposable income turned the Thames into a playground for the new middle classes. Many riverside towns saw the potential of the new leisure industry for the local economy, and developed attractions including a regatta. In a changing world, the establishment of the regatta at Henley in 1839 was just such an act, helping the town to reinvent itself as an 'inland resort'. When the Great Western Railway opened a branch line to the town in 1857, tourism flourished. One summer's day in 1888, 6,768 Londoners travelled to Henley for a return fare of three shillings and sixpence. By the 1890s the regatta was attracting crowds of 34,000 for what has been described as a 'world-celebrated water picnic' – it was almost irrelevant that competitive races were being rowed. Photographs show the river densely packed with small craft – rowing boats and punts – and Oxford college barges moved downstream for the week to provide grandstands for the favoured. Similar, though less popular, scenes were repeated at towns all along the river.

'Messing about on the river' became an accepted summer pastime. In 1804 the Thames Commissioners had passed a by-law to address complaints from 'gentlemen and others, navigating on the river for pleasure'. As interest in sport flourished, the Oxford and Cambridge University Boat Race was first rowed at Henley in 1829, moving to the current course from Putney to Mortlake in 1839 where it quickly became an annual highlight even for those who had not been to the universities. Rowing became a popular means of exercise and several rowing clubs sprang up, such as the City of London Rowing Club founded in 1860. Before long, every town had boats for hire by the hour, and the railways brought most of the Thames valley within easy reach of the capital. The social and economic importance of this new attitude was recognised in the Thames Preservation Act of 1855 which stated with apparent surprise that the Thames 'has largely come to be used as a place of public recreation and resort; and it is expedient that provision should be made that it should be preserved as a place of regulated public recreation'.

By the end of the nineteenth century 30,000 Londoners belonged to angling clubs. Swimming was another popular watery activity. In the seventeenth century, thousands reputedly bathed regularly in the Thames above London, though the popularity of river bathing must have declined as pollution increased. With its currents, locks, weirs and shipping, the river could be an unpredictable and dangerous place to swim: a memorial beside the weir known as Sandford Lasher commemorates five Oxford undergraduates drowned there on different occasions. The three swimming ponds on Hampstead Heath were created as part of the water supply system, but since at least the 1860s they have attracted the hardy for year-round swimming. The Serpentine in Hyde Park is another open-air pool that still attracted bathers, and the Serpentine Swimming Club staged its first Christmas Day Race in 1864.

Henry W. Taunt was an Oxford-based photographer. Born in 1842 to 'poor but respectable' parents, he was an ambitious young man who established his own business in 1868. Despite (or perhaps because of) financial difficulties, he continued to work until his death in 1922. Very much the Victorian, he was a self-made entrepreneur. In addition to the usual studio portraits, he was quick to grasp the potential of tourism, publishing local views and postcards, and over fifty books and tourist guides, as well a daily leaflet summarising the results of the Oxford 'Bumps'. His firm branched out to include bicycle repairs, presumably inspired by the tourists who bought his guidebooks. Perhaps his best-known book was *A New Map of the Thames* (first published 1872), which went through six editions and on the strength of which he was elected a Fellow of the Royal Geographical Society. The *New Map* was a guidebook for visitors to and on the river, and included photographs of many of the sights. But it was also a handbook for someone planning to sail down the Thames.

Jerome K. Jerome's classic novel, *Three Men in a Boat*, parodied the new public Taunt was writing for. After tossing around ideas for a holiday, the three friends decide on sailing up the river from Kingston to Oxford. This, it is felt, would offer 'fresh air, exercise, and quiet; the constant change of scene would occupy our minds

... and the hard work would give us a good appetite, and make us sleep well'. It sounds idyllic: at night 'we run our little boat into some quiet nook, and the tent is pitched, and the frugal supper cooked and eaten. Then the big pipes are filled and lighted, and the pleasant talk goes round in musical undertone; while, in the pauses of our talk, the river, playing round the boat, prattles strange old tales and secrets.' Adding a touch of realism, Harris asks, 'How about when it rained?'

Kenneth Graham's parallel evocation of the Edwardian Thames, *The Wind in the Willows*, was based in the landscape around his home at Cookham and his own days spent on the water. Quarry Wood was the model for the Wild Wood. With its sculling water rat and river bank picnics, its world is not that far from *Three Men in a Boat*. The beautiful 'Piper at the Gates of Dawn', a nature spirit playing ethereal music and protecting the young otter, sat comfortably with the spiritual imagination of the age.

11

The Preserved River

Preserving the Thames Valley

Protecting the Thames Valley

In 1926 the Council for the Preservation of Rural England was founded, with a brief to advocate sensible and effective planning control. The years after the First World War had seen a boom in suburban living. Rail, London Underground and private car ownership opened up an ever-larger radius around each urban centre. In the 1920s and 1930s an average of 300,000 new houses were built each year in Britain, covering 60,000 acres of countryside. Undoubtedly these homes were needed, and spacious suburban living was more attractive than urban overcrowding – but there was a cost which some felt was too heavy.

The Thames valley was obviously an area under threat, so as early as 1929 the CPRE commissioned a report, *The Thames Valley from Cricklade to Staines: A Survey of its Existing State and Some Suggestions for its Future Preservation*. In his foreword the chairman declared, 'The Thames Valley Branch of the Council for the Preservation of Rural England is trying to save for posterity some of the scenery, peace, and amenities of an accessible, historic, and beautiful part of England.' The authors enlarged upon the theme: 'The amenities of the Thames are worthy of special consideration, not only for the enjoyment that the river affords to the congested population of London and neighbouring towns, but also on account of its historic interest, which attracts visitors to the river every year from more distant places.' However, they were not unrealistic: 'The object of preservation is by no means to insist upon the river and its banks remaining in the precise condition they are at present. Development and growth must take place, but the task of the Thames Valley Branch should be to devise some means whereby it may be guided along the right lines.'

Some inappropriate developments were singled out, such as an encampment of old railway carriages at Bablock Hythe, 'two bungalows of incongruous temporary materials' near Appleton, and several cases of ribbon development. They also noted that houses had been built on the floodplain where flooding was almost inevitable. The report went on to make a number of suggestions, central to which was a scheme for zoning the region according to permitted development, if any.

Ribbon development was a particular problem. It was far cheaper to build along existing roads than to create housing estates where the developer would bear the cost of the new infrastructure. The young architect Clough Williams-Ellis, creator of the architectural fantasy that is Porthmerion, was galvanised by this spectre of uncontrolled development. *England and the Octopus* (1928) was a polemical book written by a spirited and angry young man, but in its way it helped to transform public opinion. The 'octopus' in question was London but could have been any metropolis, its tentacles stretching out into a countryside fast losing its integrity and identity. Ribbon development was his main target, together with a range of issues including roadside advertising hoardings (for example, lining the Bath Road between London and Maidenhead), high-tension power lines and unsightly petrol stations.

During the nineteenth century the face of Britain was transformed to an unprecedented degree. Huge acreages of farmland were swallowed up and many remote areas were scarred by the extraction and processing of essential raw materials. As the century drew to a close, thinkers began to question the spiritual costs involved in this economic progress: what was being lost was not just amenity value, but our very identity. Often their search for values harked back to an idealised past before (or after) industrialisation. For example, the main character in William Morris's utopian novel *News from Nowhere* goes to bed in 1890s Hammersmith and wakes up in a future in which the industrial Thames has given way to a rural and social paradise. The idyllic river on which his characters sail to a house very like Morris's country retreat, the seventeenth-century Kelmscott Manor (near Lechlade, Gloucestershire), is unrecognisable as that portrayed by his contemporary, Jerome K. Jerome. In this intellectual climate, a number of organisations were spawned, many with the intention of preserving the natural landscape or the relics of the past, all of which were now seen as being threatened by uncontrolled economic opportunism, and with them the essence of Britishness.

As early as 1865 the housing boom around London began to threaten the survival of the ancient commons. The newly formed Commons Preservation Society led the battle to save such important green spaces as Wimbledon Common from the developer. Soon even the historic Epping Forest was at risk. Within a few years, Octavia Hill, later to be one of the founders of the National Trust, began to campaign for smaller open spaces – green lungs – within the metropolitan area. In 1877 the Society for the Protection of Ancient Buildings was founded by William Morris and fellow Pre-Raphaelites. Two of its early projects were just a few miles away from Morris's home beside the Thames at Kelmscott, the tithe barn at Great Coxwell and Inglesham church. In 1882 the Ancient Monuments Protection Act gave the first tentative legal protection to the manmade heritage. The Survey for the Memorials of Greater London was begun in 1894, and the Victoria County History series was launched in 1899, both seeking to record the nation's heritage before it was lost. 1895 saw the foundation of the National Trust, while the Society for the Promotion of Nature Reserves (later the Wildlife Trust movement) started in 1912 with the purpose of protecting wildlife habitats rather than single species. Most of these initiatives faltered with the outbreak of war in 1914, but on their return many people realised the need to safeguard the land they had fought for.

Since at least the eighteenth century the view south and west from Richmond Hill had been recognised as one of the outstanding vistas in the south of England. Consequently, when in 1896 the Earl of Dysart, as lord of the manor, submitted a private member's Bill to Parliament to enclose nearly 200 acres of common land in Ham, known as Ham Fields, for a housing scheme, opposition was galvanised. The wealthy residents of Richmond were not prepared to stand by and see their precious view destroyed in this way. The

Bill was heavily defeated as it conflicted with the Metropolitan Commons Acts (1866 and 1878) which had outlawed the enclosure of commons within 15 miles of Charing Cross.

A new threat emerged in 1900, when an article dealing with the history of gardening in the magazine *Country Life* mentioned, almost in passing, that Marble Hill House and estate were on the market and likely to be developed for housing. Once again the view was endangered. A conglomerate of local authorities was able to purchase the property and manage it as a public park. Today both house and park are administered by English Heritage. Similar threats were seen off at Cambridge Park and Lebanon Park. In 1927 the neighbouring property to Marble Hill was bought by a private donor to prevent industrial development.

Lord Dysart had not given up. The 1896 Bill was resubmitted with minor changes to increase public access. Under a new and deliberately misleading title, the Richmond Hill (Preservation of View) Bill, it was passed in 1902. Meanwhile, the local authorities had acquired several pieces of land within the view, including the important Petersham Ait. Then in 1930 the authorities entered into a Deed of Covenant to restrict development on certain plots, paying compensation to their owners. Richmond Hill has the reputation of being the only view in the country 'protected by law'. As can be seen, however, protection has been achieved by a lattice of means and not by one single Act.

That other famous Thames view, of Oxford from Boars Hill, was praised by Matthew Arnold in his poem *Thyrsis* (1865):

> And that sweet City with her dreaming spires
> She needs not June for beauty's heightening.

At that date Oxford was still a largely non-industrial town, dominated by the university. Its skyline was as it had always been, unmarred by belching chimneys. In *The Scholar Gypsy*, Arnold expanded on the rural idyll of the Thames around Oxford. This was, for him, a traditional world which hardly changed amid the turmoil of Victorian England, a world in which 200 years could pass unnoticed. A world viewed through the lens of his own student memories. He would not recognise it today.

Flood Control

The Thames has always been unpredictable. Even today the river cannot be tamed, no matter how much faith is placed in engineering solutions, but will break out when and where it is least expected. This unpredictability may have contributed to its role in the spiritual life of communities in prehistory as they tried to respond to its moods. Archaeological excavation frequently finds evidence of flood damage, for example the destructive floods from which Roman Staines never really recovered. Many settlements along the Lower Thames constructed embankments as flood defences, though the river often had the last word: despite its river defences, throughout the Middle Ages Woolwich was periodically flooded and lives lost.

The riverside towns are all prone to flooding: the river was both their reason for existence and their nemesis. The worst recorded flood at Maidenhead was in 1894, though earlier severe flooding was probably not recorded in detail. In March 1947 the Thames burst its banks for a fortnight, and other smaller floods have frequently occurred. The 7-mile-long Jubilee River was opened in 2002, part of the Maidenhead–Eton–Windsor Flood Alleviation Scheme, and it has already proved its worth.

Although London was built on a low river bluff, parts of the City are low-lying, as are the East End and Southwark. Serious flooding has claimed lives on several occasions, with significant events over the last two centuries in 1809, 1823, 1849, 1852, 1877, 1894 and 1947. In the nineteenth century, some areas of poorer housing in London flooded on an almost annual basis. The last time central London was badly affected was 1928, claiming fourteen lives. Westminster is equally vulnerable. In 1236 it was said that boats could pass through the Great Hall of Westminster Palace. The palace was again flooded in 1555. For the diarist Samuel Pepys, a seventeenth-century top civil servant, a flood in Whitehall was a calamity. His diary entry for 7 December 1663 notes, 'There was last night the greatest tide that ever was remembered in England to have been in this river, all Whitehall having been drowned.'[1]

The floods that devastated the east coast on the night of 31 January 1953 inundated Canvey Island, killing fifty-eight, but

London was spared. Even so, with an estimated 60 square miles of the capital lying below the high-tide level, the government has been prepared to invest heavily. The greatest threat, as in 1953 – and even in 1099 – is a storm surge coinciding with a spring tide. The Thames Barrier opened in 1984 at a cost of £534 million. The Barking Flood Barrier at the mouth of the River Roding was a result of the same fear. Little by little global warming is reducing the effectiveness of these defences.[2]

Tideless Thames

Many schemes to solve the Thames's ills have been proposed by private individuals, usually from a very particular perspective. One such visionary was J. H. O. Bunge. In his book *Tideless Thames in Future London*, Bunge advocated a very different barrage across the river at Woolwich to that which was eventually built between New Charlton and Silvertown. He believed his scheme offered many advantages, including the aesthetic and public health benefits of stopping the foul river mud from being exposed twice daily on the tides, and the commercial benefit of maintaining a constant deep-water channel for shipping. The barrage would combine locks for shipping with a much-needed eastern bridging point to relieve congestion on the roads. It would also allow better control of river levels and so minimise the risk of flooding. Published in 1944, the proposal must be seen in the light of post-war plans for a utopian Britain, alongside the setting up of the welfare system. A heavily bombed London may have looked to a dreamer like a blank slate, as it had done to Wren and others following the Great Fire of 1666. Even so, it was a bold suggestion and would have created a very different river from the one we now enjoy.

Drinking the River

Visual and recreational amenity are nice to have, but providing a clean and reliable water supply for London long taxed the ingenuity of businessmen and politicians alike. Roman wells have been excavated at a number of sites in the City, often timber-lined for stability. Private wells continued to be a source of water for domestic use into the nineteenth century, while public pumps also drew water up from the aquifer. This, however, could not meet the growing need.

In the Middle Ages the solution was for public benefactors to provide fountains.[3] One Gilbert de Sanford made a gift of running water to the City of London. By a deed of gift, confirmed by King Henry III, he allowed the water of the Tyburn and associated springs to be piped to a cistern in Cheapside, a distance of nearly 3 miles. It appears that this water was available freely to private citizens but that commercial users paid a charge. In 1439 the Abbot of Westminster granted a second water supply in return for a nominal annual fee of 2 lb of pepper (an exotic spice) payable on the Feast of St Peter ad Vincula. This conduit ran from a fountain-head on his manor of Paddington. A third public conduit was granted in 1491 by Sir John Fortescue from his lands at 'Mewes Close' for an annual fee of 4 pounds. By the late sixteenth century, further conduits served different areas of the City, but the supply of fresh water remained a serious problem, as did the related issue of waste disposal. John Stow lists numerous conduits and public pumps in his *Survey of London* (1603).

The next step forward came with the introduction of a new pumping technology from Germany in the late sixteenth century. One Peter Morris used a waterwheel driven by the power of the Thames to pump river water through pipes to a public fountain in Cornhill and to the houses of subscribers in Thames Street, New Fish Street and Grasse Street. Initially just one, and later three, waterwheels were erected in arches under London Bridge, and pumping began on Christmas Eve 1582. To compensate for the effect of the tides which meant that the rate of pumping was not constant, a tower with a header tank was required. During the intensely cold winters when the river was frozen for weeks on end and frost fairs were held, ice constantly had to be cleared from around the three water wheels under the bridge. Although the waterworks was destroyed during the Fire of London, it was rebuilt and continued into the nineteenth century until the bridge itself was replaced in 1831. By this date other companies were supplying water on both sides of the river, usually by means of pumping from depth, but as late as 1821 the London Bridge Waterworks still supplied nearly 4 million gallons daily.

The New River was another imaginative solution. It was a commercial venture, operated by the New River Company, designed by Sir Hugh Myddelton and opened in 1613. In recognition of its vital importance the king became a 50 per cent shareholder, helping to defuse opposition. This was an innovative undertaking at a time when Dutch engineering was just starting to drain the Cambridgeshire fens and it seemed that mastery over water had been achieved. An artificial watercourse was cut from the River Lea near Hertford to the New River Head in Clerkenwell. It was gravity-fed, an impressive piece of engineering with a drop of just 5 inches per mile over a length of around 25 miles. The New River Path has recently been developed as a riverside walk for much of its length.

The River Lea was another important source of water, quite apart from being siphoned off upstream into the New River. The East London Waterworks Company operated two oval, brick-lined reservoirs at Old Ford, filled from the river. By 1830, 5.9 million gallons a day were being drawn from the Lea to meet the needs of East London.

For centuries the concern had simply been to supply sufficient water, but by the middle of the nineteenth century questions of public health were being asked. Water quality began to be improved, using methods such as sedimentation, filtration and analysis. The cholera epidemics of 1849 and 1854 roused public feeling, and resulted in the Metropolis Water Act of 1852. This stated that after 1855 no water company should take water from the river below Teddington Lock and required that all water for domestic use should be filtered. A later amendment of the Act created the post of water examiner, who was to report periodically on the water supplied by the various companies. The Rivers Pollution Prevention Act of 1876 made it compulsory to treat sewage before it could be discharged into a river.

An important advance towards 'fitness for purpose' came in 1902 with the formation of the Metropolitan Water Board. The many different water companies were taken over and the provision of water unified across what was then greater London. The financial outlay in purchase and taking on liabilities came to over £47 million, and further investment was required to bring all parts up to standard. By the 1960s the Metropolitan Water Board and the smaller suburban water companies were taking 280 million gallons a day against a minimum summer flow of 576 million gallons a day (i.e. up to half of the river)! Since 1988 the Thames Water Ring Main has been constructed to rationalise water distribution around the metropolis. This pipe, 2.5 m in diameter, runs for 80 km to supply 300 million litres of drinking water a day to the capital from water treatment works near the Thames in West London at Ashford, Hampton, Kempton and Walton. Even this goes only some way towards meeting the daily demand of 2,000 million litres. Today, each glass of rainwater falling on the headwaters of the Thames is drunk eight times before it reaches the sea.

The demands placed on the river are often in conflict. Throughout history the Thames and its tributaries were the natural sewers for riverside communities, carrying both domestic and industrial waste of all descriptions. For centuries natural cycles had broken down this waste and aerated the water, and the river had been flushed out on the tide. By the eighteenth century this balance was beginning to be over-tipped as the population of the Thames valley, and particularly of the capital, reached a critical capacity: the river that was London's life-blood was suffering from blood poisoning. The presence of fish is a good measure of a river's condition. As the level of pollution increased on the tidal river, the numbers of fish and the range of species declined. The medieval Thames had been full of fish at London, while it could still be described as a 'fishfull river' at the close of the eighteenth century. Upriver also, fishing had long been an important economic activity. It had even been a salmon river. This changed quickly in the early years of the nineteenth century.

Public health was another significant victim of London's sewage disposal problem: the situation was never as serious higher up the river, though every town experienced difficulties. Domestic cess pits cut the water table all over the City while sewers drained into the river. This same water was then pumped back for domestic use from the Thames or out of the water table. Four major cholera epidemics hit the capital in the nineteenth century – in 1832, 1849, 1854 and 1865. In a pioneering piece of 'medical geography', Dr John Snow plotted the occurrences during the 1854 outbreak and noticed that they were mostly within a short distance of a public water pump in Soho. When the authorities sealed off the pump, the outbreak ceased. This demonstrated a clear link between water and the spread of certain diseases. Even so, Parliament dragged its heels.

The collective mind of Parliament was finally focused on the problem under their windows by the 'Great Stink' of 1858. It was an unusually hot summer, and the bacteria in the Thames thrived. The dissolved oxygen was removed from the water, reducing the naturally occurring sulphates to sulphides, creating the gas hydrogen sulphide and turning the water black with iron sulphide. In the House of Commons, the curtains were soaked in chloride of lime in a vain attempt to counter the overwhelming smell. Plans were made to evacuate Parliament to Hampton Court and the Law Courts to Oxford and St Albans. The crisis passed when heavy rains ended the heatwave and freshened the river, but the lesson had been taken to heart. A House of Commons Select Committee was appointed to make recommendations to solve the problem.

Contrary to popular perception, emptying waste into the river did not dispose of it. With the competing effects of tides and currents, it took several weeks for the contents of the river to make their way from London Bridge to the sea. One of the responsibilities of the Metropolitan Board of Works, created in 1856, was to prevent sewage flowing into the Thames, where it would languish. At the same time the Thames Conservators were given powers to prohibit the discharge of sewage into the Thames or its tributaries above London. After rejecting a number of proposals, the Metropolitan Board of Works accepted a scheme put forward by its own chief engineer, Joseph Bazalgette, and received an enabling Act in 1859. A system of 'intercepting sewers' collected the flow from the sewers which had previously emptied directly into the river and carried the effluent to reservoirs well to the east of London from which it could be discharged into the Thames. Four intercepting sewers were built, two parallel to the north bank and two parallel to the south, each with a fall of 2 feet per mile. Massive pumping stations were built at Deptford and at Crossness on the Erith marshes. At first raw sewage was simply discharged on the ebb to be sucked out on the tide, but in 1884 a Royal Commission recommended that crude sewage should no longer be discharged. Sewage works with huge settling tanks and filter beds were built along the Lower Thames, and the resultant sludge was dumped at sea. As part of the scheme, the Victoria, Albert and Chelsea embankments were built. As well as carrying the new sewers, these consolidated the river frontage, canalising the river so that it flowed more quickly and hygienically through the capital, and providing a further defence against flooding. A considerable area was reclaimed, allowing traffic flow to be improved and public gardens laid out. The opportunity was taken to construct the Metropolitan and District Line tunnel within made ground behind the Victoria Embankment.

The various schemes to address pollution in the Thames could barely keep pace with the rapid growth in population in the metropolis. In 1920 the Joint Advisory Committee on River Pollution found the existing authorities were no longer adequate. A further committee recommended consolidation, reducing the number of sewage works from nearly 200 (virtually one for every community) to just ten. By the 1950s twenty-eight sewage works still discharged into the Thames, while direct industrial discharge contributed 10 per cent of the river's pollution, mostly in the lower reaches. The life of the river had reached a low point, often with no dissolved oxygen between Chelsea and Tilbury during the summer months – the Lower Thames was dead.

Beginning in the 1960s, increased investment and stricter water quality standards, coupled with the decline and closure of the docks and the movement of industry out of London towards the estuary, have finally led to what may be described as the rebirth of the river. Already by 1963 every sample from the river contained at least some dissolved oxygen, and the quantity of ammonia was more than halved. Fish are returning. 125 species have been recorded: sea species such as trout, herring and sprats are found in the estuary, with freshwater fish such as chub, roach, bream and perch in the non-tidal river, and eel migrates upriver as it used to. Rare colonies of seahorse are even being monitored. Despite occasional lapses, today the Thames is cleaner than at any time in the last 500 years, and is perhaps the cleanest metropolitan river in the world.

Recently, 127 Marine Conservation Zones have been proposed around the coasts of England and Wales. These are a form of nature reserve, offering the marine environment legal protection from destructive activities and putting a management plan in place. As a network, they will help to improve as well as protect local ecosystems. Three of these Marine Conservation Zones are around the mouth of the Thames: the tidal river from Southend as far upstream as Richmond, the Medway estuary, and the Swale estuary (which lies between the Isle of Sheppey and the Kent coast). Each of these areas supports a rich variety of resources as well as one or more rare marine species. If these proposals are accepted, it will represent a huge step towards safeguarding the future health of the river and estuary.

Eternal Vigilance

To bring this part of the story up to date, successive iterations of planning and preservation legislation over many decades, starting with the Town & Country Planning Act of 1947, could be seen as an ongoing return on public pressure – though the watchword remains 'eternal vigilance'. We are fortunate to have a range of dedicated campaigning organisations in this country, such as the National Trust, the various Wildlife Trusts and other conservation organisations and charities, together with local amenity societies, backed by millions of supporters and thousands of dedicated volunteers, who ensure that every development proposal is properly examined, while local authorities regard the Thames as integral to their tourism strategies. The Berkshire, Buckinghamshire & Oxfordshire Wildlife Trust manages numerous nature reserves along the Upper and Middle Thames valley, while the Essex, Kent and London Wildlife Trusts manage reserves down river. The Thames Path was declared a National Trail in 1989 as the end result of a long process, recognising the importance of the Thames to the nation. As more people enjoy the path every year, or engage with trusts and charities, its centrality is cemented.

12

The Once and Future River

Enduring Themes

The history of society's dealings with the Thames, and indeed any river, is a progression from propitiation to control to taking it for granted. But the river has the last laugh.

Throughout the history of the River Thames a number of themes have kept surfacing. The river has often been imbued with a spiritual content in the broadest sense, from veneration to preservation. It has been a military river: a frontier, a barrier, a routeway. It has been both a workhorse and a playground, a liquid slum and a utopian idyll. The conflict between the demands of long-distance transport and the needs of local communities has been a running sore, reflected in constant changes in jurisdiction and administration. River crossings have been an ongoing theme, as fords, ferries, bridges and tunnels have jostled with economic and strategic considerations.

For 2,000 years it has been London's river, and the pull of the capital has almost been a constant since the Romans first established its lowest bridging point. The river made London. But it has been – and continues to be – much more than an adjunct to its largest town. It has been England's river, at the heart of much that has shaped the nation. As John Buchan said in his foreword to the CPRE report, 'For the whole space of our history the valley has been the heart of English life.'[1] And it is also a local river, a river of three parts, each with its own distinctive and enduring character.

It has been constantly shaped both by natural forces and by human action. From its glacial past to its globally warmed future, it is a part of planet earth. On a smaller scale, it has been shaped and modelled for human ends. Its banks have been stabilised and reclaimed by local communities and landowners, while transport and management needs have dredged, canalised and built locks. Pollution and restoration have dominated the last two centuries: it has passed through death to emerge as a river which is cleaner than it has been for half a millennium.

Perhaps the overarching theme, the mega-theme, is change – as Heraclitus of Ephesus realised 2,500 years ago. Change is its nature, and to attempt to straightjacket the river is to attempt the impossible. If change is life, then the Thames is alive.

The history of the Thames has been one of taming the river, whether by making ritual deposits, revetting the banks, or building locks and bridges. Yet these advances did not lead to greater respect. Rather, we learned first to dominate the river then to take it for granted. Its occasional furies always come as a surprise. It took environmental disaster before the tidal Thames began to be treated properly once again. Even then, if changes in the structure of world trade had not intervened, it is doubtful whether much would have been achieved.

The future of the Thames will be more closely bound to human decisions than its past was. Today, with the threatened impact of global warming on sea level, the Thames may be standing on the cusp once again. It is being seriously suggested that coastal defence is not a good investment. The pumps could be turned off and large areas of the east coast allowed to revert to their 'natural' state: salt marsh and creeks, it is argued, are nature's way of dealing with tidal floods. It would also be good for ecological diversity. If a policy such as this was extended to the estuary, the changes would be considerable. The river would become much wider once again, and the boundary between land and sea less clear-cut. There would be major adjustments as the Essex and Kent marshes were 'taken back' by the sea; places such as Canvey Island could be drowned after centuries of dedicated drainage.

South East England is sinking at the rate of 1–2 mm per year. The effect of rising sea levels due to global warming may double this figure. If the projections are correct, it is just a matter of time before the Thames Barrage is over-topped and central London is flooded for the first time in a century. Assuming that this would not be a permitted 'adjustment', could it be that J. H. O. Bunge's conception of a 'tideless Thames' will be dusted down?[2] A dam and lock system across the river somewhere to the east of London would be much easier to implement now that it is not necessary to accommodate the needs of a major international port. The Thames at London could instead become a tourists' playground, a vast boating lake.

While the considerations outlined above would have no direct impact above Teddington Lock, green concerns could lead to a revival of river transport upstream of London for bulky non-perishable goods. The Thames Path could serve once again as a towpath for horses, and the dark red sails of wherries might again be seen from Richmond Hill. Perhaps William Morris's dream of the future in *News from Nowhere* might start to look prophetic!

Flooding on the non-tidal river is another problem which will not go away. Greater control of land use on the floodplains may be part of the answer. This was noted by the CPRE in 1929, yet the lesson has still not been learned. By reversing the trend towards building and denuding, and instead managing and preserving, run-off would be slowed down and reduced. This may be another case of green issues serving the common good.

Clean water is another challenge for the future, and one in which the Thames is destined to play a significant role. It has been said that the next world war will be over the control of water rather than fossil fuels. Conserving supplies of water and managing waste disposal will go hand in hand to help ensure that South East England does not suffer from crippling seasonal drought.

Yet the Thames valley remains a region of several distinct characters. Its natural beauty and historical interest continue to attract visitors to the middle and upper reaches, as does its emergence over the last 150 years as a recreational river, while the London area is also tourist-rich and the towns of the estuary are well-established as holiday destinations. Many local authorities embrace this fact and invest significantly in order to earn tourist income as well as to improve quality of life for residents. Planning control and public investment are essential for the future of the Thames, but they should not be taken for granted. Official influence will weigh in on the side of the angels only as long as bureaucratic interests are served. The future of the river and its setting depend to a large extent on this Faustian pact; but if the balance in that equation shifts ...

Perhaps it is fair to suggest that each generation gets the Thames it deserves. Hopes and fears, concerns and priorities are brought to the table. In 1929 the CPRE put much faith in 'the weight of public opinion'. Today, backed by a strong conservation movement, green issues are high on the agenda; but these have to be aligned with economic realities if they are to carry popular opinion and win any particular argument. In the 1920s the CPRE recognised the need to be realistic if it was to negotiate and persuade, and today's green knights are no different. Its advocates cannot rest; the price of a healthy Thames is still eternal vigilance.

Notes

1 The Context: Climate, Environment and Human Interference

1. For a technical analysis of the geological history of the Thames valley, see Bridgland, D. R., *Quaternary of the Thames* (London: Chapman & Hall, 1994).
2. This quotation is recorded by Plato, *Cratylus*, 402a.
3. John Stow, *A Survey of London*, first published in 1598 (second edition 1603). This description of London in the reign of Elizabeth I has been reprinted several times.
4. For a discussion of sea level change, see Gaffney, V., S. Fitch and D. Smith, *Europe's Lost World: the Rediscovery of Doggerland* (York: Council for British Archaeology, 2009) (Research Report 160), and Devoy, R. J., 'Post-glacial Environmental Change and Man in the Thames Estuary: A Synopsis', in Thompson, F. H. (ed.), *Archaeology and Coastal Change* (London: Society of Antiquaries, 1980) (Occasional Paper 1, 134–48).
5. Combe, W., *An History of the River Thames* (London: J. & J. Boydell, 1794 & 1796), with aquatints by J. C. Stadler after drawings by Joseph Farington. This print is reproduced as figure 2.

2 The Ancient River: The First Inhabitants, from 500,000 to 5000 BP

1. For an excellent overview of the period covered by this chapter, see Stringer, C., *Homo Britannicus: The Incredible Story of Human Life in Britain* (London: Allen Lane, 2006).
2. Pitts, M. and M. Roberts, *Fairweather Eden: Life in Britain Half*

a Million Years Ago as Revealed by the Excavations at Boxgrove (London: Arrow Books, 1998).

3. After Wymer, J. J., *The Lower Palaeolithic Occupation of Britain* (Salisbury: Wessex Archaeology & English Heritage 1999), table 2.
4. Stringer, C. and C. Gamble, *In Search of the Neanderthals: Solving the Puzzle of Human Origins* (London: Thames & Hudson, 1994).

3 The Sacred River: Ritual, Ceremony and Power from the Neolithic to the Iron Age

1. York, J., 'The Life Cycle of Bronze Age Metalwork from the Thames', *Oxford Journal of Archaeology* 21:1 (2002), 77–92.
2. Bradley, R. and K. Gordon, 'Human Skulls from the River Thames, their Dating and Significance', *Antiquity* 62 (1988), 503–9.
3. Reported in Heard, K., H. Sheldon and P. Thompson, 'Mapping Roman Southwark', *Antiquity* 64 (1990), 608–19.

4 The Quiet River: Roman Conquest and Provincial Life

1. Cassius Dio, *Roman History*, Book 60, Chapters 19–23.
2. Tacitus, *Annals*, Book 14, Chapter 33.
3. Strabo, *Geography*, Book 4, Chapter 5.2 and 5.3.
4. *Ibid.*

5 The Harried River: The Struggle for Anglo-Saxon England

1. Winterbottom, M. (trans.), *Gildas: the Ruin of Britain and Other Works* (London: Phillimore, 1978), Chapter 25.
2. Gildas, *The Ruin of Britain*, Chapters 28–29.
3. Gildas, *The Ruin of Britain*, Chapter 16.
4. For references to the Anglo-Saxon Chronicle see Garmonsway, G. N. (trans.), *The Anglo-Saxon Chronicle* (London: J. M. Dent, 1954).
5. For a translation of *The Ruin* see Alexander, M. (trans.), *The Earliest English Poems* (second edition) (Harmondsworth: Penguin Books, 1977).
6. For references to the Venerable Bede see Sherley-Price, L. (trans.), *Bede: A History of the English Church and People* (Harmondsworth: Penguin Books, 1955).

6 The Meandering River: The Creation of England and the Middle Ages

1. Clauses taken from Davis, G. R. C., *Magna Carta* (London: British Museum, 1963).
2. Tatton-Brown, T., 'Excavations at the Custom House Site, City of London, 1973', *Transactions of the London & Middx Archaeological Society* 25 (1974), 117–219, quoted from 141.

7 The Broken River: From the Tudors to the Great Fire of London

1. Victoria County History, *A History of the County of Oxford: Volume 16, Henley-on-Thames and Environs* (Woodbridge: Boydell & Brewer, 2011), 127.
2. For references to Samuel Pepys's diary, see Latham, R. and W. Matthews (eds), *Samuel Pepys's Diary* (London: Bell & Hyman, 1974).
3. Quoted from Chandler, J. (ed.), *Travels Through Stuart Britain: The Adventures of John Taylor, the Water Poet* (Stroud: Sutton, 1999).
4. See the poems: Robert Herrick, 'His Tears to Thamasis', and Francis Quarles, 'My Beloved is Mine and I am His'.

8 The Working River: Industry and Empire, Seventeenth Century to the Present

1. Wrigley, E. A. and R. S. Schofield, *The Population History of England, 1541–1871: A Reconstruction* (London: Edward Arnold, 1981).
2. Conrad, J., *Nigger of the Narcissus* (London: William Heinemann, 1897 and subsequent editions).
3. Henry Mayhew's newspaper articles were reprinted in Mayhew, H., *The Morning Chronicle Survey of Labour and the Poor: The Metropolitan Districts, Volume 1* (Firle, Sussex: Caliban Books, 1980).
4. Quoted in Cox, A., *Docklands in the Making: The Redevelopment of the Isle of Dogs, 1981–1995* (London: Survey of London/Athlone Press, 1995), 8.
5. From John Betjeman's poem 'Middlesex', reproduced in *John Betjeman's Collected Poems* (enlarged edition) (London: John Murray, 1970).
6. *Ibid.*

10 The Recreational River: Frost Fairs, Pleasure Gardens and Poetry

1. Collected magazine articles, first published in book form as Dickens, C., *Sketches by 'Boz': Illustrations of Every-Day Life and Every-Day People* (London: John Macrone, 1836).

11 The Preserved River: Preserving the Thames Valley

1. For references to Samuel Pepys's diary, see Latham, R. & W. Matthews (eds), *Samuel Pepys's Diary* (London: Bell & Hyman, 1974).
2. An unofficial website, *www.floodlondon.com*, graphically shows what could happen if a storm surge burst over the Thames Barrier. It should be noted that this is just one possible reconstruction.
3. Much information has been drawn from Dickinson, H. W., *Water Supply of Greater London* (Leamington Spa & London: Newcomen Society, 1954).

12 The Once and Future River

1. Council for the Preservation of Rural England, *The Thames Valley from Cricklade to Staines: A Survey of its Existing State and some Suggestions for its Future Preservation* (London: Univ. London Press, 1929).
2. Bunge, J. H. O., *Tideless Thames in Future London* (London: Thames Barrage Assoc., 1944).

Further Reading

Many books and articles have been referred to in writing this history. The following have been highlighted because they will give the reader an entrance into the extensive literature that the Thames and its hinterland have generated. Particular interests can be followed through the bibliographies they each contain.

Ackroyd, P., *Thames: Sacred River* (London: Chatto & Windus, 2007).

Batey, M. *et al.*, *Arcadian Thames: The River Landscape from Hampton to Kew* (London: Barn Elms Publishing, 1994).

Blair, J., *Anglo-Saxon Oxfordshire* (Stroud: Sutton 1994).

Booth, P., A. Dodd, M. Robinson and A. Smith, *The Thames Through Time: The Archaeology of the Gravel Terraces of the Upper and Middle Thames. The Early Historical Period: AD 1–1000* (Oxford: Oxford Archaeology, 2007) (Thames Valley Landscapes Monogr. 27).

Brigham, T., 'The Late Roman Waterfront in London', *Britannia*, 21 (1990), 99–183.

Cowie, R. and L. Blackmore, *Lundenwic: Excavations in Middle Saxon London 1987–2000* (London: Museum of London Archaeology, 2012) (MoLA Monogr. 63).

Cox, A., *Docklands in the Making: The Redevelopment of the Isle of Dogs, 1981–1995* (London: Survey of London/Athlone Press, 1995).

Foreman, S. *et al.*, *Gathering the People, Settling the Land: The Archaeology of a Middle Thames Landscape: Anglo-Saxon and Post-Medieval* (Oxford: Oxford Archaeology, 2002) (Thames Valley Landscapes Monogr. 14).

Hann, A., *The Medway Valley: A Kent Landscape Transformed* (Chichester: Phillimore & Co., 2009).

Hayman, G., P. Jones and R. Poulton, *Settlement Sites and Sacred Offerings: Prehistoric and Later Archaeology in the Thames Valley, Near Chertsey* (Woking: Spoil Heap Pubs, 2012) (Monogr. 4).

Further Reading

Jones, P., *The Roman and Medieval Town of Staines* (Woking: Spoil Heap Pubs, 2010) (Monogr. 2).

Marsden, P., *Ships in the Port of London: First to Eleventh Centuries AD* (London: English Heritage, 1994) (Archaeology Rep 3).

Marsden, P., *Ships in the Port of London: Twelfth to Seventeenth Centuries* (London: English Heritage, 1996) (Archaeology Rep 5).

Morigi, A. *et al.*, *The Thames Through Time: The Archaeology of the Gravel Terraces of the Upper and Middle Thames. Early Prehistory: To 1500 BC* (Oxford: Oxford Archaeology, 2011) (Thames Valley Landscapes Monogr 32).

Museum of London, *The Archaeology of Greater London: An Assessment of Archaeological Evidence for Human Presence in the Area now Covered by Greater London* (London: Museum of London, 2000).

Phillips, G., *Thames Crossings: Bridges, Tunnels and Ferries* (Newton Abbot: David & Charles, 1981).

Port of London Authority, *The Cleaner Thames 1966* (London: PLA, 1967).

Reed, N., *Frost Fairs on the Frozen Thames* (Folkestone: Lilburne Press, 2002).

Saunders, A. (ed.), *The London County Council Bomb Damage Maps 1939–1945* (London: London Topographical Society, 2005) (LTS Publication 164).

Schofield, J., *London 1100–1600: The Archaeology of a Capital City* (Sheffield: Equinix Publishing, 2011).

Sharp, D., *The Thames Path*, National Trail Guides (London: Aurum Press, 1996).

Sidell, J., K. Wilkinson, R. Scaife and N. Cameron, *The Holocene Evolution of the London Thames: Archaeological Excavations (1991–1998) for the London Underground Limited Jubilee Line Extension Project* (London: Museum of London Archaeology Service, 2000) (MoLAS Monogr. 5).

Smith, V., *Front-Line Kent: Defence Against Invasion from 1400 to the Cold War* (Maidstone: Kent County Council, 2001).

Stringer, C., *Homo Britannicus: The Incredible Story of Human Life in Britain* (London: Allen Lane, 2006).

Townley, S., *Henley-on-Thames: Town, Trade and River* (Chichester: Phillimore & Co 2009).

Tucker, J., *Ferries of the Lower Thames* (Stroud: Amberley Publishing, 2010).

Tucker, J., *Ferries of the Upper Thames* (Stroud: Amberley Publishing, 2012).

Index

Also available from Amberley Publishing

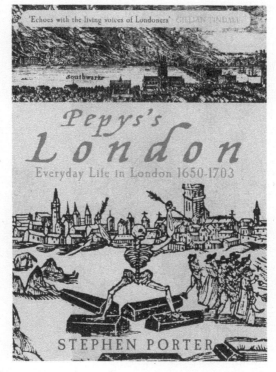

*Everyday life in the teeming metropolis during Pepys's time
in the city (c.1650-1703)*

'A fast-paced narrative with a real sense of history unfolding' GILLIAN TINDALL

Samuel Pepys's London was a turbulent, boisterous city, enduring the strains caused by foreign wars, the
Great Plague and the Great Fire, yet growing and prospering. The London of Wren, Dryden and Purcell was
also the city of Nell Gwyn, an orange seller in the theatre who became an actress and the king's mistress; of
'Colonel' Thomas Blood, who attempted to steal the crown jewels from the Tower and yet
escaped punishment; and of Titus Oates, whose invention of a Popish Plot provoked a major political crisis.

£10.99 Paperback
146 illustrations
256 pages
978-1-4456-0980-5

Also available as an ebook
Available from all good bookshops or to order direct
Please call **01453-847-800**
www.amberleybooks.com

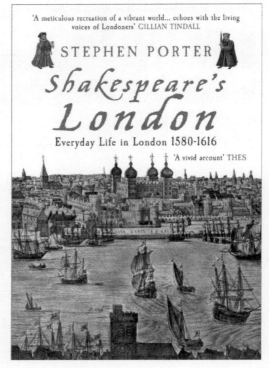